Shakespeare and the
Art of Physiognomy

Shakespeare and the Art of Physiognomy

Sibylle Baumbach

$\mathcal{HEB}$ ☼ Humanities-Ebooks, LLP

First published by *Humanities-Ebooks, LLP,*
Tirril Hall, Tirril, Penrith CA10 2JE

The Ebook (with the facility of word and phrase search) is available exclusively from http://www.humanities-ebooks.co.uk

ISBN 978-1-84760-078-3 Ebook
ISBN 978-1-84760-079-0 Paperback

Contents

PHYSIOGNOMY, n. The art of determining the character of another by the resemblances and differences between his face and our own, which is the standard of excellence.

'There is no art,' says Shakespeare, foolish man,
'To read the mind's construction in the face.'
The physiognomists his portrait scan,
And say: 'How little wisdom here we trace!
He knew his face disclosed his mind and heart,
So, in his own defence, denied our art.'

Lavatar Shunk
(Ambrose Bierce, *The Devil's Dictionary*, 1911)

1 Looking for Shakespeare's Face(s)

'Searching for Shakespeare'[1] has become a popular discipline as numerous recent publications on the life of the poet and dramatist confirm.[2] Thereby it is especially the mystery of 'Shakespeare's face'[3] which takes centre stage. The particular fascination elicited by Shakespeare's countenance is based on a strong belief in physiognomy, by which it is understood that the human face indicates a person's character as well as traces of the passions of the mind. Physiognomy, which reaches back into antiquity, was revived towards the end of the 16th century when numerous physiognomic manuals were published and the art of face-reading became popular again both as a tool for deciphering fellow-beings and as a device for self-fashioning. Taking into consideration the renaissance of physiognomic thought and theory in the late 16th and early 17th century, the following study will examine physiognomic readings in Shakespeare's oeuvre. Based on the physiognomic discourse of his time, a physiognomic inventory of his plays will be established before embarking on a close analysis of the 'art of physiognomy' (*The Rape of Lucrece* 1394f.) as it is performed in his plays. Thereby, the focus will be set on the construction, translation, and reception of 'characters', that is on the production of physiognomic data, its verbalisation or, respectively, visualisation onstage, as well as its reception by physiogno-

---

1 Searching for Shakespeare was the title of an exhibition showing Shakespeare's portraits in the National Portrait Gallery in 2006.
2 See, for instance, A. D. Nuttall, *Shakespeare: The Thinker* (New Haven et al.: Yale University Press, 2007); Bill Bryson, *Shakespeare: The World as Stage* (New York: Atlas Books / Harper Collins, 2007); Mark Anderson, *Shakespeare by Another Name* (New York: Gotham Books et al., 2005), Peter Ackroyd, *Shakespeare: The Biography* (London: Chatto and Windus, 2005); Stephen Greenblatt, *Will in the World: How Shakespeare became Shakespeare* (London: Jonathan Cape, 2004); Michael Wood, *In Search of Shakespeare* (London: BBC, 2003).
3 Stephanie Nolen, *Shakespeare's Face* (London et al.: Piatkus, 2003).

mic readers. The latter use their physiognomic competence not only to decipher their fellowmen but also to fashion their own faces and bodies, to frame their faces to all occasions, and to hide their emotions and passions behind a seemingly natural mask, which is their own face. Thus, in Shakespeare's work, faces are perceived as open books and cryptic documents, they are read, re-read, and misread and subject to manipulative forces. At the same time, the face remains the key medium for communication in Shakespeare's plays: it speaks even when words fail and precedes verbal utterances by its silent but very telling expression. The present study investigates Shakespeare's poetics of the face and his physiognomic scheme. This includes the analysis of the construction and reception of 'characters' both in the literal and metaphorical meaning of the term, as well as the tracing of the progression from characters on the page to characters on the face, which is a frequent topos in Shakespeare's plays.

Given that the limits and the potential of physiognomy are key motifs in his writings, it is almost ironic that Shakespeare's face should have become an object for abundant physiognomic (mis-) readings.[1] His plays and poems constantly tackle the question of the interrelation between seeming and being, between outer and inner man, or, more specifically, between man's physiognomy and his character from numerous different perspectives. Even though it is often suggested that 'there's no art / To find the mind's construction in the face', to quote Duncan in *Macbeth* (1.4.11f.),[2] the face eventually reveals itself as an eloquent and most telling medium for characterisation. Thereby anti-physiognomic axioms such as Duncan's emerge as instances of subversive affirmation as well as a dramatic strategy to sensitise readers and audiences to both the potentialities and the ambivalence of facial rhetoric. Quite frequently in Shakespeare, the art of face-reading is disputed only to be re-established. *Macbeth* is a case in point in that Duncan's remark sets the audience on the wrong track, belying facial eloquence, which especially in this play provides the key to the characters onstage (see Chapter 6.1).

---

1   Compare Hildegard Hammerschmidt-Hummel, *The True Face of Shakespeare* (London: Chaucer Press, 2006).

2   Unless indicated otherwise, quotations follow *The Norton Shakespeare*, ed. by Stephen Greenblatt et al. (New York/London: Norton, 1997).

Before starting our investigation of Shakespeare's physiognomic scheme, however, let us first reconsider the portrayals and readings of Shakespeare's manifold physiognomies, especially as some of these (first and foremost the Droeshout engraving) might hold the key to the way his plays should be read. Facing Shakespeare's monument in the Holy Trinity Church at Stratford-upon-Avon, the American writer Nathaniel Hawthorne, for instance, almost immediately embarks on a physiognomic-phrenologic[1] reading:

> I know not what the phrenologists say to the bust. The forehead is but moderately developed, and retreats somewhat, the upper part of the skull rising pyramidally; the eyes are prominent almost beyond the penthouse of the brow; the upper lip is so long that it must have been almost a deformity, unless the sculptor artistically exaggerated its length, in consideration, that, on the pedestal, it must be foreshortened by being looked at from below. On the whole, Shakespeare must have had a singular rather than a prepossessing face; and it is wonderful how, with this bust before its eyes, the world has persisted in maintaining an erroneous notion of his appearance, allowing painters and sculptors to foist their idealized nonsense on its all, instead of the genuine man. For my part, the Shakespeare of my mind's eye is henceforth to be a personage of a ruddy English complexion, with a reasonably capacious brow, intelligent and quickly observant eyes, a nose curved slightly outward, a long, queer upper lip, with the mouth a little unclosed beneath it, and cheeks considerably developed in the lower part and beneath the chin. But when Shakespeare was himself (for nine tenths of the time, according to all appearances, he was but the burgher of Stratford), he doubtless shone through this dull mask and transfigured it into the face of an angel.[2]

---

1 Phrenology is based on the belief that the form of the cranial bone reflects a person s character and that the development of certain areas of the brain can be felt in bumps and fissures of the skull. The term *phrenology*, however, was not coined until around 1800 when the German neuroanatomist Franz Joseph Gall introduced the study of the localisation of mental development in the form of the cranium. Therefore *phrenology*, in this study, will be categorised as being part of *physiognomy*.

2 Nathaniel Hawthorne, 'Recollection of a Gifted Woman', in George P. Lathrop ed., *The Complete Works of Nathaniel Hawthorne* (Boston et al.: Houghton, Mifflin, 1887) Vol. 7,113–47.

Deeply impressed by Shakespeare's portrait, Hawthorne chose to clear his mental gallery of all those flattering pictures and portraits, which dominated his image of the dramatist up to that time. The first to go might have been the Chandos portrait, 'the favourite likeness of Shakespeare',[1] which shows a Mediterranean, or, as J. Hain Friswell claimed, 'a decidedly Jewish physiognomy'[2]—a swarthy full-bearded man with curly hair and a golden earring. The Flower and the Droeshout portraits would have been the next to be dismissed. Both of these portraits had a great impact on the ways in which Shakespeare was perceived over the centuries even though the Flower portrait turned out to be a complete fake, or more precisely, a coloured copy of the Droeshout engraving. The most prominent feature in all of these images of Shakespeare is his broad, lofty forehead that was to become one of his main characteristics. Not only does it indicate greatness of mind but it also strengthens a possible connection to the 'genio Socratem'[3], which is implied in the epitaph engraved below the bust in the Holy Trinity Church. There are no records indicating how phrenologists or physiognomists would have judged Shakespeare's face. However, it does not seem unlikely that the bard would have met a similar fate as Socrates when it came to physiognomic readings. It is told that Zopyros, for instance, a renowned physiognomist of the time, classified the sophist as *stupidum et bardum*, as dull and imbecile by the mere look at Socrates' face, being unaware of his identity.[4]

---

1   Samuel Schoenbaum, *Shakespeare's Lives* (Oxford: Clarendon Press, 1991) 203.

2   Ibidem, *William Shakespeare: Records and Images* (London: Scolar Press, 1981) 175.

3   The Greek philosopher is also said to have had an exceptionally roomy forehead, which the physiognomist Johann Caspar Lavater regards as a key indicator of an intelligent, strong-minded person. Referring to Socrates, Lavater writes, '[i]n these high and roomy arches, undoubtedly, the spirit dwells which will penetrate clouds of difficulties, and vanquish hosts of impediments.' (Cf. Johann C. Lavater, *Essays on Physiognomy*, trans. by Thomas Holcroft [London: J. Robinson, 1844] 4th ed., 177f.)

4   Compare Cicero, *De Fato* 10. The Zopyros episode is frequently referred to in Early Modern physiognomic treatises. See also Thomas Hill, *The Contemplation of Mankinde* (London: Seres, 1571) fol. x–xi, and Richard Saunders, *Physiognomie and Chiromancie, Metoposcopie* (London: Brooke, 1653) 144.

Which of the well-known Shakespeare portraits does most justice to the dramatist's physiognomy remains an open question. While some critics make a case for the authenticity of the Chandos portrait,[1] there is evidence suggesting that it is Gheerart Jannssen's bust gracing the monument at Stratford which bears the greatest resemblance to Shakespeare. Not only was it erected shortly after Shakespeare's death but it was probably also commissioned by his family. The question remains, however, why Shakespeare's relatives would have approved of a likeness that shows the dramatist with a rather unflattering podgy face with a small nose, thin moustache, 'goggle eyes and gaping mouth'[2]. The man presiding over what is assumed to be Shakespeare's grave, who overlooks his beholders with a vacuous gaze, opposes the notion of poetic grandeur and intellectual refinement. With his mouth half-opened as if awaiting some brainwave to enter the mind and guide the hand across the yet empty parchment, the bust appears more like a persiflage on divine inspiration than a homage to an exceptionally gifted writer.

'Read if thou canst': against the background of these observations, the mocking tone of the appeal engraved beneath the bust can hardly be missed. Did we misread the features on this, to speak with Hawthorne, 'singular' face and misjudge their implication? Or are these words designed to urge us to disregard the bust and move on from the face to the page and to progress from the character Shakespeare to Shakespeare's characters? There can be no doubt that Shakespeare's writings are far more revealing than his countenance, provided that we know how to read them. It is precisely the capability of interpreting these tokens correctly, however, which is disputed in the derisive dare which confronts the beholder contemplating the bust. And yet, the contemptuous tone of the phrase 'read if thou canst' fits the scintillating wit which pervades Shakespeare's work. Hence, even though the bust and the epitaph might not display the physiognomy

---

1   See Hildegard Hammerschmidt-Hummel, 'What did Shakespeare Look Like? Authentic Portraits and the Death Mask. Methods and Results of the Tests of Authenticity,' *Symbolism* 1 (2000) 41–79.
2   Clement M. Ingleby, *Shakespeare, the Man and the Book: Being a Collection of Occasional Papers on the Bard and his Writings* (London: J. Allen, 1877) Vol. 1, 79.

of a genius, they succeed in conveying Shakespeare's character.

Challenging the reading skills of its beholders, the monument not only distracts the view from its imperfections and denies its potential misapprehension of the man 'Shakespeare'. It urges the beholders to reconsider their interpretation of these hideous features which seem irreconcilable with their preconceived image of his face. Are we, like Hawthorne, willing to replace 'our' Shakespeare with a portrait that undermines our notion of a man of genius? Due to human curiosity, the search for Shakespeare's true face will in all probability never come to a close. This is all the more remarkable as Jannssen's bust continues to serve as a gentle pointer to Shakespeare's work rather than his physiognomy. In its respect, it is in line with the preface of the first Folio edition and Ben Jonson's poem, which asks the reader 'to look not at his picture but the book'[1] before allowing him to begin the collected works.

The picture Jonson refers to, and which he bids the reader to neglect in favour of Shakespeare's oeuvre, is the Droeshout engraving, which adorns the edition. In contrast to Jannssen's bust that seems to depict Shakespeare as a writer, which is indicated by the blank parchment he is clinging to, the Droeshout image portrays the actor Shakespeare. In addition to the characteristic enlarged, almost colossal forehead, the visage depicted in the Droeshout engraving appears somewhat detachable, almost mask-like, as if it could be swapped at any moment for another persona and one of those characters that the reader is about to encounter. Furthermore, it emphasises the fact that the plays printed in the edition are but scripts and blueprints that are meant to be performed, translated, and viewed in a theatre. It is onstage that the mask falls, and is recreated in a more natural but not necessarily less deceptive appearance as is suggested by Mercutio's remark 'a visor for a visor' (*Romeo and Juliet* 1.4.30). Ever since the static visor disappeared from the theatre,[2] the face is at the centre of a play. Considering the extensive mobility of facial features and their volatility in expression, the human countenance could be regarded as

---

1   Ben Jonson, 'To the Reader', *William Shakespeares Comedies, Histories & Tragedies* (London: Isaac Iaggard and Ed. Blount, 1623).
2   Compare Meg Twycross and Sarah Carpenter, *Masks and Masking in Medieval and Early Tudor England* (Aldershot: Ashgate, 2002).

a stage within a stage, upon which temporary states of mind, moods, and emotions can be communicated without delay.

Especially in the Globe theatre, the spectators had a full view of the actors. They could peruse their faces and were highly susceptible to non-verbal communication, through which the actors succeeded in steering their audience's emotion. Following a performance of *Othello* in September 1610, a spectator recalls the gripping effect of Desdemona's silent play:

> They had tragedies (too) which they acted with skill and decorum and in which some things, both speech and action, brought forth tears. – Moreover, that famous Desdemona killed before us by her husband, although she always acted her whole part supremely well, yet when she was killed she was even more moving, for when she fell back upon the bed she implored the pity of the spectators by her very face.[1]

Just as the spectators were able to read the actors' faces, the actors could peruse the countenances of their audience. Thus, they could anticipate the success of their performance and possibly adjust their play to the facial feedback they received. Considering that actors did not receive the full script of the play and probably used the script of their parts as a guideline, the play itself might have changed quite dramatically between the processes of rehearsal and enactment. Due to the lack of sufficient records that might provide substantial evidence of schemes of non–verbal communication in Early Modern theatre, however, we are obliged to return to the book and, complying with Jonson's appeal, consult the written script, which holds numerous clues pointing to a complex, multi-layered, and multi-faceted physiognomic sub- or paratext, whose implications for the reading of Shakespeare's work have not yet been explored.

Despite the body-boom and the 'corporeal turn',[2] which has pervaded literary research over the past decade and has become very

---

1   Gamini Salgado, *Eyewitnesses of Shakespeare: First Hand Accounts of Performances 1590–1890* (London: Sussex University Press, 1975) 30.

2   Keir Elam, '"In What Chapter of His Bosom?": Reading Shakespeare's Bodies', in Terence Hawkes ed., *Alternative Shakespeares* (London/New York: Routledge, 1996) Vol. 2, 140–63, 143.

notable especially in Shakespeare studies,[1] the poetics of the human face have remained largely untouched. This is all the more astonishing since physiognomic thought and theories experienced a renaissance towards the end of the 16th century and thus can be assumed to have had a considerable impact on early modern drama. Considering the rise of portraiture and autobiographical writings,[2] the advent of anatomic theatre[3] and a growing awareness of individuality towards the end of the 16th century, physiognomy emerges as a key concept in the Early Modern era. In the increasing desire for self-fashioning, it becomes a central device for the art of simulation and dissimulation. While the former is concerned with the enactment of something that does not exist, the latter aims at hiding certain features whose existence are to be concealed. In both cases, physiognomy becomes an indispensible tool in that it provides the means to 'frame [the] face to all occasions' (*3 Henry VI* 3.2.185) and suggests ways to 'look like the innocent flower / But be the serpent under't' (*Macbeth* 1.5.63f.).

Supporting the presentation of the self[4] as well as assisting the deciphering of fellow-beings, physiognomy can be seen as central to the early modern era in which concepts of individuality and the presentation of the self take centre stage to be continually questioned and contested. Even though the claim by the historian Jacob Burckhardt

1   See Maurizio Calbi, *Approximate Bodies: Gender and Power in Early Modern Drama and Anatomy* (London/New York: Routledge, 2005); Ewan Fernie, *Shame in Shakespeare* (London/New York: Routledge, 2002); Carol Chillington Rutter, *Enter the Body* (London/New York: Routledge, 2001); Lynn Enterline, *The Rhetoric of the Body from Ovid to Shakespeare* (Cambridge: Cambridge University Press, 2000); Jonathan Sawday, *The Body Emblazoned: Dissection and the Human Body in Renaissance Culture* (London: Routledge, 1995).

2   Compare Karl Enenkel et al. ed., *Modelling the Individual: Biography and Portrait in the Renaissance* (Amsterdam/Atlanta: Rodopi, 1998) as well as Nicholas Mann and Luke Syson ed., *The Image of the Individual: Portraits in the Renaissance* (London: British Museum Press, 1998).

3   Jonathan Sawday, *The Body Emblazoned: Dissection and the Human Body in Renaissance Culture* (London/New York: Routledge, 1995) esp. 129–40.

4   For concepts of the self and the notion of inwardness in early modern theatre and literature see esp. Katharine Eisaman Maus, *Inwardness and Theatre in the English Renaissance* (Chicago et al.: University of Chicago Press, 1995); Anne Ferry, *The Inward Language: Sonnets of Wyatt, Sidney, Shakespeare, Donne* (Chicago et al.: University of Chicago Press, 1983); for the notion of the self in Shakespeare see esp. John Lee, *Shakespeare's Hamlet and the Controversies of Self* (Oxford et al.: Clarendon Press, 2000).

about the rise and discovery of the individual appears too ambitious, since notions of individuality and selfhood are not phenomena reserved to the early modern period, there seems to have been a growing awareness of possible formations and (re-)fashionings of the 'self' in Shakespeare's era. Alongside a firm belief in a world order in which the principle of correspondence between psyche and body was still valid, this heightened notion of self-confidence opened new perspectives and called for a revision of the Paracelsic semiotic system by granting the individual co-authorship in the book of nature. Thereby physiognomy serves to reinforce the creative role of man in the design of 'his' world in that it provides the tools not only to decipher and understand but also to alter, rewrite, or even reinvent the signatures in the book of nature by offering ways of re-fashioning the body.

As well as being the most complex, versatile, and most eloquent non-verbal communicator, the face is at the same time a 'non-verbal liar'[1] in that it can withhold information and simulate expressions which are completely psychologically unfounded. Thus it is not surprising that the activities of the face have been the main focus of rhetoric since antiquity. Furthermore, the expressions conveyed by the countenance often precede and even more often exceed verbal communication:

> But the face is sovereign. It is this makes us humble, threatening, flattening, sad, cheerful, proud, or submissive; men hang on this; men fix their gaze on this; this is watched even before we start to speak; [...] this makes us understand many things; this often replaces words altogether.[2]

Moreover, the face continues to 'speak' long after speech has died and continues to communicate whenever words fail. Due to its highly flexible and sensitive features, the face has become the chief target of physiognomy and is the main focus of this book. Like the

---

1 Paul Ekman, Wallace V. Friesen, Phoebe Ellsworth, 'Conceptual ambiguities', in Paul Ekman ed., *Emotion in the Human Face* (Cambridge: Cambridge University Press, 1982) 7–22, 18.

2 Quintilian, *The Orator's Education* XI 3.72, trans. and ed. by Donald A. Russell (Cambridge [Mass]: Harvard University Press, 2001) 123. Compare also Cicero, *De Oratore* III 69.220f.

skilled orator, the capable actor is expected to emphasise a passionate speech by an appropriate physiognomic subtext. Thus it is asserted by Thomas Overbury in his portrait of the 'Excellent Actor': 'whatsoever is commendable in the grave Orator, is most exquisitely perfect in him; for by a full and significant action of the body, he charmes our attention.'[1] Conveying certain emotions via facial expressions and creating signs that move silently between the stage and the theatre audience, the actor succeeds in both catching the attention of his spectators and stirring their emotions. It is the manipulative power involved in the process of *movere* and *persuadere*, which even in antiquity raised suspicion about the validity of bodily eloquence. As an area where impression and expression collide, the human visage can be regarded as a very revealing and, at the same time, utterly unstable document, whose legibility greatly depends not only on the acting skill of its owner but also on the reading proficiency of its beholder. While it reveals certain traits of character insofar as they are engraved upon its surface, its dynamic features are constantly at risk of being manipulated, which can impede its analysis and put a challenge to its beholder. Both the dissimulating deceiver and the simulating courtier[2] can apply the tools provided by physiognomy in order to belie their true characters. At the same time, however, they can be 'unmasked' by vigilant observers, who are aware of the physiognomic scheme and base their 'readings' of their opponents on certain expressions that are thought to be beyond human control.

The potential danger of misreadings, however, could not impair the popularity of this 'lawdable science'[3]. After all, in everyday life, we constantly examine and interpret faces and thus either consciously or instinctively apply physiognomic axioms for deciphering our vis-à-vis. Facial features are intuitively connected to certain passions of the mind. Furthermore, the language of the body is universal and accessible to everybody, disregarding their education or nationality. As it was attested by Charles Darwin, many pathological reac-

---

1 Wilfrid J. Paylor ed., *The Overburian Characters: To which is added A Wife by Sir Thomas Overbury* (Oxford: Blackwell, 1936) 76.
2 Cf. for instance Baldassare Castiglione, *The Booke of the Courtier,* translated by Thomas Hoby (London: D. Nutt, 1900).
3 Thomas Hill, *The Contemplation of Mankinde* (London: Seres, 1571) 2.

tions that become visible in the human face are the same worldwide and follow the same communicative patterns. It is striking that in order to substantiate his claims regarding the expression of emotions, Darwin refers to Shakespeare's plays. To support his observations of expressions of rage, Darwin cites Henry's battle speech, which infuses 'a terrible aspect' into the eyes of his soldiers, urging them to 'set the teeth, and stretch the nostrils wide', to 'stiffen the sinews' and 'summon up the blood' (*Henry V* 3.1.7–15). And in *King John*, for instance, he diagnoses typical signs of wonder and astonishment.[1] Nonetheless, Shakespeare, whom Darwin praises as 'an excellent judge' that shows a 'wonderful knowledge of the human mind'[2] does not always comply with science. Commenting on Juliet's claim that her blushing is prevented by the darkness surrounding her, Darwin distances himself from his favourite source, claiming, 'Shakespeare […] erred.'[3] Like paling, blushing, thus Darwin argues, is an involuntary, cross-cultural somatic action, which can neither be repressed nor generated by an act of will wherefore especially women, 'who are great blushers'[4], are thought to even blush in the dark.

One could argue, of course, that Shakespeare, in this particular instance, referred to Romeo's and the spectators' perspective, who, in the logic of the play, could not see Juliet's face (even though they did since the scene was acted in daylight). This explanation would certainly exculpate him from Darwin's accusation. In Darwin's view, however, this particular instance becomes a welcome opportunity to confirm his role as scientist, to distance himself from his literary 'mentor', and thereby to authorise his own work, which emerges victorious in the combat between literature and science. And yet it is Shakespeare, or rather, Hamlet who has the final say in Darwin's treatise. Quite remarkably, Darwin chooses the Hecuba scene to round off a study that claims that most emotions and facial expressions are not culturally determined but biological in origin:

---

1   Charles Darwin, *The Expression of Emotions in Man and Animals*, ed. by Francis Darwin (London: Pickering, 1989) 184f., 218f.
2   Ibidem 285.
3   Ibidem 262f.
4   Ibidem 262.

> Is it not monstrous that this player here,
> But in a fiction, in a dream of passion,
> Could force his soul so to his own conceit
> That from her working all his visage wann'd
> A broken voice, and his whole function suiting,
> Which forms to his conceit? And all for nothing!
> > *Hamlet*, ii, 2[1]

In contrast to Darwin's findings, which support his assumptions that the emergence of emotions on the bodily surface resists man's control, the monstrous acting of the First Player suggests that some passions, such as anger, disgust, surprise, happiness and even tears can be feigned. At first glance, therefore, this particular quotation from *Hamlet* seems to undermine rather than support Darwin's findings. The scientist, however, has shortened Hamlet's speech according to his purposes. It is not 'for nothing' but 'for Hecuba' that the player's eyes fill with tears. Taking into account the empathic dimension of playing, crying *for* Hecuba equals crying *with* Hecuba. To produce tears, sorrow has to be evoked as *com*passion, a suffering with someone else, and thus has to be truly felt in order to emerge on the surface. Hence, Darwin can refer to this passage without undermining his main argument, which stresses the involuntary translation of the passions. As it will also become apparent in the reading of Shakespeare's plays, in most cases, weeping has to be counted among the truthful expressions of emotions. However, tears can be simulated on occasion. Thereby it is especially the female body that seems capable of this art as it was regarded as having more liquid at its disposal than its male counterpart and thus was especially prone to spontaneous overflows. To squeeze artificial tears out of the male body, however, is a task that can only be fulfilled by a highly skilled performer or by employing external devices. The boy actor in *The Taming of the Shrew*, whose acting skills have yet to develop, for instance, is advised to have an onion at hand in order to produce tears on command (Induction 1, 120–24). The great effect weeping can have on fellow men constitutes the necessity to find tools and tricks

---

1   Charles Darwin, *The Expression of Emotions in Man and Animals*, ed. by Francis Darwin (London: Pickering, 1989) 285.

to evoke this reaction in the body. Ovid already emphasised the eloquence attributed to tears, which carry weight especially when dealing with women. In his *Ars Amatoria*, he advises men in courtship to carry a vial with them so they could soften their beloved by producing 'tears' whenever necessary.[1] Ovid's love rhetoric yet again points to the ambivalence of facial features, which challenges their beholder and probes their perceptive skills. As already suggested, however, weeping in Shakespeare is presented as an emotion which tends to be reliable and genuine.[2]

As Darwin's reliance on Shakespeare suggests, literature heavily draws from non-verbal signifiers when sketching character types or describing certain emotions and passions of the mind. For expounding the problems of physiognomic inference, drama emerges as a particularly apt genre. First, the theatre provides a space for counter-discourse by drawing from social discourses of the time and re-enacting them in front of an audience, who are encouraged to carefully probe and critically reflect upon their validity and applicability. Thus, at the theatre, the debate evolving from the contested pseudo-science of physiognomy can be performed, contested, and discussed both onstage as part of the action and beyond, by urging the audience to participate in the debate. Secondly, by enacting face-readings onstage, a metatheatrical level is opened up, which holds up a mirror not only to life but also to drama and to the theatre *per se*. In every face-reading, regardless of its success, we are constantly reminded that not only the actors onstage but all men and women, including the audience in front of the stage, are merely players. Against this meta-dramatic and self-reflexive tapestry, two notions of performance come into view, namely the theatrical and social *personae*. Etymologically, the term *persona* refers to a theatrical visor, but this meaning was already obsolete in the Middle Ages. Referring to theatrical terminology, a *persona* denotes a metaphorical mask which has been imposed on man by his environment and denotes the *homo sociologus*, which is subjected to certain socio-cultural constraints.[3]

---

1   Compare, Ovid, *Ars Amatoria* I 659f.
2   Compare page 56f.
3   The notion of the *homo sociologus* reaches back to Cicero's *De Officiis*, 107–25.

Promoting, questioning, and ultimately challenging the communicative value of the face, the theatre opens up several different levels of perception, involving the audience in a physiognomic panopticon in which masks are adopted, altered, and begin to crumble under the discerning gaze of their beholders. Especially in Shakespeare's plays, the countenance becomes a battlefield upon which concepts of simulation and dissimulation are being challenged and physiognomic axioms claiming a sympathetic relation between body and mind come under scrutiny. As this study will demonstrate, it is not so much the descriptions of faces and the interpretation of individual facial features which make Shakespeare's physiognomic scheme an interesting field to be explored but rather the performance of face-readings, their preparation, execution, and reception, which deserves closer attention. The questions of who 'translates' and verbalises physiognomies in a play and who is subjected to face-readings can shed some new light on Shakespeare's mode of characterisation, especially with regard to the (de)construction of masculinity and femininity. Rather than merely presenting Shakespeare's physiognomic armamentarium, the present study demonstrates how Shakespeare does things with physiognomy and focuses on the performances of physiognomic readings. The physiognomic inventory that will be established (chapter 4) shall serve as a starting point, providing the tools for a closer analysis of selected plays, which concentrates on the ways physiognomic readings are enacted.

Putting two or more *dramatis personae* onstage to face or outface each other, Shakespeare stages physiognomic readings and attains an interesting effect. Not only does he direct the spectators' view to specific characters, which are read out onstage, but he explores ways in which characters are established in the encounter of 'self' and 'other'. Thereby, he inaugurates a meta-dramatic discourse which involves the audience in the process of facing, deciphering, and stereotyping a particular *persona*. Physiognomic readings in which figures are subjected to the 'eye' of both the theatre-goers and their counterparts onstage, often mark a focal point in the individual plays when certain roles are confirmed, power relations are established, and masks become brittle.

Being aware of the ambivalence connected to specific facial features and potential misreadings, which might arise from anti-physiognomic axioms that are uttered by *dramatis personae* such as Duncan, the audience is encouraged to participate in the character readings which are performed onstage and either confirm or challenge their interpretation. In many instances, the audience will comply with the explanations given by the figures onstage not only because the principle of word scenery obliges them to assent but also because the character proposing the reading seems reliable and trustworthy. Furthermore, there might not be any contradictory analyses offered, or the reading could meet common physiognomic axioms, which they are already familiar with. However, this kind of mutual agreement with regard to a face-reading is not always given. The onstage reading might turn out to be fatally misleading: Othello, for instance, blind with rage, tragically misjudges the 'fair paper' (*Othello* 4.2.73) of Desdemona's 'alabaster' (5.2.5) face, and Romeo fatally distrusts the traces of life on Julia's countenance and overlooks the 'crimson in [her] lips and in [her] cheeks' (*Romeo and Juliet* 5.3.95). Even though these two examples of lethal negligence and fatal disregard of outward indicators ultimately support the validity of physiognomic inference and promote the legibility of the human face, they have fatal consequences on the level of the plot. Beside the successful and failed face-reading, a third category emerges from Shakespeare's plays, namely the reading that fails successfully. As outside observers who observe the observers onstage observing each other,[1] the audience holds a privileged position in that they have some insight into the reliability of specific facial documents. Thus, when Richard Gloucester announces that he can 'smile, and murder whiles I smile / And wet my cheeks with artificial tears' (*3 Henry VI* 3.2.182f.), we are prepared for a facial self-fashioning, which might lead other characters astray. Therefore those face-readings that seem unsuccessful onstage may be regarded to have failed successfully if one considers the effect on the theatre audience, who are henceforth sensitized to the physiognomic subtext underlying the play.

---

1 Cf. Dietrich Schwanitz, 'Shakespeare stereoskopisch: Die Schule des Sehens und die Optik der Praxis', *Shakespeare Jahrbuch* 129 (1993) 134–49, 136f.

To further investigate the different levels of physiognomic discourse is the task of this book. Tracing face-readings in selected plays, it shall be examined how Shakespeare's plays reflect, comment on, and engage in the physiognomic debate of his time. On considering the scope of physiognomic characterisation, colour and racial differences are probably the first aspects to come to mind. Shylock, the Jew, and the figure of the Moor, namely Morocco, Aaron, and Othello, as well as distinctly foreign characters such as Caliban and also Cleopatra catch our eyes with their outward appearances, which clearly demarcate them as 'others', as alien figures that are identifiable as such at first glance. Especially in connection with these *personae*, a closer analysis of face-readings turns out to be very revealing, as it can provide some insight into the politics of ethnical identity and the question of how same- and otherness is constructed and deconstructed through the interpretation of facial signifiers. It is remarkable, for instance, that the outcome of a physiognomic portrayal is often less relevant than the politics of reading attached to it. Since physiognomic descriptions function like scenery does in Shakespearean drama in that they must be verbalized in order to materialize onstage and to be perceived by the audience, it becomes highly significant, which characters emerge as readers, who actively engage in physiognomic analyses, and which can be regarded as 'documents' that are subjected to their opponents' view. It is the *discursive body* therefore, which is at the centre of this book, the body as it is perceived, de- or prescribed by others, the body that materializes in speech and also in writing.[1] In most plays, only one figure qualifies as physiognomic reader by frequently directing the view towards facial and bodily expressions while showing a deep understanding of the manipulating forces that

---

1 Compare Bruce R. Smith, 'Prickly Characters', in David M. Bergeron ed., *Reading and Writing in Shakespeare* (Newark: University of Delaware Press, and London: Associated University Press, 1996) 25–44, 25: 'The illusion of character in the theatre, like the illusion of personhood outside the theatre, demands two things: speech and a body. Or rather, it demands just one thing: a speaking body. What an embodied speaker says about himself provides one perspective on the subject; what other embodied speakers say *to* him provides a second; what they say *about* him behind his back provides a third. The result is an illusion that is situated among three dimensions in sound just as it is among three dimensions in space.'

could influence and alter outward appearances. These 'physiognomists', as I term them, seem remarkably faceless themselves since they are only rarely, if ever at all, subjected to face readings.

The distinction between reader and document, or, respectively, physiognomic writer and script provides a fresh perspective on questions of authority and authorisation within individual plays. Making the counterpart the object of a physiognomic reading by textualising its body becomes a means of authorising the self. It is remarkable that many of those figures which *prima facie* would classify as 'documents' and favoured objects of racial or gendered readings turn out to be the most powerful and skilled 'physiognomists' onstage: they not only know how to progress from the outer to the inner man and how to infer 'that within' from external signifiers but they also very cunningly make use of their ability to fashion their faces and bodies while manipulating others in their readings and thus taking care of their own reception. In Shakespeare's globe, physiognomic encounters, however, often provide an opportunity to 'read back', to question, and to counter alienating readings by looking back at the 'reader' and thereby destabilising the latter's authority. Othello, Cleopatra, and Shylock, for instance, challenge their 'texts', which have been imposed on them by society, by performing their own physiognomic readings in which they authorize themselves to participate in the dynamics of mutual inscription while undermining their racial and ethnical 'otherness'.

Even though the decipherment of the body follows very specific rules, which are set down in physiognomic manuals, the interpretation of bodily signs ultimately depends on the recipient, who might deliberately misjudge certain features and thereby thwart the correspondence between body and psyche. Besides analysing the physiognomic catalogue employed in the individual plays and taking a closer look at the ways in which certain features contribute to the characterisation of the *personae*, it is the act of face-readings, the question of their reliability, which ties in with the question of trustworthiness of physiognomic readers and the authenticity of the 'document', which will under scrutiny in the analyses to follow. The intimate connection between physiognomy and graphology will become relevant especially with regard to concepts of authenticity and authorship. As indicated by the etymology of the word *character*, both areas are closely intertwined. In her description of Gutenberg's printing machine, Margreta de Grazia hits the mark when she humanizes the letters, which appear to show 'a body' (stem of metal) standing on 'feet' with 'shoulders' supporting a face whose physiognomy is literally its character, '*a legible face*'.[1] Thus, we constantly have to remind ourselves that a *character* is a component of a greater document in which it joins other linguistic elements to constitute meaning: 'Characters, that is, are not people, they are elements of a linguistic structure, lines in a drama, and more basically, words on a page.'[2] While being part of a greater scheme of signification, each individual character is also genuinely legible on its own, which takes us to the origin of physiognomic theory.

The concept of man as a decipherable being hearkens back to the Paracelsian doctrine of signatures, which conceives the world as a book in which every character has its assigned place and, bearing the inscription of its maker, provides some insight not only into its own innermost being but also into the greater design of the world. The latter is comprised in the *liber corporis*, to which physiognomy is the key that is available to all men, disregarding their nationality or status:

> [...] there are mystically in our faces certain Characters which carry in them the motto of our Souls, in which he that cannot read ABC may read our natures. [...] The Finger of GOD hath left an Inscription upon all His works, not graphical, composed of Letters, but of several forms, constitutions, parts, and operations, which, aptly joined together, do make one word that doth express their natures.[3]

1   Margreta de Grazia, 'Imprints: Shakespeare, Gutenberg and Descartes', in Terence Hawkes, ed., *Alternative Shakespeares* (London/New York: Routledge, 1996) Vol. 2, 63–94, 86.
2   Stephen Orgel, *The Authentic Shakespeare and Other Problems of the Early Modern Stage* (New York/London: Routledge, 2002) 8. See also Jonathan Goldberg, *Shakespeare's Hand* (Minneapolis/London: University of Minnesota Press, 2003) esp. 10–47.
3   William A. Greenhill ed., *Sir Thomas Browne's Religio Medici, Letter to a Friend and Christian Morals* (Peru: Sherwood Sugden and Company, 1990) 98.

In many of Shakespeare's plays, the connection between graphical and physiognomic *characters*, which Thomas Browne explicates here in his *Religio Medici*, is alluded to. Letters that are produced or read onstage, forged documents, and instances of misjudged handwriting prompt a reading, which often progresses from page to face. Shortly after Lady Macbeth, for instance, found some evidence of her husband's effeminate nature in his letter, which is 'full o'th'milk of human kindness' (*Macbeth* 1.5.15), the scold character enters the scene as if to provide the physiognomic text to this reading. It is with the audience that this interaction of characters involving written signs with *dramatis personae* and with the spectators in front of the stage, stands and falls since the theatre-goer is the one to challenge or confirm Lady Macbeth's judgement and consequently to identify her as 'physiognomist' of the play.

Before further engaging in the textualisation and decipherment of the body and before taking a closer look at those figures that qualify as 'physiognomists' and examining physiognomic readings in Shakespeare's plays, a brief overview of physiognomic thought, its reputation in the early modern world, and its relevance for the theatre is given. To identify physiognomic features, which become relevant in Shakespeare's scheme of characterisation, an outline of facial features and their interpretation in accordance with physiognomic manuals of the time will be provided. Following this introduction to Shakespeare's physiognomic inventory, several close readings of selected plays shall serve to illustrate the physiognomic scheme underlying Shakespeare's plays as well as differences and parallels in the function and functionalisation of physiognomy in the tragedies, comedies, and histories. While this book lays no claim to giving an exhaustive account of physiognomy on Shakespeare's stage, it aims to provide a fresh approach to some of his most popular plays in order to shed some new light on the construction of characters and the significance of non-verbal communication in Shakespeare's dramatic writings.

2 A Brief Overview of Physiognomic Thought and Theory

Physiognomy, the art (*gnomos*) to know nature (*physis*), reaches back to antiquity where it originated as a branch of medicine,[1] which is based on the inference of visible signs and symptoms. The first physiognomic treatise, the *Physiognomonica*, which dates to the fourth century, is attributed to Pseudo-Aristotle, who defines physiognomy as the analysis of 'movements, gestures of the body, colour, characteristic facial expression, the growth of the hair, the smoothness of the skin, the voice, condition of the flesh, the parts of the body, and the build of the body as a whole'[2]. From these audio-visual signs or impressions certain characteristic traits are inferred, which either by nature or by habit left their traces on man's outer appearance. The latter becomes transparent in that body and soul are closely linked to each other: 'when the character of the soul changes', writes Pseudo-Aristotle, 'it changes also the form of the body, and conversely, when the form of the body changes, it changes the character of the soul'[3]. Just like an illness might affect the soul, a melancholic mind will eventually rub off on the body.

Of all bodily parts, the face is given top priority in any characterological reading. Not only does it present itself as an area which, in Western civilisations, is usually uncovered, it also bears the most diverse, multi-faceted, and variable 'text', whose interpretation proves extremely fruitful even though it is exceptionally challenging. To a

---

1 Galen ascribes physiognomy to Hippocrates (*Anim. mor. cor. temp.* 7). For an extensive study of the history of physiognomy see Martin Porter, *Windows of the Soul: Physiognomy in European Culture 1470–1780* (Oxford: Clarendon Press, 2005).

2 Ps.-Aristotle, *Physiognomonica*, i 806a 25, in Aristotle, *Minor Works*, trans. by W. S. Hett (London/ Cambridge [Mass.]: Harvard University Press, 1936). All quotations from this work that are cited hereafter follow this edition.

3 Ps.-Aristotle, *Phyisognomonica*, i 808b.

far greater extent than the body, the face is liable to change. Stirred by emotions, its aspect can alter rapidly from one moment to the next even though its physiognomy in a strict sense remains the same. Thus, it is not surprising that the majority of the *Physiognomonica* is devoted to facial features and expressions. For their interpretation, Pseudo-Aristotle offers three different methods, the ethnological, the zoological, and the expression method, two of which he discards again almost immediately since they fall short of the purpose. The expression method is directed towards the affections, emotions, and passions that perturb the mind and is thus concerned with temporary features only. Hence, it does not necessarily provide a greater insight into man's character if the latter is understood as qualities and features that are innate and consistent. The ethnological approach is deemed just as unsuccessful. Even though it is concerned with static features, it does little more than support the assumption that the body is formed, or impressed, as it were, by ambient environmental conditions. It provides explanations why people with dark hair and skin can be found in hotter regions of the world while in the inhabitants of the northern hemisphere tend to have hair of a lighter colour and a fairer skin. These observations, however, bear only little relevance for physiognomic characterisation. The key to man's inner being is supposed to be the zoological trail, which Pseudo-Aristotle follows for most of his treatise. If men and animals are integrated in one and the same sign system and subjected to one and the same signifying force, it can be assumed that they bear the same inscriptions on their faces and bodies, which reveal their inner disposition.

And yet, this particular branch of physiognomy is also problematic. Not only because, as Pseudo-Aristotle rightly points out, nobody looks exactly like an animal but also because the characterological implications of individual animals are disputable. Even though some animals appear rather unambiguous in this respect (the lion serves as a symbol of strength, the fox represents cunning, and the magpie has genuine thieving associations), others are polyvalent and evoke different connotations, which change with their regional and cultural context. While in antiquity, for instance, the raven was considered a symbol of prudence and helpfulness,[1] it is evoked as harbinger of mischief by Shakespeare. Thus, in *Macbeth*, the hoarse croaking of the raven announces 'the fatal entrance of Duncan' (1.6.37).[2] To avoid being led astray by zoological inference, Pseudo-Aristotle suggests listing all the animals which show the same feature, in order to rule out the possibility that the quality in question is accompanied by an opposing feature which might undermine its characterological implications. Applying this method Pseudo-Aristotle comes to the conclusion that soft hair indicates cowardice whereas rough hair points to courage, a hypothesis which is confirmed, or rather: not contested by a comparison to the animal world (sheep and deer have soft hair, lions and boars rough hair). Notwithstanding this impediment, the inversion of certain characteristics from analogies in the animal world remained a popular method within the field of physiognomy and also became very prominent in the second major treatise in the art of character-reading, which is Giambattista Della Porta's *De Humana Physiognomonia* (1586).

   While physiognomic thought did not hibernate for around 2000 years to be finally awakened by Della Porta, the *Physiognomonia* is generally regarded as the most comprehensive and elaborate study of facial and bodily features since antiquity[3] and provides an extensive overview of the classical and medieval physiognomic tradition. Amongst others Pseudo-Aristotle, Galen, Philo, Polemon, Adamantius, Rhazes, Conciliator, Michael Scot, Albertus Magnus, Pietro d'Abano, and Avicenna have their share in the physiognomic readings offered and Della Porta comments on their analyses or expands on them wherever he feels the need. Even though physiognomic thought in the Middle Ages still awaits a closer analysis, its prevalence within this period seems indubitable. Physiognomies

---

1   Compare Herodot, *Historia* 4.15; Livius, *Ab Urbe Condita* 7.26.
2   Another example can be found in *Hamlet* where this image introduces the scene of murder in the performance of the *Mousetrap*: 'Come, the croaking raven doth bellow for revenge' (3.2.248). See also *A Midsummer Night's Dream* 5.1.376–78, *Much Ado About Nothing* 2.3.81–3, *1 Henry VI* 4.2.15, *Othello* 4.1.20–2, *The Rape of Lucrece* 165, and *Richard III* 4.4.507.
3   Compare Georg Gustav Fülleborn, 'Abriss einer Geschichte und Litteratur der Physiognomik', in ibidem, *Beyträge zur Geschichte der Philosophie* (Züllichau/Freystadt: Frommann, 1797) 1–188, 124.

were transmitted through Latin translations of Arabic writings, which amongst others secured the reception of the *Physiognomonica*. Furthermore, biblical references, such as Ecclesiastes 8:1: 'a man's wisdom maketh his face to shine', or Isaiah 3:9: 'the shew of their countenance doth witness against them', as well as literary sources, such as Chaucer's *Canterbury Tales*, which comprise numerous physiognomic descriptions, bear witness to a general awareness of this pseudo-science and the notion of the body's legibility. Last but not least, in the Late Middle Ages, physiognomy was part of the curriculum at numerous universities across Europe.[1]

With the advent of the printing press, the art of character reading became available to an even wider audience, which is one reason for the success of Della Porta's treatise. Another reason could have been his fresh approach to physiognomy as a science that was presented as being largely independent from its affiliated disciplines of chiromancy and metoposcopy, which outshone it throughout preceding centuries.[2] Furthermore, in Della Porta's treatise, physiognomy was to a great extent disconnected from astronomy. Unlike in other physiognomies that circulated in 17th century Britain such as John ab Indagine's, Richard Saunders', and Pierre de la Chambre's writings, the influence of the stars on man's disposition is factored out in the *Physiognomonia* in favour of a more rational, epistemological, and scientific approach. This might have been the reason why Della Porta's writings were not deemed as promoting mantic arts like other physiognomies of the time. Under the cloak of *scientia*, Della Porta's treatise was spared from being put on the *index auctorum et librorum prohibitorum*, which listed Bartolommeo della Rocca Cocles', Juan Huarte's, and John ab Indagine's physiognomical and chiromantical works. Although not named explicitly, however, the *Physiognomonia* undoubtedly fell into the category of occult writings as it was defined in the decree issued in 1559 by Paul IV, which forbade '*libri omnes et scripta chiromantiae, physionomiae, aeromantiae, gemantiae, hydromantiae, onomantiae, pyromantiae, vel necromantae*'.[3] This

---

1 Compare Martin Porter, *Windows of the Soul: Physiognomy in European Culture 1470–1780* (Oxford: Clarendon Press, 2005) 75.

2 Compare Fülleborn, 1–188, 6.

3 Franz Heinrich Reusch ed., *Die Indices librorum prohibitorum des sechzehnten*

interdict was reinforced by Sixtus V in 1590. Even though in the revised decree, physiognomy was no longer listed amongst the forbidden arts, some individual treatises still got banned.

Despite its popularity, however, physiognomy continued to be discredited as occult science elsewhere and was at times even associated with witchcraft as for instance in James' *First Daemonologie* (1597):

> For he [*Sathan*] will oblish himselfe to teach them artes and sciences [...] the thought none knows but GOD; except so far as yee may ghesse by their countenance, as one who is doubtleslie learned inough in the *Physiognomie*: Yea, he will make his schollers to creepe in credite with Princes, by fore-telling them mannie greate thinges [...]. And yet are all these thinges but deluding of the senses, and no waies true in substance.[1]

In the same year in which the *Daemonologie* was published, the 'Acte for Punyshment of Rogues Vagabonde and Sturdy Beggars' was passed, which prohibited the practice of all divinatory arts, including physiognomy:

> [...] all idle psons going about in any Cuntry eyther begging or using any subtile Crafte or unlawfull Games and Playes, or fayning themselves to have knowledge in Phisiognomye Palmestry or other like crafty Scyence, or ptending that they can tell Destenyes Fortunes or such other like fantasticall Ymagynacons [...] shalbe taken adjudged and deemed Rogues Vagabonde and Sturdy Beggers, and [...] be stripped naked from the middle upwarde and shall be openly whipped untill his or her body be bloudye [...].[2]

Notwithstanding Queen Elizabeth's decree, a strong interest in physiognomy persisted as various treatises circulating at the time attest. In fact, the bad press the pseudo-science received could have sparked a novel enthusiasm for face-readings and brought physiognomy centre stage. The theatre, in any case, discovered the controver-

---

Jahrhunderts (Nieuwkoop: de Graaf, 1970 [1886]) 196f.

1 King James, *The first Daemonologie* (1597), ed. by George B. Harrison (Edinburgh: Edinburgh University Press, 1966) 21f.

2 39° Elizabeth c. 3,4 (1597).

sial discipline for itself. Condemned as occult art, defended as natural science, and often applied as an appreciated tool for self-fashioning not least by the Queen herself, who monitored her portrayals and dug deep into the paint-pot to let her face appear youthful, spotless, and unwrinkled until old age,[1] physiognomy was a subject that seemed particularly apt to be discussed, challenged, and possibly resurrected onstage. But before turning to the theatre, let us focus on another work published towards the end of the 16th century, which became seminal for the English speaking world, namely Thomas Hill's *The Contemplation of Mankinde*.

Hill's treatise, which appeared fifteen years prior to the first edition of the *Physiognomonia* connects to Della Porta's physiognomic manual insofar as it pursues a similar 'scientific' approach with one exception: two small chapters on metoposcopy and chiromancy remain as relics of Cocles' *A Brief Epitome of the Whole Arte of Physiognomy*, which Hill translated in 1556 and which his *Contemplation* is modelled on. Covering 236 pages, the manual offers a detailed catalogue of physiognomic features, which, like Della Porta's, also draws from other sources, mainly Italian writers. The analyses of facial and bodily features are carried out with great diligence whereby every single element is examined in considerable depth. Giving consideration to the origin of physiognomic inference in Greek medicine, Hill devotes the first chapters to the theory of the four humours and addresses the hot, cold, dry, and moist as well as the temperate and distemperate body before moving on to the colour of the body being the main indicator of a sanguine, melancholic, choleric, or phlegmatic disposition. In the physiognomic catalogue that follows, Hill adheres to physiognomic conventions insofar as facial features are at the centre of his study: 'no part there is of mans bodie, which like expresseth and uttereth the passion of the minde, as the face properly doth' (f. 93). The colour and shape of the eyes, the form of the nose, size of the nostrills, the mouth, the lips, the teeth, the chin, and even the condition of the tongue as well as the tone of

---

1   Compare Susan P. Cerasano and Marion Wynne-Davies ed., *Gloriana's Face: Women, Public and Private, in the English Renaissance* (Detroit: Wayne State University Press, 1992).

voice, and more specific features such as the frequency, volume, and pitch of laughter are scrutinised before Hill attends to the rest of the body, gradually progressing from the throat and the condition of the backbone and the belly to the shape of the feet and the ankles.

In complexity and elaborateness, the *Brief Epitome* resembles the *Physiognomonia*. Its catalogue follows the same structure, scanning the body from the head to the toes, whereby the implications of a specific shape, colour, or texture are meticulously spelt out. In addition to the analyses of physiognomic features, however, Della Porta not only offers a more complex introduction to the art of character reading by providing the theoretical background to the interaction of body and soul, but also includes a catalogue of characters. In the Theophrastian tradition, the coward, the shameless, the galoot, and forty other character-types are sketched in a separate book, which is the last of the four books comprised in the treatise. But unlike Theophrast, Della Porta derives his portrayals exclusively from physical qualities. In compliance with his catalogue of physiognomic features, the face is given the most attention. Its pre-eminence over the rest of the body, the shoulders, breast, the extremities and finally the abdominal area, springs from its immediate vicinity to the mind, which, as Della Porta reminds us, is attested by Aristotle and Galen.

The predominance of facial features is reflected in the structure of the study: whilst the first book provides the theoretical framework by considering the correspondence between body and mind, the second book is concerned with the analyses of individual features, two thirds of which are connected to the face. The third chapter is devoted to the most complex and diverse element of the face (and body): the eyes. Due to their closeness to the mind, the eyes are often referred to as as *speculum animi*, as 'windows to the soul', and offer vast data to the physiognomist. Thus Hill comments not only on their size, form, and colour but also on their moisture, shine, movement, and on the frequency of blinking as well as on the symmetry of the pupils. Some of these observations seem more obvious than others. Whereas the common viewer might associate a cloudy, misty expression of the eyes with a dull mind, he will probably miss the nuance between misty eyes or, even worse, small and misty eyes, which point to a malignant and evil mind, and eyes which appear somewhat cloudy due to their light colour, which indicates a timorous character. Before one starts to wonder what conclusions can be drawn from small and light eyes, or, indeed, light and misty eyes, it should be added here that many analyses proposed in Della Porta's treatise, remain slightly vague. A certain ambiguity, however, does not rule out the applicability of physiognomic axioms as such but merely stresses the precautionary approach that should be taken in any face- or body-reading. While individual features are significant in their characterological implications, it is their interaction with other features which eventually constitutes a character.

Leaving some room for interpretation, Hill's *Contemplation* follows the *Physiognomonia* insofar as it does not claim conclusive authority with regard to the interpretations provided but opens up a polyphonic forum bringing together numerous voices from antiquity and the Middle Ages. From the outset of the treatise it is emphasised that man's disposition cannot be deduced from a single though seemingly very telling feature. He is a compound of many individual observations which can be combined into a character portrait and pieced together like a jigsaw. Considering Galen's remark that even physiognomists will err if they rely on but one particular token, a remark which is referred to in the *Physiognomonia*,[1] misreadings are bound to happen. In Hill's *Contemplation of Mankinde*, the potential failure of physiognomic analyses is made even more explicit: not only does the author acknowledge, 'that the bodily notes of Phisiognomating by the naturall conditions of men doe procure and cause a great probablenesse, although no necessitie'[2]. In the preface, he addresses an apologia to the reader, asking for his lenience if the analyses proposed do not hold true:

> [...] if thou canst not attaine unto the certaine knowledge thereof: yet let not thine yll fortune condemne the iudgements and experiences of a number well learned and practised in this Arte: neyther thinke yll on me, who wisheth unto thee well, and have taken the paynes altogether for thy sake.

---

1   Giambattista Della Porta, *De Humana Physiognomonia* (Vici Aequensis, 1586) book 1, chapter 16.
2   Thomas Hill, *The Contemplation of Mankinde* (London: Seres, 1571) f.4.

Hill's *captatio benevolentiae* does not miss its target, especially since it puts the responsibility for the accurateness of physiognomic inference on the reader, who by his 'own iudgement, and experience', it is implied, would not deem this art wrong unless he is met by 'yll fortune'. Thus, it would be considered a case of considerable misfortune, for instance, to come across Socrates and to be asked to judge him by his face. While other sources refer to Zopyros as the one to have called Socrates dull and simple-minded, Hill names Phylemon in this context. On scrutinising Socrates' features, Hill reports, the famous physiognomist pronounced him 'a leacherous person, subtill, a deceyver, covetous, and given to wickednesse'[1]. As it is highly unlikely, however, that Hill's reader would face another Socrates, who constitutes the exception to the rule, the preface succeeds in reinforcing the validity of physiognomic inference.

While the shape and design of the visage, which count among the constant features of the face, are regarded as providing the greatest insight into a particular character, physiognomic readings also consider movable features of the face. In the volatile expressions on the face, temporary emotions and passions of the mind come into view. At this stage, it seems appropriate to briefly leap into the 18th century and review the distinction between the study of static and movable features of the body and thus explicate the distinction between physiognomy and pathognomy. The Zurich pastor Johann Caspar Lavater, who is often, though erroneously, regarded as the founder of physiognomic theory, was the first to offer a definition distinguishing the two branches of physiognomy: 'Die Physiognomik zeigt, was der Mensch überhaupt ist, die Pathognomik, was er im gegenwärtigen Moment ist und welche Emotionen ihn gerade bewegen.'[2] While physiognomy illuminates man's disposition, pathognomy deals with man's temporary being and serves to disclose his current emotional state. Whereas physiognomy is directed to bodily features that are persistent and thus, in Lavater's view, indicative of man's innermost character, pathognomy searches for clues about man's emotions, pas-

---

1   Hill, Preface, vi.
2   Fritz Aerni ed., *Johann Caspar Lavater: Physiognomische Fragmente zur Beförderung der Menschenkenntnis und Menschenliebe – Eine Auswahl* (Waldshut-Tiengen: Aerni, 1996) 166.

sions, and feelings and the ways in which they translate onto one's outer appearance.

Lavater made the distinction following a dispute with the scientist Georg Christoph Lichtenberg, who strongly opposed the rigid focus on innate physical contour to determine a person's character. It is not the shape of the body, the straightness of the back, nor the size of the nose, nor the colour of hair, he argues, which can provide a truthful insight into man's moral character. Far more relevant in his view are the traces left on the face and body in the course of one's life, by one's habits and behaviour. To prove his point, he comes up with a provocative suggestion: if physiognomic inference were to be applied, children whose bodies and faces show some tokens of criminal character must immediately be hanged as a precautionary act on the sheer grounds of their bodily appearance.[1] This prospect of a physiognomic auto-da-fé was not the only criticism Lavater was to take. Lichtenberg published numerous pamphlets, including a *Fragment von Schwänzen / A Fragment of Tails* (1783), which is a characterological analysis of animal tails, to expose the preposterousness of the assumptions made by what seems from his point of view an entirely unlawful, highly speculative, and utterly inflexible science.

Although the awareness of the two branches of physiognomy reaches back to antiquity, the term *pathognomy* was not coined until the late 18th century when it first appeared in Thomas Holcroft's translation of Lavater's *Physiognomische Fragmente*, or *Essays on Physiognomy*, published in 1789. Taking into consideration that early modern 'physiognomy' comprised both the study of the body's constant features and its temporary movements, the term *physiognomy* as it is used in the present study, unless indicated otherwise, will encompass both physiognomic and pathognomic features. Despite the lack of terminological differentiation, moveable features have always played a leading role in the assessment of a particular character, which, as suggested in the Pseudo-Aristotelian treatise, 'took as its basis the characteristic facial expression which are observed to accompany different conditions of mind, such as anger, fear, erotic

---

1   Georg Christoph Lichtenberg, 'Sudelbücher' F.521, in Wolfgang Promies ed.,
     G. C. Lichtenberg: Schriften und Briefe (München: Hanser, 1971) 532.

excitement, and all other passions'.[1] Furthermore, repetitive actions of a particular pathognomic expression are prone to inscribe themselves into one's physiognomy. Somebody who is constantly furrowing his brow will eventually develop the *frons caperata*, a forehead with deep wrinkles indicating a grave and pensive mind.[2] A similar analogy can be drawn with regard to complexion. In accord with Pseudo-Aristotle, Della Porta assigns timidity as the reason for wan skin colour since a person who is frightened involuntarily turns pale almost immediately. People of a fearful disposition, he adds, can be likened to a chameleon, which is of a wan colour and the most timid of all animals, which is why it constantly changes appearance. These examples suggest that even though in his introductory chapter (book 1, chapter 11) Della Porta advises against overestimating temporary features, pathognomic impulses nonetheless inform some of the readings offered in his *Physiognomonia*.

The reference to the animal world, which, in this particular instance, serves to support the link between fear and paleness of skin, is no singular case. Far more frequently than Thomas Hill, Della Porta enters comparative physiognomy and thereby adheres to his predecessors, first and foremost Pseudo-Aristotle. Furthermore, he picks up the zoological method and takes it one step further than his model by including 29 woodcuts in his treatise. Most of these images show a human face next to an animal head, revealing a striking resemblance between their physiognomies, whereby the analogy often arises from one particular feature.

Dull and languid is the gaze of the ox-man, whose flat and bulky nose sticks out his face even more clearly when flanked by his animal counterpart, indicating brazenness and imbecility (Della Porta, 76). Another figure shows a man with a full-bearded face, whose forehead seems overgrown by scalp hair reaching for the nose. This portrait, which is reminiscent of images of Zeus is adequately placed next to the lion (Della Porta, 34), whose presence indicates grandeur, magnanimity, and heroism. Quite a few of Della Porta's archetypical analo-

---

1   Ps.-Aristotle, *Physiognomonica*, i 805a 20–5.
2   Giambattista della Porta, *De Humana Physiognomonia* (Vici Aequensis, 1586) book 2, chapter 4.

gies are linked to personages of rank and fame. We find Socrates next to a deer head (86), whose flat and short muzzle, which mirrors the nose of the philosopher in shape, points to a lewd, bawdy character. Plato's counterpart is a hound (53), whose wide-stretched forehead, which Della Porta also ascribes to Dante Alighieri,[1] indicates a strong sense and an intelligent mind.

While zoomorphism has always been a common method for deducting certain characteristic traits by relating animal features to human begins on the basis of physical similarities,[2] some of the images offered by Della Porta appear rather overdrawn and the resemblance of the two physiognomies so blatantly obvious, especially those which are linked to celebrities, that one cannot help suspecting a certain ironic twist here. One could argue that the exaggeration of the features in question was indispensable for providing unequivocal illustrations of particular characters. And yet in the attempt of investigating and imitating nature's emblematic architecture and its underlying semiological system, a certain playfulness suggests itself, which corresponds to the *lusus scientiae*, which seems indicative of seventeenth century natural science.[3] Mirroring nature's mimeses, Della Porta's woodcuts sum up the *lusus naturae* and, adhering to the grammar underlying the book of nature, provide the key to an efficacious reading of it. The Mannerist painter Giuseppe Arcimboldo (1527–1593) carried this playful scientific approach and the concept of physiognomic readability to extremes. Be it in his depiction of the four elements, the seasons, or in his portrayal of specific professions, faces are metamorphosed into clusters of objects indicative of the 'character' he aims to depict. Thus an assortment of fruits and vegetables resembles autumn, a selection of bare branches are joined together to a profile of an old, weary man with the name of 'winter', and a

---

1 Giambattista della Porta, *De Humana Physiognomonia* (Vici Aequensis, 1586) book 1, chapter 4.
2 Especially Charles Le Brun refers to the analogies between human and animal physiognomy in his *Conférence sur l'expression générale et particulière* held at the Académie Royale in the 1670s. Compare Jennifer Montagu, *The Expression of the Passions* (London: Yale University Press, 1994).
3 Compare Paula Findlen, 'Jokes of Nature and Jokes of Knowledge: The Playfulness of Scientific Discourse in Early Modern Europe', *Renaissance Quarterly* 43/2 (1990) 292–331.

carefully compiled collection of books, graced by glasses in place of eyes, stand in for the librarian. It is this sense of playfulness attached to physiognomic portrayal and physiognomic readings, especially those which are zoologically informed, which also suggests itself in some of Shakespeare's plays and which makes physiognomy a particularly popular and suitable subject to be raised, twisted, and scrutinised on the early modern stage.

Not surprisingly, most of the illustrations in Della Porta's and in Hill's treatises show male faces. Physiognomic reading is highly differentiated according to gender. In reference to the Pseudo-Aristotelian *Physiognomonica*, Della Porta distinguishes the male from the female body. In this, he supports his observations by drawing parallels to the animal world. A broad face, broad shoulders and breast, strong back and arms, big feet and hands, which fit the figure of a lion and are typical features of a man's physiognomy, indicate magnanimity, justice, intrepidness and a desire for victory. A slender face with a narrow forehead, a cramped chest, large hips, a weak back, thin arms and fleshy loins, however, which are assembled in the body of a female panther, point to a narrow-minded, thieving, insidious, irascible, bold, though at the same time timid, and generally disagreeable mind such as a woman's. These highly misogynistic sketches are taken as the foundation, as the basic, innate character, which can be adjusted for better or for worse in closer readings of the bodies under scrutiny, which might alter in the course of one's life. In order to change them for the better, however, one should adhere to Della Porta's advice and exercise caution in the choice of a nurse. For children, he writes, will drink and digest good or bad habits with their milk.[1]

As will be shown in the present study, the predominantly masculine physiognomating eye and patriarchal perspective, which becomes apparent in most treatises on the art of face-reading, is challenged in Shakespeare's plays where it is the female characters that emerge as the most diligent and most enthusiastic physiognomic readers. While those actors, who take over a woman's role onstage,

---

1   Giambattista della Porta, *De Humana Physiognomonia* (Vici Aequensis, 1586) book 1, chapter 15.

might be granted a greater ability to form and perform their faces
and bodies than men playing men, the subjection of the male body
to the female physiognomic eye sheds new light on early modern
gender discourse on both the theatrical and the social stage. As stated
above, physiognomy is a twofold art. While providing the means for
interpreting bodily expressions, it also offers the tools to feign certain
characteristic traits. Thus, it not only instructs the actor how to act his
part and the audience how to 'see', but also teaches people how to
perform themselves and conduct their public behaviour. One of the
treatises encouraging this mode of facial self-fashioning is Thomas
Wright's *The Passions of the Minde* (1601), which closely examines the
body's liability to passions whose translation onto the bodily surface
lies beyond man's control but at the same time provides a manual on
how to feign their external signs. The latter is too scarcely practised,
laments Wright in his 'Preface to the Reader', before pronouncing
the aim of his writing, which is to teach his countrymen, who show
a 'naturall inclination to Vertue and honestie', the necessary tools to
enable them to compete with 'those brazen and darke countenances'
that dwell in hotter climates and to adopt some of the techniques
of the inhabitants of the southern hemisphere, 'who never change
themselves although they commit, yea, and be reprehended of
enormous offences'[1]. Thus, for 'the good of [his] Countrie', Wright
feels appointed to teach his readers 'a certain politique craftinesse'
and instruct them in the art of facial rhetoric and ways to control and
alter their countenance 'by wit and will'[2]. The learned eye and skilled
physiognomist, however, will still be able to catch a glimpse of the
true character, which might shine through the adopted mask.

Similar to Thomas Wright, Thomas Hill does not deny that man
might interfere in the natural translation of the inner disposition onto
the bodily surface. Legible, 'outwarde notes' become apparent espe-
cially 'in those, which lyve after their affection and appetites, rather
than governing themselves by reason', and yet, Hill adds, 'none of
the wise and godly (which is by an inwarde working of the spirite) do

---

1 Thomas Wright, *The Passions of the Minde in Generall* (London: Helme, 1620)
   Preface, no page numbers.
2 Ibidem, 149.

lyve after reason'.[1] This hypothesis is as presumptuous as it is wrong. Nonetheless, with regard to physiognomic inference, it can hold its ground since beauty, which is regarded to accompany a wise, godly mind,[2] has no need for deception though it may deceive. Even physiognomists question an uncritical approach to the Neoplatonic concept of *kalokagathia*. Della Porta, for instance, refers to Alcibiades, who was regarded attractive but cantankerous, and Helen, who was notorious for her infidelity. While most physiognomists seem to agree that especially beauty which occurs in a female body should be handled with care, the divergence of beauty and goodness remains the exception to the rule. Thus Della Porta adds to these examples that they are but exceptions to the rule.

Deformity, however, is quite a different case and predominantly regarded as a reliable indicator of moral corruption. 'Deformed persons are commonly even with nature', Francis Bacon asserts, 'for as nature hath done ill by them, so do they by nature.'[3] Bacon regards the soul as being trapped in the body and thus predisposed to (de-)form itself according to the space it inhabits. This reasoning is based on the belief that virtue can only develop in an agreeable *physis* whereas a misshapen body causes a corruption of the mind. This concept of human predestination is shared by Levinus Lemnius, whose treatise entitled *The Secret Miracles of Nature* provides an aid for self-diagnoses in order to maintain a healthy body and a healthy mind:

> For where there is an errour about some principle part, there the mind partakes of some inconvenience, and cannot perfectly perform her offices. So they that are deformed with a bunch-back, so it be a natural Infirmity, and not accidental, nor come by any fall or blow, are commonly wicked and malicious.[4]

---

1   Thomas Hill, *The Contemplation of Mankinde* (London: Seres, 1571) f. 2
2   Compare Baldassare Castiglione, *The Booke of the Courtier*, trans. by Thomas Hoby (London: D. Nutt, 1900) 348.
3   *The Works of Francis Bacon*, ed. by James Spedding et al. (London: Longman et al, 1857) Vol. 3, 367f.
4   Levinus Lemnius, *The Secret Miracles of Nature* (London: Jo. Streater, 1658) 131. Compare Baldassare Castiglione, *The Book of the Courtier*, trans. by Thomas Hoby (London: D. Nutt, 1900) 349.

Physical deformity cannot be hidden, nor covered up by cunning play and thus counts as an unambiguous indicator of a malignant mind. However, there are exceptions to the rule. Not unlike a beautiful face, an unattractive countenance might mislead the beholder and prompt overhasty judgements. The most famous example illustrating the potential disparity between body and mind is the often cited Socrates. His bulbous nose, protuberant eyes, and rather bulky lips contribute to a grotesque, derisory exterior, which Alcibiades compared to Silenus' appearance.[1] A physiognomist's judgement of his face can only be damning. However, Socrates himself did not object to Zopyros' unfavourable reading of his character as imbecile and dull.[2] Instead, he is said to have confessed to these vices, claiming that nature had indeed entrenched these properties in him but he has successfully beaten them by reason. The intervention in, and alteration of a character, which is suggested by Socrates, challenges the belief in man's physical and moral predisposition. What is more, it defies the foundation of physiognomic reasoning, which ultimately relies on the inference of certain characteristic traits from specific visible signs and denies a potential disparity of body and mind. And yet, physio-gnomists have always been aware of this problem and confronted it in their manuals by referring to the paradox of Socrates.

Rather than refuting physiognomic axioms and invalidating the claim of the body's legibility (after all, Socrates himself is said to have employed images asserting the correspondence of body and mind)[3], Socrates' Silenic appearance illustrates man's co-authorship in his character. On the assumption that man naturally strives for goodness, the case of Socrates is cited as evidence proving that 'the imperfections of nature may be reformed by Vertue, and that a man may in some sort resist his Destiny, if he be wise'.[4] Notwithstanding man's

---

1 Plato, *Symposion* 215b.
2 Plato, *Apology* 21a.
3 Socrates' metaphor of the human soul, which is told in Plato's *Phaidros*, comprises an image of virtue and vice, which are represented as two horses that while being put to the same carriage are very different in their appearance: the one being slender and beautiful, the other plump, misshapen, and black-skinned (Plato, *Phaidros* 253d-e).
4 Richard Saunders, *Physiognomie and Chiromancie, Metoposcopie* (London: Brooke, 1653) 144. Cf. Thomas Hill, *The Contemplation of Mankinde* (London:

capability of intervening in his *liber corporis*, the divergence of body
and mind such as it is embodied in Socrates remains the exception to
the rule. Thus referring to the sophist, Montaigne, in his essay 'On
Physiognomie' claims that 'nature did him wrong', and Lavater sees
Socrates as one of nature's mistakes, which occur from time to time
but which carry no more weight and could no more destroy the legi-
bility of the human face than ten, twenty, thirty misprints could make
a book illegible.[1]

The potential discrepancy between *physis* and *psyche* has always
been a popular motif in literature. In Homer's *Odyssey*, the gods are
said to compensate for the unjust distribution of qualities amongst
men. Whoever is physically disadvantaged, will be granted other val-
uable skills, such as an outstanding eloquence that is detained from
the beautiful. Nonetheless, these 'misprints' of nature cannot out-
weigh other physiognomies that display a genuine correspondence of
body and mind. Again, it is especially the deformed body, which is
regarded as a trustworthy image of the mind. The figure of the 'born
devil' (*Tempest* 4.1.188) has remained a popular topos since antiq-
uity. Under the rule of Hadrian, for instance, a *mala physiognomia*
was taken as an indication of a criminal mind and could be a crucial
factor for one's conviction in court.[2] Biblical references such as Jesaia
3,9 confirm the connection between a deformed body and a corrupted
soul, which has prevailed until modernity when Cesare Lombroso
published his treatise *L'Uomo Delinquente* (1876). Presenting a por-
trait gallery of delinquents and closely examining their facial fea-
tures, Lombroso sought to prove the existence of a criminal phy-
siognomy. A short, bulky neck, a hooked nose, bleary eyes, and
above all a hunchback were regarded as unmistakable indicators of

Seres, 1571) f. x–xi.

1   John Florio ed., *Montaigne's Essays* (London/New York: Dent, 1910) Vol. 3,
    314. Johann Caspar Lavater, *Physiognomische Fragmente, zur Beförderung
    der Menschenkenntnis und Menschenliebe* (Leipzig/Winterthur: Weidmanns,
    1775) Vol. 1, 65.

2   Cf. Manfred Schneider, 'Die Beobachtung des Zeugen nach Artikel 71 der
    Carolina: Der Aufbau eines Codes der Glaubwürdigkeit 1532–1850', in Manfred
    Campe ed., *Geschichte der Physiognomik* (Freiburg: Rombach, 1996) 153–84,
    164f.

profound malice, a claim that Lichtenberg had tried to counteract.[1] Despite the spurious connotations connected with a *mala physiognomia*, prototypes of physical and moral deformity lived on and, as the gruesome events of past century testify, still inflame racist degradation and discrimination. In the literary realm, the image of the 'born devil' has never lost its attraction even though its validity might be questioned just as often as it is confirmed. For the ambivalence of external tokens, Shakespeare's plays offer several examples. While in *Troilus and Cressida*, Thersites enters as the classical prototype of a villain, both in body and in mind, the black Othello and the Jewish Shylock both play against their stigmatised external appearance. The most prominent example of deformity in Shakespeare's plays, however, is Richard Gloucester, even though his monstrous body is the result of a metamorphoses *post mortem*. The hunch-back attributed to him in Shakespeare's play harks back to Tudor writers, who by this physical deformity intended to emphasize their image of Richard as a vicious, unscrupulous character even though there is no evidence to support the notion of his having a malformed body.

As these examples indicate, literature and physiognomy are closely interlinked and their relationship is one of mutual influence. Literary portrayals heavily rely on the readability of the human body since they delineate a character via his or her external appearance whereby '[t]he presentation of the bodily appearance of a character, particularly, if it is accompanied by an interpretation, becomes the application of physiognomy, the art of revealing character traits via physical features'[2]. Characterological sketches as they are defined here by Edmund Heier can already be found in classical literature, in Lucian, Suetonius, Pliny, Apuleius, Horace, Homer, for instance, and especially in Ovid, all of whom Della Porta refers to in order to strengthen his reading of certain physical features. As Elizabeth Evans has pointed out, not only classical epic and lyric poetry have strong physiognomic overtones, but also the descriptive schemes in drama adhere to physiognomic theories of the time. Thus Seneca's plays, for instance, seem to con-

---

1   Compare page 26
2   Edmund Heier, 'The Literary Portrait as a Device of Characterization', *Neophilologus* 60 (1976), 321–33, 321.

nect to the *Physiognomonica*, because the focus is set on temporary facial expressions, on movements that are generated by passions of the mind.[1] Likewise, in Greek drama, the momentary appearance seems to prevail over icon-like descriptions of individual people.[2] Furthermore, characters were expressed in the actor's mask, which often carried very distinct features pointing to certain types of character and adhered to Julius Pollux' cata-logues of masks.[3] Sketching specific types such as the *senex*, the braggart soldier, or the shrewd wife, Pollux gives particulars of the colour and style of hair, forehead, beard, cheeks, brows, complexion, and sometimes even includes an expression of a specific emotional state.[4] Whether a character was small-minded or loud-mouthed could hence be derived from the design of the mask. Amongst the 44 masks of New Comedy, for instance, the perfect young man shows a ruddy complexion signifying haste as well as a good disposition and a somewhat wrinkled forehead, which is regarded as indicating courage. The mask of the old woman depicts a withered and deeply wrinkled skin face, which Pseudo-Aristotle interprets as indicators of sulkiness, with a yellowish complexion and roving eyes and overall communicates a somewhat wolfish appearance. Whether Shakespeare thought of Pollux' masks, however, when he let Lear curse Gonerill's 'wolvish visage' (*King Lear* 1.4.285) remains open to speculation. Nonetheless, one can assume that he was familiar with these type-characters, which together with Theophrast's *Charakteres Ethikoi*,[5] Thomas Overbury's *Characters*, and the numerous physiognomic manuals circulating at the time, were a major source for physical and moral portrayals in literature.

---

1   Elizabeth C. Evans, *Physiognomics in the Ancient World* (Philadelphia: The American Philosophical Society, 1969) 28–33.
2   Ibidem 35.
3   Compare David Wiles, *The Masks of Menander: Sign and Meaning in Greek and Roman Performance* (Cambridge et al.: Cambridge University Press, 1991).
4   Compare Evans, *Physiognomics*, 37f. For an extensive description of tragic and comic masks see Arthur W. Pickard-Cambridge, *The Dramatic Festivals of Athens* (Oxford: Oxford University Press, 1968) 177–212.
5   While Theophrast's character-sketches concentrate on moral features, some references to outward appearance are being made. Thus, for instance, the abhorrent man has a bedraggled, hairy body, and cankered teeth, and the slanderer is apparent as such at first glance due to his repellent exterior (cf. Theophrast, *Charaktere*, trans. by Dietrich Klose [Stuttgart: Reclam, 1970] 49 and 69).

3 Shakespeare's Physiognomic Characters

3.1 Physiognomic Types and Character-(Re)Writings

For the mutual interaction between character-writings and literature, Theophrast is a good example in that it remains disputable not only from where he drew his characters, but also to whom the treatise was addressed. Was it composed as a mockery of every day life, or was it meant to serve as a compendium for poets and dramatists, which was inspired by characters Theophrast encountered in literature? It would probably be best to strike a balance between these potential addressees. It seems quite plausible to regard the *Charakteres* as a body of *personae* drawn from precedent literary works, which undoubtedly inspired later (character-)writers. The same applies to Shakespeare's plays, whose relation to character-writings is undoubtedly an ambivalent one. While some of his figures, especially the *personae* of the comedies, show certain parallels to character types as they have been defined for New Comedy, they undoubtedly had an impact on contemporary authors, who took them as models for their literary portraits. Thomas Overbury's melancholic man, for instance, is strongly reminiscent of Shakespeare's Hamlet:

> He carries a cloud in his face, never faire weather: his outside is framed ot his inside in that he keeps a *Decorum*, both unseemly. Speake to him, he heares with his eyes, eares follow the minde, and that's not leasure. He thinks busines, but never does any: he is all contemplation no action. [...] His spirits and the sunne are enemies, the sun bright and warme, his humor black and cold [...].[1]

While this affinity could simply be explained by the fact that both portraits refer to one and the same persona, namely melancholy man, the connection exceeds a coincidental recurrence on melancholic stere-

---

1   Wilfrid. J. Paylor ed., *The Overburian Characters: To which is added A Wife by Sir Thomas Overbury* (Oxford: Blackwell, 1936) 22.

otypes. The cloudy face is the first feature of Hamlet, which we 'see' when he enters the stage and is greeted by Claudius with the slight reproach, 'How is it that the clouds still hang on you?' (*Hamlet* 1.2.66). Gertrude further develops this image by commenting on his 'nightly colour' (1.2.68) and his 'vailèd lids' (1.2.70), which are equally unseemly in her view. Finally, the image of the sun, an important element in Overbury's sketch, is semantically charged in Shakespeare's play where Hamlet realises that he is 'too much i'th'sun' (1.2.67). Alluding to the upheaval and the new successor to the crown, who strives to replace Old Hamlet by placing himself in the centre of Denmark and thereby adopting the prince ('think of us / As of a father' 1.2.107f.), Hamlet's remark, which plays upon the homophonic *son* and *sun*, foreshadows his future knowledge of the true circumstances that led to his father's death. In addition to the Platonic metaphor, this passage can be read in a metadramatic context as an implicit aside to the audience by the protagonist, who will be in the spotlight for the remainder of the hourglass, giving them the opportunity to carefully scrutinise his persona, which is introduced as melancholic, but cannot be summed up merely with the words 'all contemplation no action'. As the play develops, Hamlet not only instructs the players how to act but also emerges as author and director of a play. As such he carefully supervises its translation from the page, the script that he himself has (re-)written, to the stage, calling the players into their roles: 'Begin, murderer' (3.2.246). Even though Hamlet remains 'passive' in that he does not appear on the stage-within-the-stage *in persona* but merely provides the blueprint and theoretical background to the art of playing, both the plotting and observing entail a certain drive, which neither opposes a contemplative mind nor negates Hamlet's restraint by moral scruple but nonetheless adds yet another feature to the melancholic man, which challenges the notion of utter passivity. The melancholic disposition connected to the pensive, bookish student from Wittenberg is but one feature of this multi-faceted character, who, as numerous books and volumes devoted to the analysis of Hamlet and the exposure of 'that within' (1.2.85) confirm, is one of Shakespeare's most complex figures.

It is Hamlet's unfeasibility which becomes his most prominent feature. In the course of the play, he seems affiliated with several different personae, none of which he can secure for himself: the lover, the avenger, the heir to the throne, the quirky scholar, the passionate player are parts that are snatched from him by other characters, by the First Player, by Polonius, but first and foremost by Laertes, his semblance and mirror, which confronting Hamlet eventually breaks him. The 'glass of fashion' (3.1.152) that is obliged to frequently refashion itself according to the images confronting it and 'the mould of form' (3.1.152), which produces personae without materialising almost like the stumps in Gutenberg's printing press, to a certain degree lacks a visible character of its own. Hamlet's multi-faceted playing, especially his 'antic disposition' (1.5.173), which together with his melancholic mind is the only role that is successfully and convincingly staged, make it impossible to typecast and classify his character. It is not until the final scene and only in retrospect, after his final appearance onstage, that Hamlet's role can be assessed. In the last act of the play, he emerges as an actor *sui generis*. Fortinbras' obituary underscores this impression. Asserting the prince's kingly qualities, '[f]or he was likely, had he been put on, / To have proved most royally' (5.2.341f.), Fortinbras eventually takes on the part that was designed for Hamlet, who failed to adopt it, and becomes successor to the crown.

With regard to the multifaceted masking at work in *Hamlet* and also in Hamlet, it is not surprising that physiognomy becomes very prominent at the court of Denmark. The face does not only prompt characterological readings (Hamlet's clouded features) and is subject to dissimulation and disguise (especially in connection with Hamlet's old-fashioned disposition), but it is also consulted as a document bearing witness to one's conscience (as is indicated by Hamlet's impatient expectation of Claudius' reaction to the staging of the Mousetrap).[1]

The somehow bewildering unfeasibility of his persona, however, makes Hamlet a prime example of the ways in which especially the tragic characters in Shakespeare oppose stereotypical patterns as they

---

1   For the impact of physiognomic sub-texts in *Hamlet* see pages 108–12. See also Sibylle Baumbach, *Let me behold thy face: Physiognomik und Gesichtslektüren in Shakespeares Tragödien* (Winter: Heidelberg, 2007) 261–80.

have been set down in manuals such as Overbury's or Theophrast's treatises. Even though some figures might show certain affinities to specific type-characters, more often than not, they ultimately resist categorisation. Furthermore, this resistance is often conveyed by a physiognomic counter-reading: Othello immediately comes to mind, who, prior to his first appearance onstage, is painted black by Iago but eventually reveals himself as a 'noble Moor', whose dark complexion belies the fair soul beneath it. While the implications of black skin in early modern thought remain contentious,[1] Iago's deprecatory image of 'a black ram' (*Othello* 1.1.88) suggests a profound aversion to what was commonly regarded a bestial hue. The predominantly negative connotation of blackness springs not least from the fact that a black face lacks any visible emotion in that it can neither blush nor grow pale and thus seems to defy the laws of nature. Its immunity against these physiological reactions is a 'quality' which Aaron takes great pride in when mocking the visages of Chiron and Demetrius as 'whitelimed walls' and 'alehouse painted signs' (*Titus Andronius* 4.2.97). In contrast to their countenances, which openly communicate the passions of their minds, translating their innermost thoughts and feelings onto the bodily surface for others to perceive, Aaron's face is colour-proof and as such superior to the 'treacherous hue, that will betray with blushing / The close enacts and counsels of the heart' (4.2.116f.).

While in *Titus Andronicus*, Shakespeare taps the full scope of stereotypes connected with blackness in the figure of the pathologically evil Aaron, who shows but a mite of human kindness towards his own offspring whose face bears the Moor's 'stamp' (4.3.69), his treatment of this highly charged colour gains in complexity and polyphony in his later plays. Notwithstanding Iago's denunciation, Othello turns out to be one of the fairest characters of the play if judged with regard to his mind and morals rather than to his complexion. Similarly, Marocco in *The Merchant of Venice* emerges as unblemished or, viewed from Portia's perspective, just as repulsive as any of the other (European) suitors wooing for her love, and Cleopatra's tawny com-

---

1   Compare Ania Loomba, *Shakespeare, Race, and Colonialism* (Oxford: Oxford University Press, 2002) esp. 1–3 and 49–59.

plexion, whose degree of blackness is disputable, is but a welcome opportunity for the Romans to degrade her character. While Aaron exploits this dissimulative potential of blackness, Othello incorporates a radical break between outer seeming and inner being.

The way in which colour is presented and discussed especially in *Titus Andronicus*, *Othello*, and *The Merchant of Venice* is illuminating in view of the different connotations attached to blackness. While in *Titus Andronicus* the dark colour is indicative of a murky character, this notion is challenged though not refuted in *The Merchant of Venice* as Morocco's appeal to Portia, 'mislike me not for my complexion' (2.1.1.) is countered by Portia's sneer 'let all of his complexion choose me so' (2.7.79). In *Othello*, the appeal for colour blindness is much more emphatic. Desdemona presents Othello's face as an obstacle that is to be transcended in order to obtain a clear view of the true inner being. Her claim, 'I saw Othello's visage in his mind' (1.3.251), urges the bystanders to disregard the external appearance, which according to her judgement belies a fair soul. It is striking that none other than Brabanzio's daughter, who herself serves as a prime example of physiognomic legibility with her 'alabaster' (5.2.5.) skin and her correspondingly untainted 'within', steps forward to question the connection between body and psyche and promote an inversion of the physiognomic mode. The two conflicting concepts of the decoding of a particular character prove to be seminal for the further development of the plot and prepare the fatal misreading in the final scene. By the end of the play, the concept of 'otherness' as far as it connects to Othello's blackness has been successfully subverted and stereotypical connotations which might have been stirred in the mind of an early modern audience facing a black or blackened man onstage have to be revised.

In the comedies, character types seem most prevalent even though they are not necessarily bound to physiognomic description. However, there are instances when the face comes into view for stereotyping. In *As You Like It*, for instance, Rosalind's portrayal of a man in love accrues from external features (3.2.338–42), Orlando's panegyric praise of Rosalind's beauty lists stereotypical qualities, and Jacques' 'masks' of the seven ages of man entail references to external appearances. Distinctive, physiognomic (in the strictest sense) features are referred to for the following reasons: first, they create 'antibodies', that is, characters that are opposed to each other by their sheer external appearance such as small, dark-haired Hermia and tall, blond Helena, who is supposed to exceed Hermia by some inches; she is, after all, a 'painted maypole' (*A Midsummer Night's Dream* 3.2.297). As in this particular case, the combat these antibodies enter in is not restricted to the level of external appearance. The two women, for instance, are rivals in love as well as in physiognomy. Secondly, physiognomic features serve to establish genealogic relations whereby the fatherly imprint is discovered in a particular face and finally, certain features are exposed to evoke an *anagnorisis*. The latter is often accompanied by a face-reading. When Mariana refuses to show her face 'until my husband bid me' (*Measure for Measure* 5.1.169), Angelo finally acknowledges his engagement to her. Far more effective and exposed is the *anagnorisis* in *Twelfth Night* when Viola and Sebastian confirm their family bond through a mole which they remember to have graced their father's brow.

Notwithstanding a greater adherence to stereotyping, many characters in the comedies seem to play against their masks rather than complying with them. Amidst the dynamics of code-making and code-breaking, however, which is fuelled by cross-dressing, masking, and disguises onstage, physiognomic clues become even more significant insofar as they might reveal a character's true identity, which shines through an adopted persona. Viola's face, for instance, retains its soft features beneath her disguise, which does not escape Orsino, who scrutinises her exterior:

> For they shall yet belie thy happy years
> That say thou art a man. Diana's lip
> Is not more smooth and rubious; thy small pipe
> Is as the maiden's organ, shrill and sound.
> And all is semblative a woman's part.
> (*Twelfth Night* 1.4.29–33)

What attract Orsino are the womanly features which can be discerned in the countenance of the boy-actor playing the part. The face behind the mask, which displays the womanly features, in *As You Like It* is exposed in a similar manner when Phoebe detects a distinctly feminine physiognomy in Ganymede's countenance:

> [...] The best thing in him
> Is his complexion [...]
> There was a pretty redness in his lip,
> A little riper and more lusty-red
> Than that mixed in his cheek.
>
> (*As You Like It* 3.5.116–23)

Both readings arouse a homoerotic desire. In Phoebe's portrayal of Rosalind-as-Ganymede, a woman falls in love with a face, whose red lips and white cheeks display the 'silent war of lilies and of roses' (*The Rape of Lucrece* 71) and thus bears distinctively female features. Orsino's mistaking of a woman's face for a man's countenance, however, draws its homoerotic effect from a meta-theatrical perspective and the audience's awareness that the persona Viola-cum-Cesario, just as 'Ganymede' is incorporated by a boy-actor. Thus, the unmistakably female features not only pose a threat to Viola's performance as Cesario and also to Rosalind's disguise as Ganymede but also, on a meta-theatrical level, hints at the perilous play of the boy-actor embodying the two sexes.

Adopting a female role, the young actors were thought to expose themselves to the destructive power of effeminisation, which opponents to the theatre saw lurking onstage.[1] 'A woman's garment being put on a man', argues John Rainolds, 'doth vehemently touch and move him with the remembrance and imagination of a woman'.[2] Men that carelessly jeopardized their masculine self by dressing like a woman were regarded 'lascivious [...] dishonest and ignominious'[3]. The soft, smooth, and beardless face of the boy actor seems particularly vulnerable and susceptible to feminine imprints. Not surpris-

---

1   Compare Laura Levine, *Men in Women's Clothing: Anti-Theatricality and Effeminization, 1579–1642* (Cambridge: Cambridge University Press, 1994) 1–25.

2   John Rainolds, *The Overthrow of Stage-Plays* (Middleburgh: Schilders, 1599) 97.

3   Thomas Beard, *Theatre of God's Iudgements [...]* (London: Sparke, 1631) 419f.

ingly, physiognomic readings quite often embark on gender trouble within the theatrical realm. Thus Cleopatra, for instance, dreads to be represented by a young actor with a 'squeaking' voice (*Antony and Cleopatra* 5.2.216). The highly volatile tone of voice, which cannot be controlled, however, not only threatens but at the same time retains the masculine self of the boy-actor insofar as it can be identified as a masculine feature. It is not unlikely, however, that the voice of the actor incorporating Cleopatra broke at this 'complaint' about the ill-pitched tone of the young player, which would contribute to the comic effect of this scene.

Doubling the cross-dressing by staging male actors playing women disguised as men, Shakespeare's plays unveil the physiognomy of the theatre. The squeaking voice of 'Cleopatra', the growing beard, which Flute puts forward in order to prove his incapability to 'play a woman' (*A Midsummer Night's Dream* 1.2.39), the soft features of the actor, who plays Viola playing Cesario and not to forget the afore mentioned onion, whose acid odour was employed to replace female lacrimal gland reveal different ways in which gender could be performed and, at the same time, be revealed as performance. Within the cross- and double-cross-dressing, physiognomy can serve as a tool, which enables the audience to look, as it were, behind the scenes and lift the actors' masks.

Shakespeare's approach to type characters serves a similar aim in that it reveals the inventory of the theatre, sometimes even hearkening back to Pollux' catalogues of masks, in order to critically reflect and transgress the boundaries of the stage and thereby exceed the limited leeway attached to traditional character-writings. While the *Overburian Characters* seem to draw from Shakespeare's plays, it seems likely that Shakespeare was familiar with character-writings such as Hall's *Characters of Virtues and Vices* (1608), which dates to the same year as *Coriolanus* and might have inspired Menenius' portrayal of the protagonist:

> The tartness of his face sours ripe grapes. When he walks, he moves like an engine, and the ground shrinks before his treading. He is able to pierce a corslet with his eye, talks like a knell, and his 'hmh!' is a battery. He sits in his state as a thing made

for Alexander. What he bids be done is finished with his bidding.
He wants nothing of a god but eternity and a heaven to throne in.
(*Coriolanus* 5.4.14–20)

'I paint him in the character' (5.4.22), thus Menenius replies to the
question whether his sketch does justice to Coriolanus. His answer is
tailored to his addressee, Sicinius, who unlike the audience has not
witnessed the preceding scene where the seemingly relentless killing
machine has been moved to tears ('Mine eyes [...] sweat compassion'
[5.3.197]) by his family's plea for mercy. The ironic side-swipe of
Menenius at the fast-developing genre of character-writing, which can
be identified in the rather doubtful conviction that this is Coriolanus'
character while just a moment ago the audience got quite a different
picture of him, is not only another example of Shakespeare's criti-
cal approach to stereotypical classifications: it also underscores the
significant role of the physiognomic reader. Characterological por-
trayals are highly subjective insofar as they are subjected to the ana-
lytic skills of the beholder, who can alter and amend 'his' document
according to his own purpose and discretion. As will become appar-
ent in the course of this study, in Shakespeare's plays there is usually
one figure in each play that qualifies as 'physiognomist' by numer-
ous face-readings as well as outstanding physiognomical awareness.
In *Coriolanus*, this part is taken on by Menenius, who already in the
very first scene provides a sample of his proficiency in rhetoric when
he succeeds in pacifying the rebels with the parable of the belly ('I
may make the belly smile as well as speak' [1.1.92]) and the members
of the body. Menenius quite obviously relies on the legibility of man.
He himself seems a case in point with regard to the correspondence
between body and psyche and emphasises the physiological activities
of the face which provide an insight into the body when he claims: 'if
the drink you give me touch my palate adversely, I make a crooked
face at it' [2.1.50f.]). At the same time, he directs his physiognomic
eye to his opponents, the tribunes, who 'make faces like mummers'
(2.1.67) in the attempt to hide their disagreeable character: 'they
lie deadly that tell you have good faces' (2.1.55f.). Furthermore, he
dares others to perform a counter-reading of 'the map of [his] micro-
cosm', an allusion to the Paracelsian concept of the legibility of the

universe: 'If you see this in the map of my microcosm, follows it that I am known well enough too?' (2.1.56f.).

3.2 Outperforming Performance

Non-verbal communication takes centre stage in *Coriolanus*, which in accordance with Volumnia's axiom might be themed 'action is eloquence' (3.2.76). As the action develops and the body politic and the body natural break apart, a programme, or rather an anti-programme of physiognomic self-fashioning is pronounced: the citizens complain about the ritual connected with the display of Coriolanus' wounds, in which the open body is expected to 'speak' for itself, or rather to incline the watching crowd to speak for it (2.3.5–7). It is Coriolanus' reluctance to cast away his disposition and consequently corrupt his mind, his refusal to perform a part and submit to the projection cast upon him by others that eventually lead to his downfall on the social stage and his untimely exit from the play, which is coupled with his alienation from any kind of performance: 'I have forgot my part' (5.3.41). Behind this self-reflection of social and theatrical self-fashioning and the rejection of the play in favour of an authentic appearance, a plea for a naturalistic play on Shakespeare's stage suggests itself,[1] which is underscored by the preceding reunion scene when Coriolanus is moved to tears that seem to undo his character.

Undoubtedly, the actor playing Coriolanus would not forget his part but provide an impressive example of a first class performance, stirring emotions while, as theatre critics have repeatedly deplored, 'infecting' the spectators with his tears and thus bridging the gap between actors and spectators. And yet, the self-reflection of the anti-actor Coriolanus, who leaves what consequently seems a play-within-a-play, evokes a sense of stage reality, which opposes any notions of stylised and hyperbolic acting and does indeed seem to hold the

---

1   The notion of natural acting on Shakespeare's stage is also expressed in *Hamlet* and the remark of the prince that 'anything so o'erdone is from the purpose of playing' (3.2.20). The mere identification of hack-acting suggests a preference of natural acting, an 'acting [that appears] recognizably close to human behavior' (Marvin Rosenberg, 'Elizabethan Actors: Men or Marionettes?', in Gerald E. Bentley ed., *The Seventeenth Century Stage* [Chicago/London: University of Chicago Press,1968] 94–110, 106).

mirror up to nature. As far as tears can be regarded as part of facial rhetoric and weeping can be counted amongst pathognomic features, *Coriolanus* serves as one example to suggest that physiognomic devices as they are employed on Shakespeare's stage might contribute to bridging the gap between the *theatrum mundi*, the theatre of the world, and the world of the theatre not only because they involve the spectators in character-readings but also because paradoxically their performance seems to exceed the boundaries of the stage.

In *Coriolanus*, the notion of 'authentic play' arises first and foremost from the production of tears onstage for it was generally assumed that 'tears cannot be counterfetted, because they rise not of any action or facultie voluntarie, but naturall'.[1] The fact that weeping can be feigned, however, does not diminish let alone negate their validity as physical signifiers of – and there's the rub – sorrow *or* overwhelming joy for both can trigger tears. In *Coriolanus*, they could indeed indicate either, a regretful mourning of the valiant soldier, who has turned away from his family and his *polis* as well as an expression of utter happiness at the prospect of the unexpected reunion. More important than the polyvalence of weeping in this context, however, is the effect of this particular gesture on the audience, who would have been aware of the impossibility of weeping on demand. Shakespeare alludes to the unfeasibility of this highly effective expression in *The Taming of the Shrew* where the boy-actor is urged to always have an onion up his sleeve 'if the boy have not a woman's gift / To rain a shower of commanded tears' (Induction 1, 120f.). Due to its alleged abundance of bodily liquids, the female body was prone to (excessive) weeping, and boy actors would thus quite regularly face the difficult task of producing tears. Not least their frequency contributes to the disregard and alleged insignificance of women's tears, which are often suspected to be too easily produced to be carrying great weight. Male weeping, however, is a different matter. As Shakespeare's onion indicates, to squeeze forced tears from the male body is an almost impossible venture. This observation ties in with my initial claim that male weeping onstage might narrow the gap between the theatrical and the

---

1   Timothy Bright, *Treatise on Melancholie* (1586) (Amsterdam/New York: Da Capo, 1969) 148.

worldly stage. With neither an onion nor Ovid's vial to hand, tears must be generated within the body, which means that they have to be preceded by strong emotions, which are caused by sorrow, anger, fear, joy, or any other kind of emotional stress. To 'feign' tears is to imitate one of these passions. This takes us to the two often conflated concepts of *enargeia* and *energeia*, which are concerned with the vividness of style and expression:

> [...] one to satisfie & delight th'eare onely by a goodly outward shew set upon the matter with wordes, and speaches smothly and tunably running: another by certaine intendments or sence of such wordes & speaches inwardly working a stirre to the mynde: that first qualitie the Greeks called *Enargia*, of this word *argos,* because it geveth a glorious lustre and light. This latter they called *Energia,* of *ergon,* because it wrought with a strong and vertuous operation.[1]

To strengthen the emotional involvement of the audience, the actor has to apply the principle of *enargeia* or *hypotyposis* and imagine a particular emotion or passion, which he has to show himself first before the spark can jump over to the audience. To move himself to tears, he has to arouse the corresponding emotions by force of his vivid imagination. While these passions lack outside stimuli, they are felt and suffered, which is the prerequisite for the eyes to fill with tears. This is the monstrosity Hamlet refers to when he witnesses the First Player, who 'could force his soul so to his whole conceit' (*Hamlet* 2.2.530), bringing forth tears to accompany his speech and thus not only to weep as Hecuba but also *with*, and as Hamlet implies, *for* her.[2] It is this self-induction of emotions, which is linked to the Horacian dictum *si vis me flere, dolendum est primum ipsi tibi*,[3] the key to a successful performance. When in the final scenes of *Coriolanus*, the protagonist, who throughout the play has revealed his reluctance

---

1   George Puttenham, *The Arte of English Poesie* (1589), ed. by Gladys D. Willcock and Alice Walker (Cambridge: Cambridge University Press, 1936) 142f.
2   For a detailed reading of this scene and performances of mourning in Shakespeare's drama see Tobias Döring, *Performances of Mourning in Shakespearean Theatre and Early Modern Culture* (Basingstoke: Palgrave, 2006) esp. 118–48.
3   Horace, *Ars Poetica* 101–3.

'to perform a part', let alone a part that does not connect to his persona, 'a part / That I shall blush in acting' (2.2.141f.), melts into tears whilst scolding this 'unnatural' scene, the performance is consummate in that the actor behind the figure Coriolanus seems to evaporate. In this respect, *Coriolanus* closely connects to *Hamlet* where the metatheatrical discourse has a similar effect insofar as it mourns the death of an actor playing no other than himself and performing the part of an actor who 'had he been put on' (*Hamlet* 5.2.341) would have proved to play his role to uttermost perfection. By reflecting on the actor's qualities within the world of the play, the personae seem to be outperforming performance and thereby connect the world of the stage to the worldly stage, reinforcing the intimate bond between actors and audience, and thereby supporting the dynamic interaction between personae and theatregoers.

3.3 Physiognomic Reflections

As indicated by this example, physiognomic clues and descriptions play a central part in the triangle of theatrical communication, which emerges in the interaction between actors, *dramatis personae* and theatregoers, while evoking a sense of a natural rather than a stylised art of playing. With regard to physiognomic expressions, it can be assumed that actors endeavoured to provide a suitable visual picture to the verbal text. John Russell Brown convincingly argues that the actor incorporating the apothecary in *Romeo and Juliet*, for example, whose face is marked by starvation ('famine is in thy cheeks, / Need and oppression starveth in thy eyes' [5.1.69f.]), 'will join with Romeo's words to give the impression of a world of hunger and vagrancy'.[1] Physical descriptions exceed verbal scenery in that they were designed not only to be imagined but also to be enacted. A failure to provide the corresponding physical text would not pass unnoticed by the audience, who had a full view of the actors onstage. As John Styan has argued, 'there would be many moments when the Elizabethan actor would be working as if under a microscope.'[2] Save

1 John R. Brown, *Shakespeare and the Theatrical Event* (Basingstoke/New York: Palgrave, 2002) 182.
2 John Styan, *Shakespeare's Stagecraft* (Cambridge: Cambridge University Press,

the expressions of blushing and paling,[1] we can thus assume that the face could be framed to almost all occasions. But how were static physiognomic (*stricto sensu*) features dealt with?

The majority of Shakespeare's characters seem to have been created with specific actors in mind. Considering Shakespeare's mode of type-*writing*, a type-*casting* such as it is staged in *The Return from Parnassus* (1606) would not have been necessary except for comic purposes (one might think of the casting for *Pyramus and Thisbe* in *A Midsummer Night's Dream*, for instance). In *The Return from Parnassus*, the casting has quite a comic effect, especially since it is none other than Richard Burbage who is in charge of the selection of talented actors. His criteria of evaluation are very distinct: 'I like your face', he says to the student Philomusus, 'and the proportion of your body for *Richard* the 3' (2.1.1835f.). His ugliness as well as his deformed body seems to qualify him for this persona. While it was certainly not his body that made Shakespeare attribute the part of Richard Gloucester to Burbage, his key roles seemed tailor-made for him. One might even speculate whether Burbage's mature age was the reason why Shakespeare's main characters, Hamlet, Othello, Lear, and Antony, grew older as the years went by until John Lowin, who joined the King's Men in 1603, brought a young choleric character such as Coriolanus back onto the stage.[2] Whether the age difference of about eight years was indeed the decisive factor here, however, is far from beyond dispute.

Nonetheless there are clues suggesting that certain roles were tailored in consideration of the 'physical property' available amongst Shakespeare's players: The emaciated figure of the apothecary, which is reminiscent of the First Beadle in *2 Henry IV*, whom Mistress Quickly affronts as 'starved bloodhound' (5.4.25) and 'atomy' (5.4.27), could have been catered to a specific actor. The same applies to Shakespeare's 'antibodies'. Matching the statures of Helena and Hermia, the descriptions of Rosalind and Celia alias Aliena also point

---

1967) 16.
1   Compare chapter 4.4.
2   Gary Taylor, 'Shakespeare Plays on Renaissance Stages', in Stanley Wells and Sarah Stanton ed., *The Cambridge Companion to Shakespeare on Stage* (Cambridge: Cambridge University Press, 2002) 1–20, 5.

to two boy-actors, one being 'more than commonly tall' (*As You Like It* 1.3.109), the other rather 'low' (4.3.86). Shakespeare's acting company indeed comprised two boys, one tall and cheeky, and the other rather small and reserved, who fitted the parts perfectly.[1] Furthermore, in *Much Ado About Nothing* the latter could have played Hero, whom Benedick describes as 'too low for a high praise, too brown for a fair praise, and too little for a great praise' (1.1.138–40), while Beatrice like Helena calls for an actor, who is fair and tall.[2] In film versions such as Kenneth Branagh's adaptation from 1993, these physical oppositions or 'antibodies' can be played out quite effectively.

While this is not the place for an in-depth discussion of the reception and implementing of physical clues in adaptations of Shakespeare's plays, a brief digression to Richard Loncraine's film version of *Richard III* (1995) seems appropriate to outline the ways in which physiognomy becomes a means of critical self-reflection in the age of mechanical reproduction, extending the metadramatic dialogue opened up within the plays in order to scrutinise their transference and translation into other media.

In the opening scene of *Richard III*, we encounter the protagonist in a mirror. Richard continues his first monologue, which he began as a public speech, after retreating to the bathroom, face-to-face with his own image that is 'rudely stamped', 'deformed', and 'unfinished' just like himself and thus reinforces his disdain of the world and his determination 'to prove a villain' (1.1.16, 20, 30). What suggests itself in this scene is a threefold reflection in which the historical Richard, Shakespeare's villain, and Loncraine's adaptation enter into dialogue. Thereby, physiognomy provides the key. Even though there is some dispute over Richard's outer appearance, the image of the physically deformed and morally corrupt king, with a withered arm, has prevailed. While there is some controversy about which shoulder was supposed to have been crooked, both Thomas More

---

1 Compare Helmut Castrop, 'Das elisabethanische Theater', in Ina Schabert ed., *Shakespeare Handbuch: Die Zeit – Der Mensch – Das Werk – Die Nachwelt* (Stuttgart: Kröner, 2000) 72–117, 111.

2 Compare John C. Meagher, *Pursuing Shakespeare's Dramaturgy: Some Contexts, Resources, and Strategies in His Playmaking* (London: Fairleigh Dickinson University Press, 2003) 183.

and Raphael Hollinshed, which are amongst Shakespeare's imme-
diate sources, claim that the left was 'much higher than the right'[1].
The mirror image in Loncraine's adaptation accounts for this. Ian
McKellan as Richard, however, does not. The self-reflection where
the actor carefully examines his likeness, tracing the lineaments of
'his' face, is staged as a metatheatrical encounter not only between
actor and role but also between Shakespeare's Richard and King
Richard as he is portrayed in the chronicles, between drama, histo-
riography, and history. This scene of looking for Richard abruptly
comes to an end when actor and role merge on catching sight, so it
seems, of us, the spectators, who have been silently observing the
spectacle and to whom Ian MacKellan as Richard now turns to fur-
ther explicate his plan of action: 'I am determinèd to prove a villain'
(*Richard III* 1.1.30). Determined by whom, one might ask: by histori-
ography that endowed him with a hunchback and deformed his body?
By Shakespeare, who seized this suggestion to create an archetypical
villain, as despicable in body as in mind? In any case, it was hardly
nature which 'rudely stamped' (*Richard III* 1.1.16) his character for
the historical Richard seems to have had an agreeable appearance.

The portrait in the preface to the *Royal and Noble Authors*, for
instance, depicts a handsome young man with a rather compelling
countenance, which is why Horace Walpole, for instance, resentfully
demands, 'Cannot a foul soul inhabit a fair body?'[2] It is this paradoxi-
cal combination of beauty and vice which Shakespeare challenges
in many of his plays and probably even in *Richard III* provided that
the 'determination' proclaimed by the protagonist is read as refer-
ring not so much to the historical king but to his persona as it has
been fashioned by Tudor historiography. Loncraine's confrontation
of the two Richards serves as a gentle reminder of the physiogno-
mic controversy attached to this particular figure. The hanging left
shoulder of Loncraine's protagonist seems to connect to the origin of
the 'myth', more precisely to the account of John Rous, who is said
to have invented the story of Richard's monstrous birth. According

---

1   Thomas More, *History of King Richard III*, ed. by R.S. Sylvester (Yale: Yale
    University Press, 1963) 7.
2   Horace Walpole, *Historic Doubts on the Life and Reign of King Richard the Third*
    (New Haven/London: Yale University Press, 1768) 103.

to Rous, Richard entered this world as a two year-old boy, ghastly haired and already toothed. Although Loncraine might have thought of establishing a link to the 'original' myth when he composed the mirror-scene, he could just as well have tried to avoid the somewhat irrelevant controversy about which shoulder was the crooked one, a question which remains unanswered in Shakespeare's play, by representing both versions of Richard before merging them into one and thus bringing the strings together before releasing the protagonist, McKellan as Richard, into the public space.

As it becomes apparent in the case of Richard Gloucester, physiognomy can serve as a device to confront and compare Shakespeare's adaptation of a particular figure with its model, the historical, historiographical, or fictional persona. The success of this comparison greatly depends on the expectations of the audience, who would immediately and involuntarily connect a certain image with a particular name. Hence Shakespeare could rely on the fact that Thersites would evoke the image of the bandy-legged, hunchbacked, and revolting man, the ugliest amongst the Greeks, as he emerges from the second book of Homer's *Iliad*. For an audience with some previous knowledge, a few words suffice to sketch the railing detractor, whose outer appearance is but hinted upon in his quarrel with Achilles, who calls him a 'crusty botch of nature' (*Troilus and Cressida* 5.1.5) and a 'fragment' (5.1.8), which is reminiscent of the unfinished body of a Richard Gloucester.

Rather than presenting one-to-one translations of historical or mythological figures, Shakespeare leaves some semiotic gaps for the reader and spectator to fill. His creative reception of classical and Tudor sources not only allows leeway for the actor to incorporate a particular, and, to a certain degree, also predetermined, persona, but also serves to activate the audience, who, drawing from their background knowledge and their imagination, participate in the construction of the character in question. Even though it is not required for an understanding of the play, a certain familiarity with the corresponding historical or fictional persona might prove fruitful in that it can sharpen a character's profile and underscore the relation, the rivalry, or friendship between the figures onstage.

Plutarch's *Vitae*, for instance, did not only provide the blueprint for the Roman plays but also offered the physiognomic material, upon which Shakespeare built some of his character sketches. In the lives of Julius Caesar and Brutus, for instance, Brutus and Cassius are reported to show a strong physical resemblance, both being ranked amongst those 'pale-visaged and carrion lean people' that Caesar despises in favour of their antibodies, 'these fat long-haired men'.[1] In *Julius Caesar*, however, Shakespeare does not provide any information on Brutus' outer appearance which underscores Cassius' role as a manipulating force in the play while simultaneously pointing to Caesar's blindness towards his son, whom he seems to completely overlook in the senate. Instead, he focuses on Cassius, whose 'lean and hungry look' (1.2.195) arouses his distrust. From Caesar's perspective, the role of the usurper is quite clearly ascribed to the cheerless, disingenuous senator, whose lean appearance contributes to the negative image: 'Would he were fatter!' (1.2.199). While it is not made explicit, a certain semblance between Cassius and Brutus is not ruled out even though their connection seems rooted in a spiritual rather than physical kinship. This notion is reinforced by the mirror-scene in the first act when Cassius declares himself to be 'your glass' which 'will modestly discover to yourself which you yet know not of' (1.2.68–70).

The glimpse into Brutus' soul his innermost thoughts, and moral disposition, however, entails a close reading of his external appearance. The 'I' that proposes to hold up the mirror to his vis-à-vis, confronting Brutus with his alleged worthiness turns out to be the physiognomic 'eye' of the play. It is Cassius who performs the strongest face-readings and eventually prevails over Caesar's role as diligent reader and 'great observer' (1.2.203). Not only that Cassius is the first figure in the play to perform a physiognomic reading, his attempts to decipher his opponents are also more refined than those of his contesters. In the encounter with Brutus and his reading of Caska, whose pale face bears witness to his fearful submission to the forces of nature and the tokens sent by thundering gods (1.3.3–13

---

1   Terence Spencer, ed., *Shakespeare's Plutarch* (Harmondsworth: Penguin, 1964) 85 and 109.

and 45–52), Cassius seems to concentrate on the individual, inferring certain characteristics from outward features or at least, with regard to Brutus, cunningly pretending to do so and thereby fashioning the likeness that he is supposed to merely reflect. Caesar, however, is stereotyping: '*Such* men are dangerous [...]. *Such* men as he be never at heart's ease' (1.2.196, 209). His reading rests on a classificatory system relating to a world order which Cassius already challenged in the preceding scene by underlining man's power of fashioning his self, his public persona and the environment around him. While Caesar shows a certain interest in the human face, his very first reading, the encounter with the soothsayer, whom he calls into view ('look upon Caesar' [1.2.23]), is unsuccessful insofar as he disregards him as a 'dreamer' (1.2.26) even though dreams turn out to foreshadow the future. Calpurnia's vision of her husband turned into a fountain of blood in which the Romans bathe their hands will eventually materialise onstage. Whereas the contempt of mantic sciences expressed by the dismissal of the soothsayer might be regarded as an attempt to clear physiognomy from any connection to the occult, Caesar eventually pays for his neglect of the warning to 'beware the ides of March' (1.2.19) with his life. Even though his reading of Cassius is accurate, there are certain predicaments concerning Caesar's skills as physiognomist. Firstly, it is not Cassius but rather Brutus who turns out to be bereft of sleep and therefore falls into Caesar's category of dangerous creatures. Furthermore, Caesar fails to act as reader at a crucial point of the play: on his way to the senate, he is approached by Artemidorus but fatally ignores the letter entrusted to him, whose content might have saved his life.

The intimate connection between written characters that appear on the page and physiognomic expressions or 'characters' on the face as well as the link between the ability or willingness to read and a deeper understanding of the book of nature, which become noticeable in *Julius Caesar*, are played out even more radically in other Shakespearean plays. In *King Lear*, for instance, Edgar's forging of the letter and Gloucester's misreading of his son's handwriting closely correspond to their insights into the characters surrounding them. In *Julius Caesar*, Caesar's disregard of written characters foreshadows his downfall as physiognomist and his loss of authority in a world whose changing signs have already become liable to the manipulatory forces of its microcosms and have been subjected to man's co-authorship which he fails to acknowledge.

With regard to their individual physiognomic competence and their own physiognomic portrayal, the triangle readership of Caesar, Cassius, and Brutus points to the complexity of physiognomic discourse in Shakespeare's plays. While descriptions of faces and figures can be employed as means of establishing a link to historical and mythological sources and thus provide some insight into Shakespeare's construction and deconstruction of certain type characters, it is the act of physiognomic reading as well as the composition and reception of signs, which discloses the power relations within the play. It is striking that Caesar and Cassius sketch each other's character[1] whereas the reading of Brutus seems one-sided: he becomes the object of a face-reading in which his countenance is not deciphered but rather inscribed. Even though Brutus will be the one to raise his hand against Caesar, Cassius is pulling the strings, which is indicated by Brutus' submission to Cassius' character-reading. However, as the play develops, Brutus enters the physiognomic triangle not only as document but grows in physiognomic competence. Directed by Cassius, he develops a sense for semiotic surfaces and on his part starts to turn his view towards other countenances. In the presence of his 'glass' (1.2.70), he marks an 'angry spot' (1.2.184) on Caesar's brow, observes Calpurnia's pale cheeks (1.2.186), and notices Cicero's 'fiery eyes' (1.2.187), establishing the physiognomic scenery, which suggests some altercation in the senate. The mirror scene therefore marks the entry of a third physiognomist, who, as Lavater suggests, requires a reflection and confrontation with an other, which can reassure his self in its existence and thereby enable him to become an observer and connoisseur of mankind – a physiognomist:

---

1   Both readers construe each other's character *in absentia* of the described, which heightens the opaqueness pervading this play where faces are hidden and feelings concealed: Caesar expresses his mistrust of Cassius to Antony while Cassius describes Caesar's weak and feeble temper to Brutus.

O! Leser [...] wenn du keinen Freund hast, dem du's gestehen darfst – keinen Freund, dem du dich ganz zeigen darfst, der dir sich ganz zeigen darf, dem du Repräsentant des Menschengeschlechts und der Gottheit bist; – in dem du dich erspiegeln kannst, der sich in dir erspiegeln kann; – wenn du nicht ein guter Mensch bist – so wirst du kein guter, würdiger Menschenbeobachter, Menschenkenner, Physiognomist werden.[1]

Even though Brutus' mirror is flawed, from its encounter he emerges as a third physiognomic reader of the play and gradually begins to supersede Cassius. Not only that Brutus eventually directs Cassius' view ('Look how he makes to Caesar. Mark him' [3.1.18]), by the fourth act, the relation of *reflectio* and *reflectans* has changed. Finally, it is Brutus who confronts his companion with his weaknesses before the reflection comes full circle in a last face-to-face encounter:

Brutus: If we do meet again, why, we shall smile.
           If not, why then this parting was well made.
Cassius: [...] If we do meet again, we'll smile indeed:
           If not, 'tis true this parting was well made.
           (5.1.118–22)

Complementing each other verbally and, thus it is implied, also visually, the mirror image is brought to perfection. Ian Richardson, as Cassius, tapped the full potential of this scene when he for the first and only time in the play started to smile when speaking these words.[2] The effect must have been electrifying not only because he thereby indicated that this encounter was indeed their last but also because this particular expression is highly ambiguous: a smile can be welcoming, friendly, kind as well as deceitful, cruel, or mocking. Especially in *Julius Caesar*, it seems to be devoid of joy and hope, especially as it is abused by Brutus as an expression to hide murderous intentions. Conspiracy, he claims, needs no mask to cover her 'monstrous visage' but it can 'hide [...] in smiles and affability'

---

1   Johann Caspar Lavater, *Physiognomische Fragmente, zur Beförderung der Menschenkenntnis und Menschenliebe* (Waldshut-Tiengen: Aerni, 1996) 177.
2   Cf. David Daniell ed., *William Shakespeare: Julius Caesar*, The Arden Shakespeare (Walton-on-Thames: Thomas Nelson, 1998) 306, n. 120.

(2.1.52f.). While most of Shakespeare's villains take advantage of this particular expression, which is easily enacted (and especially the smile of Richard Gloucester was one that could be called up easily and frequently in performance), the scene in *Julius Caesar* seems to be exceptionally powerful with regard to the physiognomic sub-text that might or might not accompany the conspirators' speeches onstage. The actor and director have to make a choice as to whether they intend to underscore, challenge, or counteract Cassius' speech by having him, or Brutus, or indeed both smile in this particular scene and thereby heighten their mutual reflection. Since Shakespeare's audience was sensitised to non-verbal communication and the ambivalence attached to it, the actor must have taken great caution in framing his face to his speech. While the ways in which physiognomic clues were translated onstage and diversions to performances of individual plays might prove fruitful to further assess the significance of physiognomic devices, let us return to the ways in which the face materialises in the plays' scripts.

4 A Physiognomic Inventory

A closer consideration of Shakespeare's physiognomic inventory, that is the references to individual physiognomic features that occur in his plays, is indispensable in a study dealing with facial eloquence. The following catalogue is by no means exhaustive. It is designed as an introduction to physiognomy, which offers the tools required for embarking on a closer reading of facial rhetoric. Hence, only features which are discussed in Shakespeare's writings are included. In comparison to other physiognomic inventories, the catalogue presented here will be highly selective.

For, as a glance into the classical and early modern manuals confirms, there is virtually nothing in the human face or body which does not contribute to the act of communication. Every lineament, every single movement is attributed meaning, which is rarely unequivocal. While the dynamic and highly volatile interplay of facial features requires a skilled physiognomic reader, the interpretation of individual elements of the face often requires nothing more than common sense. As Darwin's findings have confirmed, the language of the body is universal across cultures. It is therefore accessible even for the illiterate. The reading enthusiasm set off by the body's texture is as intriguing as it is perilous as it entices its beholders to drawing overhasty conclusions. For, even though the text can potentially be read by anybody, it requires an attentive observer to reveal its meaning. As Thomas Hill reminds his readers, it is crucial to 'first consider and view all the parts of man, and not to judge rashly by any one member alone'.[1] Viewed individually, certain features of the human face can entail a complex and sometimes even contrastive characterological implication. Just as in everyday communication, however, faces are usually perceived as an entity rather than as the sum of their individual elements. Instead of focussing on a certain part of

---

1 Thomas Hill, *The Contemplation of Mankinde* (London: Seres, 1571) xi.

the countenance, people tend to extrapolate from a certain expression dominating the appearance of the face at a certain moment. Thus, a certain emotion, passion, or indeed a specific character is conveyed. Therefore, before embarking on the analysis of individual features, it seems adequate to first approach the face as a whole, as an area whereupon multiple individual movements conflate in one prevailing expression, which can be grasped at a glance before dissecting this highly semantically charged medium of communication and considering its individual components. Be it in the theatre or in everyday communication, faces are perceived as pleasant or abhorrent, attractive or deformed, congenial or repulsive and, last but not least, as legible or inscrutable whereby individual elements more often than not do not come into view. Thereby, the terminology used can shed some light on the degree of legibility that is attributed to the face under scrutiny. Beside the terms *brow* and *eye*, which are often used as synecdoches, in Shakespeare's writings the *face* is also referred to as *visage* and *countenance* whereby different degrees of legibility are implied.

Whereas 'face' or *facies* points to the making (*facere*) of the face, that is its design which, according to Lavater, is god-given, paying testimony to a person's inborn character, the 'countenance' or mien comprises temporary, volatile (e)motions and as such is the object of pathognomy. The term *countenance* derives from the Latin word *vultus* or *velle* and thus points to the potential exertion of influence by human volition.[1] The difference between *face* and *countenance* is explained in Thomas Hill's *Contemplation of Mankinde*. While Hill, in a highly speculative manner and against common etymology, derives the term *countenance* from the Latin verb *volare* instead of *velle*, the differentiation he offers to distinguish the two expressions is pertinent:

> The face is often taken, and that simplie, for the naturall looke of any: but the countinaunce signifieth the qualities of the minde. [...] In a man the face remayneth, but the countenaunce doth

---

1   For the etymology of the term *countenance* see Davide Stimilli, *The Face of Immortality: Physiognomy and Criticism* (Albany: State University of New York Press, 2005) 71–5.

alter: so that the countinaunce is named of the Latine worde
Volando, which properly in Englishe signifieth a flying or van-
ishing away.[1]

Hence, when Kent mentions his dislike of Oswald's countenance
(*King Lear* 2.2.82) and adds 'I have seen better faces' (2.2.85), he first
refers to the temporary aspect of Oswald's face, namely the disgrun-
tled, aggressive aspect in his mien, and then generalises his appear-
ance by focussing on the static area, which bears the character and
inborn disposition. The latter, thus it is implied, perfectly agrees with
the countenance as it was conveyed in their first encounter. Insofar
as the countenance derives from the verb *velle*, it suggests the possi-
bility of performance, of staging and imitating certain expressions in
order to fashion facial features even though the passions of the mind
are thought typically to emerge involuntarily. In any case, the term
'countenance' is used to point to temporary features. Horatio, for
instance, refers to the mien when he reports the looks of Old Hamlet,
who shows 'a countenance more / In sorrow than in anger' (*Hamlet*
1.2.228f.). Likewise Ophelia alludes to temporary expressions on
Hamlet's face when she claims that he has 'given countenance to
his speech' (1.3.113). And Edmund directs the attention to the relin-
quishing of momentary passions when he asks his brother Edgar if
he found 'no displeasure in him, by word nor countenance' (*King
Lear* 1.2.142f.). In this context it is significant that Kent, who is the
only one to differentiate between temporary and static features (on
recapitulating his encounter with Oswald), does not locate signs of
'authority' (1.4.27) and kingship not in Lear's *face* but in his 'coun-
tenance' (1.4.24). The lack of royal character in Lear's face points to
the loss of the *body politic* that Lear has jeopardised by giving away
his power and his land to his greedy and invidious daughters Goneril
and Regan.

However, even though the reference to pathognomic features dom-
inates when it comes to the employment of the term, there are excep-
tions to the rule: when Eros shortly before his suicide bids Antony
to avert 'that noble countenance / Wherein the worship of the whole

---

1   Thomas Hill, *The Contemplation of Mankinde* (London: Seres, 1571) f. 85 and
     90.

world lies' (*Antony and Cleopatra* 4.15.85f.) he seems to allude to its physiognomic (*stricto sensu*) rather than to its pathognomic aspect. Likewise, when Valeria recognises in the young Marcus the 'confirmed countenance' (*Coriolanus* 1.3.56) of his father, it remains questionable whether she refers to temporary features. The term *face*, however, opens up a much broader range of possible meanings. Lear's fool, for instance, can only refer to a temporary expression on pretending to have been silenced by Goneril's looks: 'I will hold my tongue; so your face bids me, though you say nothing' (*King Lear* 1.4.170f.). The face as main agent of non-verbal communication and bearer of immediate feedback is also alluded to in *Macbeth* when Lady Macbeth rebukes her husband by demanding to know why he makes 'such faces' (3.4.66). In the same play, however, the face is also referred in a strict physiognomic sense: Lady Macduff's exclamation 'what are these faces' (4.2.79) unmistakably points to the characters and, one might assume, unfavourable looks of the murderers invading her castle. Hence, the term *face* is used even more ambivalently as the expression *countenance* and can refer to both physiognomic and pathognomic features, depending on the context.

The phrase *visage*, however, is often though not necessarily at all times connected to the motif of masking and as the *Oxford English Dictionary* reveals, denotes 'an assumed appearance, an outward show; a pretence or semblance'. Thus Hamlet refers to 'the dejected haviour of the visage' (*Hamlet* 1.2.81) when distancing him from the mere appearance of faces that lack a corresponding interior. Furthermore, bestial features are coupled to a 'visage' such as Goneril's, whom Lear ascribes a 'wolvish visage' (*King Lear* 1.4.285). Antony uses the term on alleging Cleopatra's dishonesty: 'let / Patient Octavia plough thy visage up / With her preparèd nails' (*Antony and Cleopatra* 4.13.37–9) and Mercutio does not speak of a *face* but a *visage* when getting ready for the masked ball and hiding his natural appearance by an artificial guise: 'Give me a case to put my visage in / A visor for a visor' (*Romeo and Juliet* 1.4.29f.). Simulation results in a masked face or 'a visor' as it is indicated in *Othello* (1.1.50), in *Timon of Athens* (2.1.28f.), in *Love's Labour's Lost* where one agrees to meet again 'with visages displayed to talk and greet' (5.2.143) or in *Hamlet* when Polonius instructs his son in the art of self-fashioning which entails the concealment of unfavourable aspects 'with devotion's visage' (3.1.49). Desdemona's claim to have seen 'Othello's visage in his mind' (*Othello* 1.3.251) is no exception. The image of the covered face is merely inverted whereby the mask becomes extracted from the interior of man with the objective of enclosing Othello's naturally black face by what seems a more favourable aspect. The allegation of masquerade is taken up by Othello, who approaches Desdemona and ponders on the divine appearance of her face which seems 'as fresh / As Dian's visage' (3.3.391f.) while suspecting a mask where there is none.

Even though faces are usually perceived as entities, the question remains what constitutes an overall impression of a countenance, a face, a visage. As mentioned above, it is typically one particular feature, which catches the eye of the beholder and inscribes itself into their memory, which becomes remembered as the predominant expression of the face. Furthermore, many of Shakespeare's characters are demarcated by one or two specific physiognomic elements, which is why, in the following discussion, the face shall be split into its segments in order to scrutinise individual features before eventually combining the pieces again to a physiognomic text. Thereby it is important to bear in mind that their meaning ultimately depends on both the physiognomic and the receptive contexts, first and foremost, however, on the objectives of their interpreter. Hence, the interpretations offered in the following physiognomic catalogue have to be regarded as tentative readings, which are often polyphonic but adhere to physiognomic knowledge as it is conveyed through Early Modern physiognomic manuals.

4.1 A Title-leaf to the Face

Considering the face as 'a book where men / May read strange matters' (*Macbeth* 1.5.60f.) and perceive their fortune and their misery, the forehead serves as an index providing a comprehensible overview of a particular character. Thus Northumberland introduces Morton, claiming that 'this man's brow, like to a title leaf, / Foretells the nature of a tragic volume' (1.1.60f.), which makes him an apt figure to set off the second part of *Henry IV*. Similarly, the chorus in *Henry VIII* announces at the outset of the play that hard times are dawning: 'Things now / That bear a weighty and a serious brow' (1.1.1f.). From a phrenological perspective, the constitution and measurement of the forehead, which in Shakespeare's plays is often referred to as 'brow', point to the design and quality of the human brain. Consequently, a high forehead is regarded to point to a great mind. The lower and smaller this particular area, the more confined and narrower the brain – this simple reasoning is based on the belief that great thoughts cannot unfold in a restricted area such as the messenger in *Antony and Cleopatra* ascribes to Octavia (3.3.33f.). Her forehead is strikingly disproportionate to Caesar's 'broad-fronted' (1.5.29) character, indicating her intellectual inferiority. Furthermore, it can be assumed, it also falls short of Cleopatra's brow, which expands by effect of her rival's unfavourable image, which the messenger most probably tailors to the expectations of his mistress. Rosaline's 'high forehead' (*Romeo and Juliet* 2.1.18), however, displays an ideal of beauty and intelligence, which, however, becomes a utopia as it never appears onstage. Duke Vincentio claims to discover signs of 'honesty and constancy' (*Measure for Measure* 4.2.143) written in Provost's brow and King Henry is concerned about the 'riot and dishonour' (*1 Henry IV* 1.1.84) staining the forehead of his son.

Where the index seems incomplete, its immediate amendment is being called for. Thereby it is predominantly the female face, which is perceived as being somehow imperfect and left unfinished, suggesting the subjection of the female body to the authority and authorising power of the male. Lear implores nature to mark Gonerill according to her character: 'Let it stamp wrinkle in her brow of youth;/ With cadent tears fret channels in her cheeks' (*King Lear* 1.4.261). While it is disputable whether at Shakespeare's time criminals and prostitutes were still branded,[1] Hamlet pretends to see a blister on Gertrude's 'fair forehead' (*Hamlet* 3.4.42) and in *The Comedy of Errors* Adriana refers to 'the stained skin' of a 'harlot brow' (2.2.136).

---

1   Compare Standish Henning, 'Branding Harlots on the Brow', *Shakespeare Quarterly* 51/1 (2000) 86–9.

Besides static, physiognomic features also temporary, pathogno-
mic emotions can be communicated on this particular surface, whose
wrinkles pronounce grief and anger when the brow is perceived as
'clouded' or 'knitted'. [1] The latter image is used by Claudius, who
pronounces himself and his subalterns to be 'contracted in one brow
of woe' (*Hamlet* 1.2.4), as a symbol of both grief for Old Hamlet's
death and national cohesion, as a shared expression that ties together
the king and the people of Denmark in times of sorrow and in times
of war. However, as Northumberland's reading indicates, which pro-
ceeds from the brow to a more complex physiognomic analyses,
the forehead marks but the index, which one beholds before further
engaging in the book.

4.2 Windows to the Soul

The most expressive and, at the same time, most complex facial fea-
tures are the eyes. Due to their proximity to the heart, the locus of
reason, and in allusion to their moist and glossy surface, they were
referred to as *speculum animi* and 'direct *Index* of the *Minde*'[2]. A
glance into the *Harvard Concordance*, which lists more than 1300
entries under the lexeme 'eye' confirms that Shakespeare extensively
draws from the rhetoric of this particular feature. It is the eyes whose
expression Cassius takes as a starting point for his 'reading' of Brutus,
claiming that he had 'not from your eyes that gentleness / And show
of love' (*Julius Caesar* 1.2.35f.) that he was used to. While the 'show'
that Cassius is missing could point to a certain deceitfulness of the
eye, it first and foremost ties in with the mirror image evoked in this
particular scene and reflects the fake image that Cassius is about to
impose onto his counterpart. What he pretends to extract from Brutus'
face is in fact a reflection of himself, which he beholds in the glassy
surface of the eyes he looks into. Thus it is not him but rather Brutus,
who serves as mirror for the 'eye' to see itself (cf. 1.2.54).

In this context, it yet again becomes very apparent that it is the

---

1   See *Julius Caesar* 1.2.184; *Taming of the Shrew* 5.2.140; *2 Henry VI* 3.1.15 and
3.1.155.
2   John Davies of Hereford, *Microcosmos: The Discovery of the Little World, with
the Government thereof* (Oxford: Barnes, 1603) 91.

reading of faces rather than the face *per se*, which is important in Shakespeare's plays. The 'art of physiognomy', which is referred to in *The Rape of Lucrece* (1394f.) not only points to the pseudo-science itself but first and foremost to the artifice of the face and body as well the artistry of reading, which have to be taken into account in order to secure a successful decipherment of the physiognomies presented onstage. Concentrating on the readings of facial features, Shakespeare is not obliged to question the validity of physiognomy at any moment. Instead, he shifts the fallibility of this pseudo-science to the 'translator' and the process of translating. Not the 'eye' delivers false information but the person describing the visual phenomenon with his or her own words. This also applies to the mirror scene discussed above: it is the task of the reader to spot the clues laid out for him, to question and review the reading presented by Cassius, and if applicable, to counter it with his or her own interpretation of the features he beholds onstage. When it comes to the expression of or in the eyes, however, the task might prove an unfeasible venture simply because the distance between spectators and actors would not allow for such scrutiny. Even the actors onstage would not always be able to scrutinise the eyes' and infer a certain emotional expression from their looks. When the approaching servant in *Macbeth* is greeted with the remark, 'what haste looks through his eyes' (1.2.46), this 'observation' is but a theatrical device to admit the messenger to the floor.[1] Even if the spectators cannot see the *speculum animi* themselves, comments on the look into one's eyes' serve to sensitise them for the expressiveness of the human face and urge them to sharpen their view for other physiognomic features.

More often than not in Shakespeare, the eyes are considered a trustworthy token, which corresponds to *communis opinio* and to the observations made in physiognomic manuals of the time. Thus it is quite likely that together with Brutus, the audience at first are deceived by Cassius' pseudo-reflection. This is even more likely as Cassius draws from a common image when considering the eyes as

---

1   The same device is used in *Antony and Cleopatra* when the servant comes onstage and Caesar gives him the floor immediately, claiming that 'the business of this man looks out of him' (5.1.50).

a mirror, which is turned to the insight in order to reflect the inner disposition to the outside world. The reflective function of the eye is also referred to elsewhere in Shakespeare. In contrast to Cassius' reading, however, the image delivered by the eye in the following examples can be trusted. Through the *speculum animi*, King Richard, for instance, can look straight into John of Gaunt and confront him with his distress: 'Uncle, even in the glasses of thine eyes / I see thy grievèd heart' (*Richard II* 1.3.201f.). No less revealing is the look into the eyes of the Earl of Worcester, which lays open 'danger and disobedience' (*1 Henry IV* 1.3.15), and the mirror of Richard Gloucester's inside does not belie its beholder but shows a 'murderous' (*Richard III* 4.1.55) and 'deadly' (1.3.222) expression. Whether described as 'fierce' (*King Lear* 2.4.166), 'bright' (*Romeo and Juliet* 2.1.17), 'graceful' (*Antony and Cleopatra* 2.2.64), as 'so quick, so fair' (*Romeo and Juliet* 3.5.220), 'death-darting' (*Romeo and Juliet* 3.2.47), or 'wounding' (*2 Henry VI* 3.2.51), the eyes more often than not truthfully reveal a certain state of mind. And yet, it is possible that characters verbalising their expression might (often deliberately as in Cassius' case) mistake their message. In *Macbeth*, a play concerned with the art of deceitful self-fashioning amidst an opaque and gloomy world, Lady Macbeth refers to the eye as the main medium of communication, which however is not immune against manipulation. When she urges her husband to 'bear welcome in your eye, / Your hand, your tongue' (1.5.62f.), she ranks facial expression in which the eyes become representative of the countenance, higher than gesture and words,

Deliberate deceit and false speculation are rarely connected to the eyes when it comes to the comedies. As in *Romeo and Juliet*, the first part of which can be regarded as a comedy, they are primarily seen as the windows through which love can enter the mind,[1] a 'quality' which the Friar chides Romeo for: 'Young men's love then lies / Not truly in their hearts but in their eyes' (2.2.67f.). Lysander discovers in Helena's eyes '[l]ove's stories written in love's richest book' (*A Midsummer Night's Dream* 2.2.128) and Prospero contentedly observes that Miranda and Ferdinand 'have changed eyes' (*The*

---

1   Compare *Love's Labour's Lost* 4.3.296–301.

Tempest 1.2.445) at first sight. The reflective surface of the eyes which confronts the viewer not only with his or her own image but with a likeness that is his or her semblable, 'a second selfe'[1], is alluded to in *Romeo and Juliet* when the lovers remark their shared paleness:

> Juliet: Either my eyesight fails, or thou look'st pale.
> Romeo: And trust me, love, in my eye so do you.
>   Dry sorrow drinks our blood. Adieu, adieu.
>   (3.5.57–9)

In the parched bodies with their colourless skin, death casts its shadows before the parting couple. The mutual reflection in each other's *speculum* marks the crest of their relationship and intensifies the encounter of the first balcony scene when the physiognomic reading is but one-sided:

> Juliet: If they do see thee, they will murder thee.
> Romeo: Alack, there lies more peril in thine eye
>   Than twenty of their swords. Look thou but sweet
>   And I am proof against their enmity.
>   (2.1.112–15)

The danger, however, lurks on the inside, or rather in the eye of the beholder. It is striking that in this particular play, which by references to the physiognomy of nature and the Friar's adherence to botany and herbology and thus to the Paracelsian concept of natural signs, the tragic ending should be prompted by a fatal misreading of external signifiers. Even though Romeo does not overlook the marks of beauty, the crimson lips and scarlet cheeks in Juliet's face, and death, which has before revealed itself in paleness, is as unsubstantial in this scene as it was in Romeo's dream (5.1.6–9), he deems Juliet dead. Failing to consider the tokens of life, Romeo finally seals his fate that has been 'writ […] in misfortune's book' (5.3.82) by a tragic misconception of visual signifiers.

Greater certainty and a deeper insight into a particular charac-

---

1   Pierre de La Primaudaye, *The French Academy*, trans. by Thomas Bowes (London: Edmund Bollifan, 1618) II 484: […] love causeth him that doth love to engrave and imprint in his heart, that face and image which he loveth: so that the heart of him that loveth is made like a looking glasse, in which the image of the party beloved shineth and is represented.

ter, however, might be expected from the colour of the eyes. While some colourings adhere to common colour connotations, however, Shakespeare is not always consistent in their distribution. When Julia identifies Silvia's eyes as the spitting image of her own ('her eyes are grey as glass, and so are mine' [*Two Gentlemen of Verona* 4.4.184]) and Olivia attributes 'grey eyes' to herself (*Twelfth Night* 1.5.217), they draw on an established ideal of beauty. The goddess Athena was attributed the sobriquet *glaukopis*, which could be translated by 'owl-eyed', 'bright-eyed', 'grey-' or even 'blue-eyed'. However, when Mercutio in his disdain for Petrarch calls Thisbe 'a grey eye or so', it seems doubtful whether he refers to 'a synonym for beautiful or bright and radiant'[1] or whether he adheres to readings such as the one by Thomas Hill, who considers grey eyes as 'a note wicked persons'[2]. As with many other features, Shakespeare fully exploits the various meanings attached to the colour grey, whose implications have to be derived from its context rather than from its presence alone. A more obvious rival candidate to the *blazon* than Thisbe, who grey-eyed as Mercutio describes her would not contradict the Petrarchan catalogue, is Shakespeare's most mysterious figure, who is distinguished by the highly charged colour black, which can be perceived even in her eyes. Like the Dark Lady herself, her 'raven-black' (*Sonnet 127*, 9) eyes call for revising the concept of beauty:

> In the old age black was not counted fair,
> Or if it were it bore not beauty's name;
> But now is black beauty's successive heir [...].
> (*Sonnet 127*, 1–3)

Notwithstanding the fact that both Petrarch's Laura and Sidney's Stella had black eyes, the colour was indeed not counted fair. According to Della Porta it derives from exceeding heat in the brain and occurs primarily in Ethiopian countries, whose inhabitants are said to be fearful and fraudulent, which is supported by Pseudo-

---

1 Walter C. Curry, *The Middle English Ideal of Personal Beauty as Found in the Metrical Romances, Chronicles and Legends of the XIII, XIV, and XV Centuries* (Baltimore: Furst, 1916) 51.

2 Thomas Hill, *The Contemplation of Mankinde* (London: Seres, 1571) f. 69.

Aristotle and Polemon.[1] It is not until Robert Burton, who praises black as the 'most amiable, enticing and the fairest'[2] of all colours, that the turn of fashion, which is pled for in *Sonnet 127*, finds its first major advocate. The positive connotations of this particular feature, however, seem to hearken back to classical literature,[3] which might explain its re-emergence in the Early Modern era where it became fashionable to endow a figure with black eyes, a trend which Agnolo Firenzuola laments: '[...] tutti e poeti greci e latini e i nostri ancora con una voce medesima, gridino occhi neri.'[4] The great success of the Dark Lady, however, derives from her ability to provoke and thus points to a semiotic system, which has not yet fully acknowledged the beauty of blackness. Shakespeare's deviance from common norms presupposes an audience that is deeply familiar with the basic principles of physiognomy; otherwise a figure such as the Dark Lady would not prove quite as effective. By challenging the conventional meanings attached to certain features, Shakespeare raises the audience's awareness of the ambiguity of bodily signs and the fallibility of their analysis. Rather than a code of practice that must be rigidly adhered to, physiognomy becomes a fruitful subtext, whose potential is fully exploited by Shakespeare's characters, which can contradict or comply with its guidelines. Deviation from physiognomic norms, however, is not as easily achieved as one might think considering that physiognomic manuals already diverge in their assessment of some features.

The colour green as eye-colour, for instance, is as ambivalent in Shakespeare as it is in physiognomic handbooks. With reference to Patroclus, who is said to have had green eyes, Polemon regards it as an indication of strength. This notion corresponds to Elizabethan colour symbolism where the colour green is connected to joy, hopefulness,

---

1   Johannes ab Indagine, *The Book of Palmestry and Physiognomy*, trans. by Fabian Withers (London: J. Cottrel, 1651) H2, and Thomas Hill, *The Contemplation of Mankinde* (London: Seres, 1571) f. 69.

2   Robert Burton, *The Anatomy of Melancholy* (1621) (Amsterdam/New York: Da Capo, 1621) 560.

3   See Holger M. Klein, *Das weibliche Portrait in der Versdichtung der englischen Renaissance* (Munich: Munich University, 1969) 408f.

4   Agnolo Firenzuola, *Celso Dialogo delle Bellezze delle Donne (1548)*. In: *Opere*, ed. by Adriano Seroni (Florence: Sansoni, 1993) 577f.

youth, and love.¹ Other physiognomic manuals, however, attribute this feature to a knowledgeable yet guileful and above all jealous character.² The latter is alluded to in *Othello* where envy is referred to as 'the green-eyed monster' (3.3.170), an image that might have been inspired by Spenser's *The Fairie Queene* where avarice appears in a green robe.³ Which association might have been evoked in the audience when Juliet's nurse praises Paris' green eyes (*Romeo and Juliet* 3.5.220) is contentious. While one could argue that the quirky woman simply mistakes their implication, it seems more likely that she beautifies the portrait to pitch the suitor to his future bride.

Unambiguous is alone the red colour of eyes, whose implications are consistent with physiognomic theory in that they point to a hot temper, a choleric disposition or a mind enflamed by anger. The latter is emphasised by the proverbially burning eyes such as Menenius ascribes to Coriolanus (*Coriolanus* 5.1.64) and Cicero's 'fiery eyes' (*Julius Caesar* 1.2.187).

4.3 'Let him not leave out the colour of her hair'

Colour becomes significant not only with regard to the eyes, but also, of course, in connection to hair and primarily skin. According to early modern psychology, the humoral disposition, which was thought to dictate one's temperament, constitution, and complexion, would determine the colouring of the surface body. While physiognomic manuals do not imply any connection between the distribution of the humours in a body and eye-colour, for instance, Shakespeare's physiognomic scheme does allow for such a connection. The 'raven-black' eyes of the Dark Lady correspond to a melancholic mind, which is suggested by the speaker's remark that they have an expression of mourning about them (*Sonnet 127*, 10). Hair, however, seems a more immediate and far more obvious witness to a particular humour, and

---

1 Compare 'Green indeed is the colour of lovers' (*Love's Labour's Lost* 1.2.78) and *Hamlet* 1.3.101. See also Cameron Allen, 'Symbolic Colour in the Literature of the English Renaissance', *Philological Quarterly* 15 (1936) 81–92.
2 Compare Richard Saunders, *Physiognomie and Chiromancie, Metoposcopie* (London: Brooke, 1653) 173.
3 Edmund Spenser, *The Faerie Queene* I iv 25.1.

yet again there is no one-to-one connection between Shakespeare's distribution of hair colour and its implication as it is set down in physiognomic treatises.

Brown or yellowish hair is regarded as indicating a sanguine, benign, and gentle character, white or flaxen hair point to an abundance of phlegm. Hair of red colour is associated with a foul humour, and the colour black signifies a choleric or else melancholic disposition.[1] Assuming that the colours brown and blond are the most desirable, Benedick's judgement of Hero, who, to his taste, is 'too brown for a fair praise' (1.1.139), is but a witty turn-around of the positive implications of this hue. Olivia, at least, whose 'brown' hair the messenger couples with a 'low' forehead (*Antony and Cleopatra* 3.3.32f.) in an attempt to diminish her beauty, turns out to be prettier than Cleopatra would have her. In both cases, the seemingly negative connotations would be recognised as such and critically reviewed and revised by the audience. And yet, as with eye colour, there is no rule of thumb that could be applied on all occasions. Mental balance and prudence, qualities that John Huarte, in compliance with Averroes, associates with brown coloured hair,[2] can hardly account for Antony's choleric character and Antony himself offers another interpretation: rashness.

> My very hairs do mutiny, for the white
> Reprove the brown for rashness, and they them
> For fear and doting.
> (*Antony and Cleopatra* 3.11.13–15)

While white and 'silver hairs' (*Julius Caesar* 2.1.143) are commonly connected to old age and with it to venerability and wisdom, Antony weaves them into a physiological process. Fear and terror let the blood retreat to the heart, causing not only the skin but, thus it is implied, also the hair to lose its colour. Antony's physiological explanation is just another example of Shakespeare's creative expansion of common physiognomic axioms, which heightens the dra-

---

1   Compare Ruth L. Anderson, *Elizabethan Psychology and Shakespeare's Plays* (Iowa: University of Iowa Press, 1927) 40.

2   John Huarte, *Examen de Ingenios = The Examination of Mens Wits*, trans. by Richard Carew (London: Islip, 1594) 243f.

matic effect of this particular scene. In Shakespeare's physiognomic scheme, it is the changeability, the shifting and movement of particular expressions and thus primarily those features that *stricto sensu* can be termed pathognomic, which take centre stage as they provide the most fruitful material for a physiognomic reading and reasoning.

4.4 'Where is thy blush?'

Skin colour becomes relevant predominantly in pathognomic terms insofar as the changing tint of the cheeks indicates temporary passions of the mind. There is, of course, one exception, which is the black(ened) face:

> Coal-black is better than another hue
> In that it scorns to bear another hue
> (*Titus Andronicus* 4.2.98f.)

Aaron comes right to the point: the advantage and monstrosity of a black face springs from the steadiness of its colour and its resistance to the tell-tale play of white and red, which is so much a giveaway, since it is involuntary. Fear, anger, guilt, lovesickness, grief, and, most of all, shame entail a change of colour and induce blushing or pallor.[1] As with other features, Shakespeare yet again takes advantage of the broad scope of implications and the polyphonic readings arising in this context.

In *Romeo and Juliet*, the pallid face is a key feature in a plot that gradually prepares the audience for a fatal misreading of the colouring of life. Juliet's sorrow over Tybalt's loss, her lovelorn state, and anxiety in view of her and Romeo's future are expressed by her paleness, which is passed on to Romeo (3.5.57–9). The face becomes an area which holds clues about the past, present, and future. As suggested by the predominance of paleness, death is hovering above 'the story of [...] woe' (5.3.308) and takes possession of the star-crossed lovers (3.5.57–9), shortly after it conquered Tybalt ('pale,

---

1 Compare Robert Burton, *Anatomy of Melancholy* (1621) (Amsterdam/New York: Da Capo, 1971) 596. See also Ewan Fernie, *Shame in Shakespeare* (London/ New York: Routledge, 2002) esp. 74–108, *Macbeth* 4.1.101, *Romeo and Juliet* 2.1.47, 2.3.187f., 5.1.28f., and *Love's Labour's Lost* 4.3.125.

pale as ashes' [3.2.55]). The friar's portrayal of the seemingly dead
Juliet ('the roses in thy lips and cheeks shall fade / To wanny ashes,
thy eyes' windows fall / Like death when he shuts up the day of life'
[4.1.99–101]) continues the image of the dried up, cold body and fore-
shadows the tragic ending. Relying on his knowledge of physiologi-
cal processes, the Friar aims at undermining natural law and arranges
the staging of a dead body. This dissociation of signifier and signi-
fied suggested by his intervention in nature's semiotic system, serves
as a prerequisite for Romeo's fatal misreading, which disregards the
indicators of life on Juliet's face. The confusion of the implications
connected to the colours red and white in this scene, which recalls the
image of the dead Tybalt ('pale, pale as ashes, all bedaubed in blood'
[3.2.55]) eventually cumulates in the sight awaiting the Friar when he
enters the monument and beholds the two lifeless bodies of Romeo
and Juliet covered in blood.

Romeo and Juliet is not the only play to focus on skin colouring:
The much ado about nothing in Shakespeare's play of the same title
springs from a misinterpretation of Hero's complexion. Her blush
at her conviction and the charges put against her prompts conflict-
ing interpretations. While both Claudio and Leonato are convinced
that 'her blush is guiltiness, not modesty' (*Much Ado About Nothing*
4.1.40) and confesses her crime, Friar Francis deems her innocent
(4.1.157–60). The accusation, however, is ill-founded since a female
blush is generally regarded as a sign of modesty and a pure mind.[1]
Thus, at first sight, Claudio's reading of Hero seems rather implau-
sible and can be dismissed by the audience, who furthermore is
aware of the mischievous machinations of Don John, as completely
unfounded.

The Rape of Lucrece, a poem which heavily relies on the eloquence
of the human face and the rhetoric of shame, seems to be organised
around the 'silent war of lilies and of roses' (71), which is the most
remarkable characteristic of 'modest Lucrece' (123), denoting her
virtue, one that is not based on reason but to which her body and soul
are naturally inclined for the blush occurs involuntarily, as well as her

---

1   Compare Juliet's 'maiden blush' (*Romeo and Juliet* 2.1.128), 'a blush / Modest as
      morning' (*Troilus and Cressida* 1.3.226f.), 'blush of modesty' (*Hamlet* 3.4.40).

beauty, which take their turn in conquering her countenance:

> When virtue bragged, beauty would blush for shame;
> When beauty boasted blushes, in despite
> Virtue would stain that or with silver white.
> (*Lucrece* 54–56)

While sustaining Lucrece's 'modest eloquence' (563), which is rooted in nonverbal communication, the symbolically charged colours white and red serve to underscore the violation of the pure body with its 'alabaster' (419) and 'ivory' (464) skin of 'the dove' (360), which falls prey to Tarquin's heated lustre and is shamed to death. Before violating Lucrece, Tarquin shifts the blame onto Lucrece's body, more precisely: to the shade of her cheeks:

> [...] The colour in thy face –
> That even for anger makes the lily pale,
> And the red rose blush at her own disgrace,
> Shall plead for me and tell my loving tale.
> Under that colour am I come to scale
> Thy never-conquered fort. the fault is thine,
> For those thine eyes betray thee unto mine.
> (*Lucrece* 477–83)

Colouring the assault by heraldic tincture, Tarquin fashions the rape as an act of heroism, the violation of the body into a conquest. Effacing his crime, he defaces Lucrece: after the dreadful deed, her body ceases to communicate.

The focus is shifted to Tarquin's face, which has lost colour in the combat and leaves the battlefield and the tainted sheets 'with lank and lean discoloured cheek, / With heavy eye, knit brow, and strengthless pace' (708f.). Lucrece's features, however, remain in the dark. The shadows of the night seem to have swallowed up her blush even though she feels the tainting of her cheeks: 'I have no one to blush with me' (792). Blushing needs an audience. It is prompted by the presence of an other under whose gaze the face changes colour in the sudden awareness of a shameful fault that has been disclosed by the look into one's own *speculum animi*. The onlooker, however, is not necessarily to be located outside one's body. Shame can be triggered in the process of self-reflection whereby a person perceives himself as an 'other' and distances himself from his body.[1] This is what happens to Lucrece, whose shame springs from the alienation of her virtuous mind from her tainted body, which furthermore bears the blame added by Tarquin's accusation that it were her colours that prompted the deed.

The first reference to Lucrece's complexion coincides with the entrance of the maid. Even though the latter sees her mistress' face 'over-washed with woe', she dares not ask the cause of her grief. Instead, after Lucrece's long monologue of woe and misery, language is substituted by non-verbal communication: the maid joins in the flow of tears, which, as the speaker reminds us, the weaker sex all too often does (1236f.). The mirror generated by the infectious quality of tears is further developed when Lucrece finally meets somebody to blush with her.

When the messenger comes face to face with his mistress to receive her letter to Collatine, he blushes. While the reaction of the 'sour-faced groom' (1334) results from a feeling of unworthiness at the sight of his mistress' beauty (1338f.) and is clearly attributed to his 'bashful innocence' (1341), Lucrece suspects 'he blushed to see her shame' (1344). But in fact the reflection works the other way round. Lucrece's cheeks redden as she sees her servant blush, underscoring the extent of her shame, which she thinks to have been deeply engraved into her face (1091). As Tarquin's shift of blame demonstrates, the female body and mind is liable to male imprints. The inferiority of the 'waxen' (1240) disposition of women to 'marble' (1240) men entails a greater degree of physical legibility:

> Though man can cover crimes with bold, stern looks,
> Poor woman's faces are their own faults' books.
> (*Lucrece* 1252f.)

The inscrutability of male faces will manifest itself in Sinon's portrait showing 'cheeks neither red nor pale, but mingled so / That

---

1   See Ewan Fernie, *Shame in Shakespeare* (London/New York: Routledge, 2002) 68f.

blushing red no guilty instance gave, / Nor ashy pale the fear that false hearts have' (1510–12). Outraged by this deceiving image of a 'constant and confirmèd devil' (1513), Lucrece stabs the simulacrum as if to mark the traitor's smooth surface, inscribing into it those 'remorseless wrinkles' (562), which she perceived in Tarquin's countenance on realising his intentions. Lucrece's vain attempt to re-establish the congruity between body and psyche foreshadows the final scene where she raises the dagger against her own body to disclose the wounds it received. Shortly before her suicide, her face comes into view again. After Collatine's return, it has turned pale, communicating her 'deadly cares' (1593). Even though the bystanders, who arrived at the scene together with her husband, assure her that 'her body's stain her mind untainted clears' (1710), the imprint of Tarquin's assault cannot be ignored nor easily extinguished. Alluding to Lavinia's 'map of woe' (*Titus Andronicus* 3.2.12), Lucrece's countenance is likened to a 'map which deep impression bears / Of hard misfortune' (1712f.). Turning away from her husband and his friends in a gesture of shame and thereby avoiding their gazes, which are both unsettling and reassuring her self in its existence, Lucrece prepares for her self-extinction. Stabbing herself, she turns her body into a fountain of blood, which bubbling from her corpse seems to blush as if to testify its innocence and purity (1749f.) in a spectacle of unspeakable woe. As the examples from *Much Ado About Nothing* and *Lucrece* indicate, the connection of blushing and guilt has to be reconsidered, especially with regard to the female face.[1] Men's faces, however, seem to resist blushing, which is considered as proof of their irreproachability.

Thus Gloucester asserts to Suffolk that his search for a blush in his face will be in vain for 'a heart unspotted' (*2 Henry VI* 3.1.100) does not taint the countenance. The reverse, however, is not necessarily the case as a deceitful, treacherous mind might resist its translation onto the exterior. Whereas Richard II accuses Bolingbroke of disloyalty, foretelling him that 'his treasons will sit blushing in his face' (*Richard II* 3.2.47), Richard Gloucester's face lacks a document of

---

1   Even though female faces might potentially belie blushing and paling by skilfully applied make-up (cf. chapter 4.4)

guilt. Anne's appeal to his corrupted body, '[b]lush, blush, thou lump of foul deformity' (*Richard III* 1.2.57) is in vain. While the missing blush where there is cause for feelings of shame or embarrassment is perceived as unnatural, even diabolic, its occurrence in a male face is often regarded shameful as it indicates loss of face and suggests a failure to control one's emotions, which consequently take over and betray the mind (*Love's Labour's Lost* 1.2.429). Furthermore, the alienating power of the blush, which takes possession of the face to reveal 'that within', poses a threat of effeminisation to the male body. Male blushing becomes a cause for mockery: 'Come, you virtuous ass, you bashful fool, must you be blushing? Wherefore blush you now? What a maidenly man at arms are you become!' (*2 Henry IV* 2.2.61–3). Only a boy might be given credit for his blushing (the Duke of Milan in *Two Gentlemen of Verona*, for instance, takes it as an indicator of grace [5.4.162]).

4.5 'God hath given you one face, and you make yourselves another'

Even though blushing seems most telling wherever it appears, its absence does not necessarily point to an emotional void nor does it always suggest firm control over the body as it is enacted by Richard Gloucester, who claims that he can 'frame [his] face to all occasions' (*3 Henry VI* 3.2.185). While Margret is indeed deemed monstrously inhuman, 'the she-wolf', due to her 'visor-like, unchanging' countenance (*3 Henry VI* 1.4.112–17), female faces can resist the play of lilies and roses on their cheeks through skilfully applied make-up.

> If she be made of white and red
> Her faults will ne'er be known,
> For blushing cheeks by faults are bred
> And fears by pale white shown.
> Then if she fear or be to blame,
> By this you shall not know;
> For still her cheeks possess the same
> Which native she doth owe.
> (*Love's Labour's Lost* 1.2.89–96)

In *Love's Labour's Lost*, Mote quite convincingly argues 'against the reason of white and red' (1.2.98). The highly disputed practice of face-painting is in itself regarded as a shameless action in that it intervenes in the divine semiotic scheme by altering characters in the *liber naturae* and plastering them with layers of white lead.[1] Enobarbus' remark that 'there is never a fair woman has a true face' (*Antony and Cleopatra* 2.6.100) implies that a whitened face devoid of any blushing action indicates not only a lack of modesty but also a culpable soul that has sinned against god's creation. This notion is supported by Philipp Stubbes, who in his *Anatomy of Abuses* claims that the sole need for make-up points to a corrupted mind: '[…] who seeth not that their soules are thereby deformed?', he asks with regard to the women of Ailgna, who 'use to colour their faces with certain Oyles, Liquors, Unguentes, and Waters […] whereby they thinke their beautie is greatly decored'.[2] Notwithstanding its critics, the popular fashion of painting the face, whose mask-like appearance resisted the signs of age and toils of life, had a most influential advocate in Elizabeth I, whose alabaster, mask-like face soon became her hallmark.

In Shakespeare's plays, face-paining comes into focus whenever the legibility of the female countenance is at stake and marks the outset of numerous misogynous portrayals.[3] 'God hath given you one face, and you make yourselves another' (*Hamlet* 3.1.142f.), Hamlet famously chides the 'beautified' (2.2.110) face of Ophelia. A little later, he turns the spectator's attention to the unnatural colour-constancy of Gertrude's complexion: 'O shame, where is thy blush?' (3.4.72). His accusation, however, misses its target. While Gertrude's reaction, or rather her non-reaction points to her clear conscience and her ignorance of Old Hamlet's murder, Ophelia throughout the play is presented as a chaste, modest, and pure character. This notion is not contradicted but rather confirmed by the nunnery-scene, which is

---

1 Compare Tanya Pollard, *Drugs and Theatre in Early Modern England* (Oxford et al.: Oxford University Press, 2005) 84–91.

2 Philip Stubbes, *The Anatomie of Abuses* (London: Iones, 1584) 32.

3 For a detailed study of face-painting in Shakespeare and early modern drama consult Shirley Garner, '*Let Her Paint an Inch Thick*: Painted Ladies in Renaissance Drama and Society', *Renaissance Drama* 10/1 (1989) 23-39; Annette Drew-Bear, *Painted Faces on the Renaissance Stage: The Moral Significance of Face-Painting Conventions* (Lewisburg: Bucknell University Press, 1994).

all-to often reduced to its bawdy para-text: Leaving aside the bawdy suggestion of Ophelia's retreat to a brothel, Hamlet's direction 'to a nunnery, go' can be read as an attempt to preserve Ophelia's purity by detaching her from the corrupted court and thereby also to preserve her natural beauty and save her from a 'conception' (2.2.185), an insight, which taints her soul in the same way as it should and, in Hamlet's reading, as it will, Gertrude's.

The assumption that Ophelia is exempt from Hamlet's accusations is furthermore supported by the broader connotations connected with face-painting in this particular play. In *Hamlet*, facial make-up is discussed primarily as a theatrical device and hence associated not only with female characters but also with (male) actors who might take on female roles. Prepared for by Polonius' remark, which sums up the dissimulative potential of faces, 'with devotion's visage [...] we do sugar o'er / The devil himself' (3.1.49–51), and Hamlet's 'antic disposition' (2.1.173), facial make-up is presented as a prop. In the graveyard scene Hamlet stumbles over Yorrick's skull, whose constant grin mocks the theatre of the world, in which multiple roles are adopted. None of them, however, is able to disclose 'that within', which Hamlet can finally grasp when he holds in his hand the remains of a persona which approximates his 'antic disposition', the role at which he is at his best. And yet, when Hamlet realises whose skull he is scrutinising, he sends 'Yorrick' in the styling room for a makeover: 'Now get you to my lady's chamber and tell her, let her paint an inch thick' (5.1.178f.). While the colours are declared to belong to a woman, who could well be Ophelia, the face-painting theme is shifted from the female sphere to the theatrical space and thus suggests a neutral if not favourable perspective on facial make-up, which is not restricted to women only but, especially in the context of the theatre, also used by men.[1]

There is some dispute about the question whether Shakespeare's actors would have applied make-up in order to fashion their personae. It seems plausible that the boy-actors resorted to face-paint in order to support their female attire. Considering the meta-theatrical

---

1   Compare Tanya Pollard, 'Beauty's Poisonous Properties', *Shakespeare Studies* 27 (1999) 187–210, 199f.

discourse opened up by Hamlet, however, it cannot be ruled out that those figures raging against the corrupted art of face-painting wore some sort of make-up themselves so that the strongest opponents of this 'art' might have appeared onstage as its greatest advocates. Actors with painted faces could have served as subversive forces, misjudging female characters and suggesting false complexions where there is in fact no room for true faces, since both the male and female figures are liable to the same fraudulent scheme. Considering that there is no evidence for the presence or absence of face-painting onstage, one can only speculate which effect Hamlet's discussion of it might have had on an early modern audience and whether Ophelia's face provided the visual text to his allegation. If the entire cast wore make-up, however, Hamlet's accusation would have had a comic effect and prompted laughter, which seems rather inappropriate especially in his accusation of Ophelia. It is possible that only the boy-actors wore make-up, which would support Hamlet's rage even though the question whether a painted face necessarily represents a corrupted mind would remain and certainly have to be negated in view of Ophelia. Furthermore, one could argue that none of the actors wore make-up but presented a visual counter-text to Hamlet's allegations, which would similarly rehabilitate Ophelia's unspotted reputation in that she is being accused of something that she obviously lacks—a painted face.

Considering its profound meta-theatrical level, which suggests a novel assessment of face-painting that exceeds common misogynistic views, *Hamlet* is exceptional with regard to its treatment of this feature. In most readings, female faces are suspected to deceive their beholders, as, for instance, in *Macbeth*. When Macbeth expresses his amazement at the rosy colour on his wife's face, which resists paleness even at times of greatest distress, it seems obvious that 'the natural ruby' (3.4.113) of Lady Macbeth's cheeks is an artifice indebted to face-paint.

More significant than the mere description of blushing and paling is the question of who notices the changes in complexion. Juliet, for instance, is the only one who can recognise the 'maiden blush' (*Romeo and Juliet* 2.1.128) spreading over her face since the latter is enwrapped by the darkness of night surrounding her. In any case, it is quite unlikely that the audience would have perceived a colouring of her cheeks, considering that blushing like paling is counted to those emotional reactions that are beyond human control. Where these features are self-inscribed, they could point to an attempt at self-fashioning, which is not necessarily backed by a 'visible' text. Juliet's blush might be regarded a playful exploitation of love's rhetoric and allude to her part in the relationship, which exceeds the role of the passive, submissive daughter and points to a more active role than one would expect from a young girl. In fashioning herself as the inexperienced 'maiden', she fuels Romeo's love and alludes to her dominant role in their relationship, which is eventually confirmed by the closure of the story of woe, which emerges as 'the story [...] of Juliet and *her* Romeo' (5.3.309).

Far more dubious than Juliet's blush, which leaves a lot of room for interpretation, is the discolouring of Cleopatra's cheeks. 'I am pale' (*Antony and Cleopatra* 2.5.59), she confesses to Charmian. At the news of Antony and Octavia's marriage, the whitening of her face fits into the queen's scheme. As one of Shakespeare's greatest actresses, Cleopatra knows how to fashion herself on the Egyptian stage and how to communicate her distress. However, her dark skin, the 'tawny front' (1.1.6), which Cleopatra also ascribes to herself, claiming to be 'with Phoebus' amorous pinches black' (1.5.28), impairs a change of colour. Nonetheless as the adjective 'tawny' indicates, suggesting a dark rather than a coal-black face, a visible blushing of her cheeks is not improbable in principle though it might be hard to spot. Thus Caesar's remark on the changing colour in Cleopatra's face is all the more noteworthy. When he identifies signs of shame and embarrassment on Cleopatra's countenance at the discovery of her fraud, it is the first instance that her face is described. Her final subjection to a physiognomic reading coincides with the conquering of her kingdom and implies her submission to Caesar. While the persona of Cleopatra will be further examined at a later stage of this study, her self-descriptions and her reading by Caesar in the final scene, point to the fact that it is especially the question of who reads whom, which is central to the physiognomic subtext of Shakespeare's drama insofar as they shed some light not only on the construction of characters but also on power relations which are at work within a particular play.

4.6 'Soft, gentle, and low, an excellent thing in woman'

There is one feature in Shakespeare's physiognomic theatre which despite being fundamental to the play appears rather inconspicuous. Not surprisingly therefore, its physiognomic value is often overlooked and slips the audience's eye – and ear – namely the voice, which links the actor to the author's pen and dematerialises as well as embodies the script in that it translates its characters onto the stage. Shakespeare's capability to do things with words, to evoke Arden forests, create desolate islands, and construe exotic kingdoms within the wooden 'O', might belie the 'telling' voices of his characters at a first glance. Admittedly, voices play a considerably minor role in the characterisation of the *dramatis personae* if judged from the number of times their tone is referred to. Whenever the voice *is* recognised not only as a medium for communication but as an index of character, however, its implications become all the more significant.

In physiognomic manuals, the voice is ranked among the key components of man's physiognomic character[1] and it is regarded not only as the body of language but also as the most perceptible and most obvious trace of the body in language. Its tone, volume, and pitch shed light on the speaker's character. Shrillness of tone and a high-pitched voice are regarded to belong to someone who is 'prone unto the veneriall acte, unstable, and vaine' as well as 'irefull'[2]. A voice 'small and lowe' suggests 'a creature to be fearefull and envious', a loud voice denotes a 'talkative, bolde, and contencious' person, a hasty one a wicked speaker. And whoever has a 'slowe, and bigge sounde of the voyce, however, 'is iudged to be quite, tractable, gentle, merie [and] very iust'.[3]

Not only in Shakespeare's plays, but also in everyday life, the most

---

1 Cf. Thomas Hill, *The Contemplation of Mankinde* (London: Seres, 1571) f. 131–36.
2 Ibidem, f. 137.
3 Ibidem, f. 134.

immediate function of the voice, however, is identification.[1] 'Who's there?': the opening question in *Hamlet* does not require a name but only a voice. 'Long live the King!'—'Barnado?' (*Hamlet* 1.1.1–4). Especially in *Macbeth*, Shakespeare relies on the voice's kinetic quality and uses it to shroud the opening scene in darkness.

With regard to the voice's function as a means of identification, however, an actor of Shakespeare's company, embodying a certain persona onstage, would have had to face two problems: first, it was not uncommon for an actor to take on several roles in one play. The multiple identities he lent his voice to would have made recognition by voice difficult, though not impractical. And yet, the audience gathered in the Globe would not have had any difficulty identifying a particular role due to its costume, its outward appearance, and possibly even its manner of speech. It is quite likely that actors who took on a double role would have attempted to vary their tone of voice accordingly to maintain the link between voice and identity. Why else would Portia mention her 'reed voice' (*The Merchant of Venice* 3.4.67), which she will adopt together with her disguise as male doctor, with men's clothes, and 'a manly stride'? Secondly, and more significantly with regard to Shakespeare's physiognomic theatre, actors would be expected to adjust their pronunciation to avoid creating a comic gap between their own manners of speech and, for instance, the 'soft, gentle, and low' tone of voice which King Lear holds in high esteem and which distinguishes Cordelia.[2]

However, a certain deviance might not always be avoidable and, at times, even required for bridging the gap between the theatrical world and the *theatrum mundi*. Cleopatra's dreaded vision of the squeaking boy actor embodying her persona in the theatre might come true at the very instance it is expressed. For the actor playing the Egyptian queen probably had not yet reached adolescence and thus might have been struggling with an occasional breaking of his voice whereby he indeed resembled a 'squeaking Cleopatra' onstage. Considering

---

1   Compare *Julius Caesar* 1.3.41; *The Merchant of Venice* 5.1.109–12; *Twelfth Night*, 3.4.318; *Troilus and Cressida* 2.2.97; *King Lear*, 4.6.95; *Othello* 1.1.93, 5.2.129; *Romeo and Juliet* 1.5.51; *Measure for Measure* 5.1.323; *All's Well That Ends Well* 4.1.7f.
2   *King Lear* 5.3.271f.

the highly unstable voices of boy-actors, which reside in a 'vocal limbo'[1] reaching highs and lows beyond their control, it does not seem unlikely that Cleopatra was audibly aligned with her rival in Antony's love, 'shrill-tongued Fulvia' (*Antony and Cleopatra* 1.1.34) even though the latter does not appear onstage.

An ideal tone of voice, so it seems, is embodied in Cordelia, whose 'soft, gentle, and low' (*King Lear* 5.3.271f.) manner of speech is praised by her father. However, there remains some doubt over to what extent his reasoning can be trusted. The admirable triad 'soft, gentle, and low' is etiolated by the additional remark 'an excellent thing in woman'. And indeed, gender does matter when it comes to the tone colour of the human voice: due to the colder humoral disposition of the female body, women's lungs were believed to have a lower capacity than men's, which explains the shriller, weaker, and softer tone of their voices. While Lear's remark could have been received by an early modern audience as approving of the actor's skill to attune his voice to his role, it has a rather misogynistic impact. What is deemed 'an excellent thing in woman' in *King Lear* is in fact a rather unfortunate trait. Even though Thomas Hill takes a soft voice as denoting a person who is 'gentle and tractable',[2] Arcandam's assessment of the same feature is slightly less favourable: 'A soft voice [...] betokeneth meeknesse which is in sheepe.'[3] The fact that both physiognomists can refer to the same animal is owed to the highly ambivalent scheme of zoomorphic inference. Cordelia's voice, however, is not only soft and gentle, but also low. A woman with a low voice constitutes a paradox that is not accounted for in physiognomic manuals. Thus it seems likely that Shakespeare takes into account the boy actor's instable vocal chords. Through the reference to the metatheatrical scope of the play, the two bodies of Cordelia come into view. Beside the body dramatic, the actor embodying Cordelia shines through, whose body has a male rather than a female physiological inventory,

---

1   Gina Bloom, '*Thy Voice Squeaks*: Listening for Masculinity on the Early Modern Stage', *Renaissance Drama* 29 (2000) 39–71, 55.
2   Thomas Hill, *The Contemplation of Mankind*, f. 135.
3   Richard Roussat, *The most excellent, profitable, and pleasant, booke of the famous doctor and expert astrologian Arcandam [...] with an addition of phisiognomie* (London: Orwin, 1592) f. 116.

which might resonate in his voice. In *Twelfth Night* there is a similar allusion to an all-male cast in which female and male voices are blurred and become indistinct. Facing the twins Sebastian and Viola, Orsino recognises not only 'one face' and 'one habit' but also 'one voice' (5.1.208). A non-squeaking Cleopatra on Shakespeare's stage, whose voice is low and gentle, would do justice to the royal subject, treating it with respect instead of stretching the persona to the spectator's delight. Whether or not a director chooses to turn this particular scene in Antony and Cleopatra into a comic farce ultimately depends on the tone of voice.

Even though its tone and the manner of pronunciation can be controlled, altered, and skilfully employed for rhetoric purposes, the voice retains its characterological colouring. It is for this reason that Thomas Wright only touches upon the voice and refrains from further embarking upon the subject. '[…] great Oratours', he claims, 'should have in the beginning of their Orations […] a small trembling voice […] forthereby they win a certaine compassion and loving affection of their auditors.' He continues by claiming that much more could be said of this particular subject but these issues would concern 'specially physiognomie and naturall constitution of the organs and humours of the bodie, therefore I will omit it.'[1]

To hit the right tone, however, is a tricky business. It seems a given fact that a laudable voice resides in a male body. Its warm temperature enlarges its veins and ensures a strong, full voice.[2] A pleasant tone of voice, however, is not essentially desirable. As Thomas Hill remarks, '[t]he delectablenesse of voice [indicates] a dull capacitie and foolishnesse: yet a stowtnesse of courage […]'[3] and points to an effeminate body, indicating 'small wisedome or simplenesse'.[4] Thus a 'gracious voice' (*Merchant of Venice* 3.2.76) is a highly ambiguous ornament and easily disclosed as mere outward show and a pretty decoration by anybody familiar with physiognomic principles. The ideal voice refrains from extremes: it is neither high nor low, neither

---

1   Thomas Wright, *The Passions of the Minde in Generall* (London: Helme, 1620) 133.
2   Compare Hill, *The Contemplation of Mankinde,* 134.
3   Ibidem, f. 135.
4   Ibidem, f. 136.

gentle nor bold, neither loud nor quiet but somewhere in-between
and can be adjusted if need be:

> They therefore that have hoat bodyes are also of nature vari-
> able, and changeable, ready, pro[m]pt, lively, lusty and aplyable:
> of tongue, trowlyng, perfect, and perswasive, deliveryng theyr
> words distinctly, plainly and pleasauntly, with a voice thereto not
> squekinge and slender, but streinable, comly and audible.[1]

Such a voice 'of nature variable, and changeable', which enables
its owner 'to discharge and execute the parte of any personne, that
wee eyther of our selves take in hande, or which by nature and pub-
like function is to us assigned'[2], such a voice which is assigned to
male bodies is attributed to Antony[3] and makes itself heart in *Hamlet*,
or Hamlet. Even though the sound of Hamlet's voice is never explic-
itly referred to, the discourse on music in act three, scene two sug-
gests that it meets the ideal of *mediocritá*, of the desired and favour-
able 'meane voice'[4], and can move between different scales like the
flute Hamlet is holding. This prop evokes a connection to Cicero's
De Oratore, more precisely to Cicero's account of Gracchus, the
renowned orator who was always accompanied by a flute player at
the rostra. Hidden from the audience's view, the latter gave him the
proper pitch to address the audience and, as Cicero recalls, by varying
the pitch restrained or animated him when delivering his speech.[5] The
flute sets the standards: a pitch of voice which exceeds its scope is not
only perceived as highly unpleasant but derogates the natural pitch-
range of the voice, which can only reach such extremes by a great
strain wherefore Cicero advises the experienced orator to leave the
piper at home.[6] It is not unlikely that Shakespeare refers to Cicero's

---

1   Levinus Leminius, *The Touchstone of Complexions* (London: Marsh, 1581) f.
    46.
2   Ibidem, f. 100.
3   Cleopatra: 'His voice was propertied / As all the tunèd spheres, and that to
    friends' (*Antony and Cleopatra* 5.2.82f.).
4   'The meane voyce in sound and in greatnes, declareth the man to be wise, cir-
    cumspect, iust, and true.' (Richard Roussat, *The most excellent, profitable, and
    pleasant, booke of the famous doctor and expert astrologian Arcandam [...] with
    an addition of phisiognomie* [London: Orwin, 1592] f. 116).
5   Cicero, *De Oratore* III 60.224–27.
6   Ibidem, III 61.227.

De Oratore and the example of Gracchus and his flute-player when he lets Hamlet challenge Guildenstern's musical talent. After all, the skilful orator and the advanced actor share the same qualities, especially if it comes to the use of voice.

As far as Hamlet is aligned to the flute player, one can assume that he is granted the ability of tuning his voice to his role even though the *mediocritá* of his voice can only be inferred *ex negativo* from his rebuke of Guildenstern. The latter turns out to be unable to play (3.2.328), which Hamlet criticises: 'there is much music, excellent voice in this little organ, yet cannot you make it speak' (3.2.338f.). As well as exposing Guildenstern as being philistine and entirely unmusical, the rebuke is directed against his hybristic conviction to be capable of playing on people, of utilizing them for his own purposes and to his pleasure. Thus Guildenstern does not only emerge from this scene both as a dreadful, 'unman[ner]ly' (3.2.321) actor and as an incapable director. Towards the end of the audition, there is a change in instruments. If one cannot control one's own musical apparatus, one cannot let another sound. Thus it is implied in Hamlet's retort to Guildenstern: 'Call me what instrument you will, though you can fret me, you cannot play upon me' (3.2.340f.). The wind instrument is swapped for a string instrument to further mock Guildenstern's lack of talent and emphasise Hamlet's superior role as actor and director *avant la lettre*.

The comparison between a persona and a musical instrument becomes even more apparent elsewhere in Shakespeare, namely in Viola. The actor playing this particular role must live up to the name and master the highs and lows of his voice just as he might the stringed instrument. He has to perform his multiple role-play which proceeds from a man playing a woman playing a man with virtuosity, adjusting the tone of his voice to the personae he takes on.

The voice, which is the most inconspicuous physiognomic feature, yet most central to Shakespeare's plays that heavily rely on verbal scenery, concludes the foray into a physiognomic catalogue, which has been briefly sketched in this chapter in order to provide the analytic tools for a re-reading of selected plays from a physiognomist's perspective. While the catalogue listing individual features can provide some insight into the ways in which Shakespeare draws from physiognomic commonplaces and expands on certain axioms that were communicated by physiognomic manuals circulating at his time, a mere listing of facial features, as it has already been indicated in the analyses above, falls short of his 'art of physiognomy', which predominantly depends on the performances and reception of physiognomic 'texts'.

Thus equipped with the tools of the trade, let us now proceed to the physiognomic re-readings of chosen plays. The analyses made in the following chapters are by no means exhaustive, but shall provide some examples that offer a fresh approach to some of Shakespeare's art of characterisation.

5 'Let me behold thy face'—Physiognomic Readings

Physiognomy is above all an art of *reading*, of deciphering and inter-
preting a text, whose reception depends heavily on the eye of the
beholder and thus on a specific social, historical, and cultural con-
text, which informs the understanding and expectations of the docu-
ment it faces. While physiognomic treatises can provide an index of
individual components, which are meticulously spelt out, they cannot
offer full portraits nor pull together every single piece of the charac-
terological puzzle to create an image of a particular persona. Even
the character sketches, which in Della Porta's treatise, for instance,
are attached to the physiognomic catalogue, tend to focus on some
selected distinctive features rather than tracing every lineament of the
facial or bodily surface. To assemble these fragments and establish
a coherent profile, a diligent and skilled reader is required who fills
in the blanks where necessary.[1] Thereby the dramatic genre seems a
particularly suitable vehicle to probe, discuss, and question the valid-
ity of physiognomic inference in that it not only scrutinises specific
physiognomic axioms as part of the plot but also relies on the partici-
pation of the theatre-goers in the creative and interpretative process
of 'facing' some-body onstage.

   On the polyphonic and polyvisual forum provided by the thea-
tre, the dyadic interaction between reader and 'text' is doubled:
The encounter with a (facial) document onstage prompts a theatri-
cal (meta-)reading, which includes the audience in the physiognomic
event. As a place where readers read other readers reading, the thea-
tre opens up a whole spectrum of realizations of a physiognomic text,
giving consideration to its multiple layers of meaning. The audience,

---

1 For the relationship of text and reader see Wolfgang Iser, *The Act of Reading: A
   Theory of Aesthetic Response* (London: Routledge and Kegan Paul, 1978).

who also in Shakespeare's times not only came to the theatre to 'hear' but also to 'see' a play,[1] are urged to constantly reconsider, revisit, and re-evaluate textual signals which they encounter as both visual and verbal signifiers. While it seems plausible that actors did their best to provide the visual text to descriptions imposed on them by other *dramatis personae* onstage, physiognomic features, as already mentioned, should be regarded first and foremost as verbal scenery. Hence, it is all the more important to pay attention to the person who translates these facial signifiers from the visual into the verbal and performs the act of physiognomic reading.

In Shakespeare's plays, these physiognomic events are often conducted by one specific *dramatis persona*, whose refined reading competence outperforms all other figures onstage. Unlike in John Webster's *The Duchess of Malfi*, however, where Bosola with reference to the Cardinal's observations on his character poses the question 'does he study physiognomy?' (1.1.245), none of Shakespeare's *personae* is explicitly linked with this pseudo-science. The painter in *The Rape of Lucrece* is the only exception and can be neglected since he is only referred to as an agent of the 'art of physiognomy' (1394f.), which Lucrece admires in the depiction of Ulysses and Ajax, but does not appear *in persona*. The absence of a figure that is explicitly labelled physiognomist could be explained by the bad press this supposedly mantic science experienced at the time.[2] The fact that physiognomy has fallen into disrepute certainly complies with Bosola's aim of denouncing the Cardinal by insinuating his alliance with the highly disputable discipline and mock his seemingly unfounded resentment of him. At the same time, however, Bosola's remark obscures the fact that it is himself who emerges as diligent observer of facial and bodily features, taking advantage of the legible bodies surrounding him and subjecting them to his manipulative skills. His blaming of the Cardinal is therefore as contemptuous as it is deceptive and soon emerges as part of his rhetoric strategy.

Even though not always made explicit, similar instances of subver-

---

1 See Andrew Gurr, 'Hearers and Beholders in Shakespearean Drama', *Essays in Theatre* 3 (1984) 30–45.
2 See chapter 2.

sive affirmation with regard to physiognomic reasoning can be found in Shakespeare's tragedies where facial eloquence is often rejected only to be reaffirmed: Duncan's denial of physiognomic inference, for instance, is fatally misleading. Especially in *Macbeth* faces are ultimately legible and the protagonist, whose countenance bears a document of fear and enters the scene straight after Duncan's antiphysiognomic axiom as if to challenge his remark, is a case in point. A similar critical background is set up at the outset of *Othello* when Desdemona counters the antipathy to her beloved by a plea for transgression of outer appearances in favour of qualities that are hidden inside the body. Following Iago's stigmatisation of Othello, who has not yet appeared onstage, as 'black ram' (1.1.88), Desdemona reverses the hermeneutics of physiognomy by deriving the character from the inner being: 'I saw Othello's visage in his mind' (1.3.251). Notwithstanding her attempt to put physiognomy into perspective, in the further development of the plot, appearances turn out to be very revealing and, ironically, it is none other than Desdemona who serves as a main advocate of physiognomic inference. While she seems to take a critical stand towards the validity of facial features, her fair, unblemished countenance, which is even more eye-catching in the presence of Othello's black face, is a prime example of the close correspondence between body and psyche. Tragically, Othello, blinded by fury and Iago's misleading lesson in reading the human face (4.1.79–85), seems to adhere to her principle when he disregards the 'fair paper' as a cunning deceit and stabs the fair skin as if to inscribe the word 'whore' (4.2.74) upon the alabaster monument, which is in fact the home of innocence and virtue.

While no figure is explicitly labelled a physiognomist, many of Shakespeare's characters show a strong awareness of the expressive and, above all, performative quality of the human face, which qualifies them for this position. Informed by a profound insight into the potentialities of facial rhetoric, these figures are not only capable of critically reflecting documents they encounter: they can also challenge their texts by wilful and provocative misreadings, by misinterpreting visible signs, or by cunningly re-writing them and attributing to the facial surface signifiers that are not actually present. Iago, for instance, the schemer and 'great manipulator of signs'[1] uses the eloquence of the human face for his purposes, providing the other *personae* in the play with their text, not telling them how to read but instructing them what to see and thereby re-fashioning and re-inscribing surfaces in order to prompt fatal misreadings. And yet, the presence of a Machiavellian figure like Iago, who turns the semiotics of the world upside down, does not in principle negate nor annul the (founded) belief in the legibility of man. It is typical of Shakespeare's plays that physiognomy like all major themes in his oeuvre is doubly inflected. Both the potentialities and the perils of physiognomic inference are displayed, discussed, and in many instances deconstructed onstage. Reading signs, symbols, and faces becomes a challenge both for the *dramatis personae* within the world onstage and for the theatre-goers, who are often granted the privilege of a superior knowledge, supporting their roles as meta-theatrical physiognomists, and who are urged to participate in the multiple readings, counter-readings, and re-readings performed onstage. As already suggested in connection to *Othello* and the two opposing views with regard to the legibility of man, which are embodied by the two main characters of the play Desdemona and Othello, the subversion of physiognomic axioms and the instrumentalisation of facial rhetoric, however, do not necessarily undermine the validity of face-readings. The possibility of manipulating signs presupposes the existence of *signa* that are in principle both legible and decipherable. Interference in the natural translation between inner and outer man are perceived as being monstrous, unnatural, and fraudulent—both within the theatrical and the meta-theatrical space. It seems paradoxical, however, that it is especially in the theatre, in which faces are both deceiving and revealing at the same time in that they belie the identity of the actor while expressing the character of the *dramatis personae*, that faces remain utterly 'legible'. The decipherability of characters tightens the strings between dramatic figures and spectators. And yet, physiognomy not only provides the tools to decipher a character onstage, but also teaches the audience ways in which to fashion their own selves, that is their own

---

1   Stephen Greenblatt, *Renaissance Self Fashioning: From More to Shakespeare* (Chicago et al.: University of Chicago Press, 1980) 238.

social (or theatrical) role. The act of facial self-fashioning involves the re-inventing of one's own appearance by taking the divine stylus of creation into one's own hand to participate in the divine order of the world. The prerequisite for interference in the process of signification is a profound insight into the possibilities of 'characterising', of altering the divine scheme, and authorising one's self to participate in the design of the book of the world. Hamlet's encounter with the ghost, for instance, prompts such a moment of recognition of man's creative and manipulative power: 'that one may smile, and smile, and be a villain' (*Hamlet* 1.5.109). The physiognomic paradox of an inner and outer being whose disposition are at odds with each other is an insight, which provides the foundation for Hamlet's play under the mask of his 'antic disposition' (2.1.173) and becomes constitutive for his further actions. As such, he inscribes the sentence in the book and 'table of [his] memory' (1.5.98), which preserves the words of his dead father that will become the blueprint for his production of the *Mousetrap*.

The dynamic interaction of reading and writing in connection with physiognomic self-fashioning, which becomes apparent in Hamlet's mnemonic act, is often played out on Shakespeare's stage when characters seem to spring from a page to materialise in the play, which points to the close link between graphology and physiognomy. In the following chapter, the progression from the characters onstage to characters on the face, and eventually to *dramatis personae* onstage shall be unfolded in order to illustrate the interaction between the production and reception of graphological and physiognomic characters.

The connection of graphology and physiognomy is often alluded to on Shakespeare's stage. In *King Lear*, for instance, Kent degrades his opponent Oswald by reducing him to a simple and rather superfluous and meaningless 'character': 'Thou whoreson zed! thou unnecessary letter' (*King Lear* 2.2.56). As Richard Mulcaster remarks, this particular consonant was even though 'much heard amongst us, [...] seldom sene'[1]. Taking into consideration that, in many cases, the 'z' can be replaced by an 's', the former can be deemed 'unnecessary'. The asso-

---

1   Richard Mulcaster, *The first Part of the Elementarie which entreateth chefelie of the right Writing of our English Tung* (London: Vautroullier, 1582) 123.

ciation of human and written characters became even more obvious in anthropomorphising illustrations of the alphabet: while examples of figurative initials can already be found in medieval manuscripts, the first complete alphabet consisting of human bodies (Giovannio de Grassi's alphabet, which dates to the 14th century and is one of the earliest examples of these illustrations, uses animal bodies as well as human figures) was presented by the German wood engraver Peter Flötner in 1534, who assembled 24 human bodies, which were bent and twisted, their arms and legs being stretched and angled to resemble the shape of a particular letter. While Shakespeare might or might not have been aware of this tradition, he quite frequently alludes to the etymological connection between graphological and physiognomic characters especially with regard to genealogical concepts.

As pointed out by Margreta de Grazia in her description of Gutenberg's letters,[1] human characters are not only products but also instruments of impression. In other words, man is both the print-off and the printer, both the characterised and the characterising agent within the greater scheme of creation. He has been authorised by nature to participate in its signifying system and produce characters by and for himself. It is this authorisation of man, which is alluded to in Sonnet 11 in the closing couplet and the slight rebuke to the addressee, '[s]he carved thee for her seal, and meant thereby / Thou shouldst print more, not let that copy die' (*Sonnet 11* 13f.). Not until the carved strut has produced an image, does it become legible. It is only in its offspring that the individual can confirm its existence by beholding and recognising itself in its reflection, which becomes constitutive for the former. If the glass holding the image is shattered, the 'original' is cracked. 'Poor broken glass', laments Lucretius over Lucrece's lifeless body, 'from thy cheeks my image thou hast torn, / And shivered all the beauty of my glass, / That I no more can see what once I was' (*The Rape of Lucrece* 1758–64). In Shakespeare's oeuvre, the physiognomic likeness between parent and child first and foremost serves as a means of identification: beholding his son's

---

1   Margreta de Grazia, 'Imprints: Shakespeare, Gutenberg and Descartes', in Terence Hawkes ed., *Alternative Shakespeare* (London/New York: Routledge, 1996) Vol. 2, 63–94, 86.

countenance, Aaron discovers his 'seal [...] stampèd in his face' (*Titus Andronicus* 4.2.126) and in *All's Well That Ends Well*, the King of France recognises familiar features in young Bertram's visage: 'Youth, thou bear'st thy father's face' (1.2.19). The shaping of the offspring is a task always attributed to the father whereas the mother does not leave an impression on the physical appearance of her child. For example, the Countess Roussillon urges Bertram to '[...] succeed thy father / In manners as in shape' without referring to her own share in his design. The likeness between parent and child becomes most distinctive with regard to father and daughter,[1] who is commonly perceived as resembling her genitor, which, again, underscores the predominance of the male agent in the act of genealogical 'printing'.

Whereas the inscriptive power is attributed to man, who leaves his imprint on the female body,[2] generating a new life, the ability to create a character, which becomes part of the divine book of the world, is ultimately denied to woman. The female body merely serves as an interface, a passive receptor that is involved only insofar as it nourishes the offspring and gives birth to it, thus reproducing the male script. If it turns out to be a boy, a true copy of the father, his body will be firm and constant while a girl remains a block of wax in her father's hands and is subjected to his authority until she is married. Of course, the alliance is only possible with the authorisation of the family.[3] In *A Midsummer Night's Dream*, Theseus' reprimand of the insubordinate Hippolyta, who has fallen in love with Lysander against her father's wishes, is unequivocal:

> To you your father should be as a god,
> One that composed your beauties, yea, and one
> To whom you are but as a form in wax,
> By him imprinted, and within his power
> To leave the figure or disfigure it.
> (1.1.47–51)

---

1 Compare *The Winter's Tale* 2.3.100–103; *A Midsummer Night's Dream* 1.1.50.
2 Compare *The Winter's Tale* 5.1.123–25: 'Your mother was most true to wedlock, Prince, / For she did print your royal father off, / Conceiving you'
3 Alluding to the patriarchal power, Lear wishes to belatedly inscribe Goneril's deceivingly pretty features and urges nature to 'stamp wrinkles in her brow of youth: / With cadent tears fret channels in her cheeks' (*King Lear* 1.4.261f.).

While the wax metaphor is connected predominantly to woman, indicating their pliable nature, it can also imply effeminacy of a male body: 'Thy noble shape is but a form of wax' (*Romeo and Juliet* 3.3.125), chides Friar Laurence the mournful Romeo, whose body seems to melt away in his 'blubb'ring and weeping, weeping and blubb'ring' (3.3.87). The image of the waxen body is furthermore alluded to in *Antony and Cleopatra* when Antony claims of himself to be unable to 'hold this visible shape' (4.15.14) but is in severe danger of physically dissolving and disintegrating in licentious Egypt, which, having estranged him from his *polis*, has upset his identity. When Juliet's Nurse, however, refers to Paris as 'a man of wax', her words do not so much aim at degrading her suitor even though her sneering comment would strengthen her part in the initiation of her love-relationship with Romeo, but rather prepares his portrayal by Lady Capulet, who shapes Paris according to her purpose and designs him as a book of love for her daughter to immerse into:

> Read o'er the volume of young Paris' face,
> And find delight writ there with beauty's pen.
> Examine every married lineament,
> And see how one another lends content;
> [...] This precious book of love, this unbound lover,
> To beautify him only lacks a cover
> (*Romeo and Juliet* 1.3.83–90)

Lady Capulet's textualisation of Paris' body, primarily his face, challenges the gender politics commonly associated with the formation of a character and the modelling of bodily substance. Juliet's reading supports this notion of subversion. Even though Juliet seems subjected to a male text, authorised by her mother, and even though she appears to be reduced to an ornament, a cover gracing the volume by its beauty comprising neither a content of its own nor a right to exist by itself, she emerges as the more dominant of the two. Her book of love, however, is not Paris but Romeo, whom she chose by herself and for herself, defying maternal and paternal authority. The book metaphor remains central to the play. Thus it is Juliet who will eventually bring the story of two star-crossed lovers to a closure and follow Romeo into death. Furthermore, on a meta-theatrical level, her *persona* will mark the closure of the book, the script of *Romeo and Juliet*, which covers her story that, as suggested by the Prince's epilogue, should be remembered as the story of 'Juliet and *her* Romeo' (5.3.309). Introduced as a story of 'two households' (Prologue 1), the play progresses to the fusion of 'two in one' (2.5.37) in marriage until it finally focuses on one figure, which is Juliet, who is presented as the main protagonist of the story. Juliet's potential for self-fashioning has already been remarked in relation to her 'maiden blush' (2.2.128) and is supported by her choice of 'reading'. Even though she dismisses her mother's recommendation, the latter serves her as an instruction of ways to emancipate from paternal dominion. Lady Capulet's portrayal of Paris' face already challenges traditional printing politics in that her governing part in providing Juliet's script ultimately undermines male authorship. Deviating from her mother's instructions, Juliet seems to assume control in the love relationship. She is the first to lament Romeo's exile even before the exiled is met at the Friar's domicile 'blubb'ring and weeping, weeping and blubb'ring' (3.3.87), providing a mirror image to his beloved. Furthermore, whereas in the balcony scene, it was Romeo's speech that marked the beginning and the end of the lovers' encounter, the wedding night is framed by Juliet's words. Last but not least, she simulates her death in a manner that will be imitated by Romeo whereby his vial, however, will contain a lethal poison. The two lovers will finally reunite in death where they become 'two in one' when Juliet with her suicide brings the play to an end.

Insofar as 'her' story is pronounced by none other than the Prince, insofar as her persona is enacted by a male player and, last but not least, insofar as her story is told and transcribed by Shakespeare, one could argue that eventually male authorship and authority is re-established on the level of the play as well as on the metatheatrical level. On the level of plot, however, Juliet's resistance to male authority is quite remarkable, especially as the latter is emphasised both on the literal and the metaphorical level in most of Shakespeare's plays.

Thus, the subjection of the female body to male authorship forms the foundation of Leontes' praise of Florizel's mother, who adhering to her natural subordination, 'did print your royal father off, / Conceiving you' (*The Winter's Tale* 5.1.123–25). According to common genealogic concepts, the female body served as interface in the creation of offspring in that it received and embraced the male seed, which determined the physiognomy and character of the child. While Leontes' use of the verb 'conceiving' refers to the act of begetting a child, the use of *conception* elsewhere in Shakespeare is more ambivalent as it also refers to a cognitive process, which, similar to physical conception, is linked to an act of imprinting. The conception of knowledge is based on the idea that our minds contain a wax block, as it is suggested in Plato's dialogue *Theaetetus*[1], and thus have to be considered a soft surface whereupon words, experiences, and memories were inscribed, which henceforth shape one's perception. When in *The Two Gentleman of Verona*, the Duke tells Thurio of the fading picture of Julia in his mind, he alludes to this topos, claiming that his love 'is thawed' and 'like a waxen image 'gainst a fire / Bears no impression of the thing it was' (2.4.197–99). Mnemonical incision furthermore sets off the action in *Hamlet* when Hamlet announces that he will clear his mental record to make room for the encounter with the ghost, whose words he imprints on his memory from where they will henceforth be retrievable.

> [...] from the table of my memory,
> I'll wipe away all trivial fond records,
> All saws of books, all forms, all pressures past,
> That youth and observation copied there [...].
> (*Hamlet* 1.5.98–101)

Erasing all imprints that have blotted his mind, shaped his reasoning, and blurred his senses, Hamlet performs a return to a precognitive state by restoring the white paper 'unscribled with observation of the world'[2], which resembles the tabula rasa, which man is born with. Having thus cleared his mind from all parasitic influences, Hamlet takes out his mental pen not only to set down the 'commandment' of his father but also to note an observation which will set the tone of

---

1   Platon, *Theaetetus* 191D–E
2   John Earle, *Microcosmographie, or A Peece of the World Discouered in Essayes and Characters* (London: Badger, 1630) B2.

the play:

> My tables,
> My tables – meet it is I set it down
> That one may smile and smile and be a villain!
> (*Hamlet* 1.5.107–9)

The image of the smiling villain, whose most radical expression is the character of Richard Gloucester, who claims of himself 'I can smile, and murder whiles I smile' (*3 Henry VI* 3.2.182), upsets the physiognomic scheme and thwarts the correspondence between inner and outer being, between appearances and 'that within', which, as Hamlet rightly remarks, ultimately 'passeth show' (*Hamlet* 1.2.85). The anti-physiognomic stance prepares the audience for a play, in which nothing is as it seems. Hamlet's 'antic disposition' is but a mask which he adopts for the purpose of both protecting himself against the squinting members of the Danish court and holding up the mirror to a hypocritical society. The king is eventually revealed as a murderous usurper, who dastardly snatched the crown from his brother. And last but not least, as indicated by the meta-theatrical perspective, which is opened up by frequent reference to acting and underscored by the play-within-the-play, the stage is inhabited by actors incorporating personae other than themselves.

Not unlike Duncan's anti-physiognomic axiom, however, Hamlet's observation belies the significance of facial rhetoric in this particular play where it only seems as if nothing is as it seems. Not only does Hamlet enquire about the ghost's physiognomy in order to confirm his identity ('What looked he? Frowningly? [...] Pale or red? [...] His beard was grizzly, no?' [*Hamlet* 1.3.227–39]), he also prompts Rosencrantz and Guildenstern to unfold the true purpose of their visit ('You were sent for, and there is a kind of confession in your looks which your modesties have not craft enough to colour' [2.2.271–73]). Furthermore, he relies on the eloquence of the human face in his plan to reveal Claudius' part in the murder of his father. Setting up a play 'to catch the conscience of the King' (2.2.582), Hamlet pins his hopes on the surprise effect, which would evoke a spontaneous reaction on Claudius' countenance, which is why he declares: 'I mine eyes will rivet to his face' (3.2.78). To provide the appropriate visual text to the nonverbal testimony, which is displayed on Claudius' countenance at the performance of the *Mousetrap*, and to fill in the blank which is left by Hamlet, who proclaims a face-reading and insinuates to Horatio that its outcome was fruitful ('I'll take the Ghost's word for a thousand pound. Didst perceive?' [3.2.263f.]), is the task of the reader's imagination or, respectively, the audience's participation in the reading of the actors' faces. As suggested by Ophelia, who attracts attention to the king ('The King rises' [3.2.242]), it seems likely that his face displayed a very telling reaction. Ophelia's own reading skills, however, are questionable. Even though she needs an interpreter to spell out the meaning of the shows she is confronted with ('What means this, my lord?' [3.2.123]), the play seems to have made an impression on her as well. When Ophelia re-enters the stage after the Mousetrap has been performed, she is already mad. While her mental derangement seems triggered first and foremost by her father's death, Hamlet's part in the slaughter, the prince's 'banishment' from Denmark, and finally her dawning insight into the circumstances of the former king's death might also have contributed to her insanity.

   Just like Hamlet, one could suspect, she has finally conceived that 'something is rotten in the state of Denmark' (1.4.67). The double entendre of the term *conception*, is fully exploited when it comes to Ophelia, who like 'a green girl' (1.4.101) is subjected to numerous imprinting forces, to the brotherly advice of Laertes, to the patriarchal authority of Polonius and finally also to Hamlet. The latter might be the cause of her *conception* as he himself suggests to Polonius whereby he alludes to the double meaning of the term: 'Let her not walk i'th'sun. Conception is a blessing, but not as your daughter may conceive. Friend look to't' (2.2.185f.). While the homonym 'sun' / 'son', which Hamlet already alluded to in another context,[1] points to

---

1   His remark to Claudius, 'I am too much in the sun' cannot only be read as an
    expression of his disapproval of the king, who as the centre of the universe
    resembles the sun, or even as a meta-theatrical comment, suggesting that all
    eyes are upon his *persona*, both at the Danish court and on Shakespeare's
    stage, which centres him as protagonist: it can also be regarded as relating to
    his flawed role as 'son', who now faces Claudius, his mother's husband and suc-

his role as Ophelia's lover and potential progenitor of her offspring while, at the same time, questioning her purity, the term *conception* in combination with the 'sun' might be regarded as referring to Ophelia's greater insight into the incidents at the Danish court and into Hamlet's assumed madness. If interpreted as a recommendation to keep Ophelia from the sun, which resembles the source of illumination and knowledge,[1] the reminder to beware of an undesirable conception would contribute to the alternative reading of Hamlet's request to Ophelia to retreat to a nunnery. In its bawdy sense, the latter would bring about her conception whereas her entry in a 'convent' would prevent her it. The convent, however, would take her closer to the 'sun', to God or respectively, bring about a deeper knowledge and insight into the world. However, Ophelia does not retreat to any kind of 'nunnery' and thus conceives neither in the physical nor in the cognitive sense. Nonetheless she seems to be impressed by Hamlet's 'stamp' insofar as she experiences the madness which he is only pretending and reproduces the mental derangement he enacts.

Ophelia does not seem to cope with the decline of her ideals and the shattering of 'the glass of fashion and the mould of form' (3.1.152): 'O woe is me, / T'have seen what I have seen, see what I see!' (3.1.159f.). Being exposed to performances she does not participate in and to inscriptive forces she cannot control makes her vulnerable. Her role as receiver and naïve recipient rather than producer of signs is underscored by her exclusion from any kind of signifying practice. She is open to inscriptive forces, which she can neither command nor cope with. When she appears onstage as spectator and reader, she does so because Polonius provides her with a book, exploiting her persona for the purpose of staging a scene, a trap, which is designed to unmask Hamlet. Apart from being employed as a stage prop, Ophelia is never seen writing or engaging in any kind of self-fashioning. On the level of plot, her madness is real, quite unlike the 'antic disposition' displayed by Hamlet, who is not only subjected to numerous readings and becomes 'th' observ'd of all observers'

---

cessor to Old Hamlet, as 'father'.

1   Compare Plato's allegory of the cave (*The Republic* 514a–520a) and especially his metaphor of the sun (507b–509c).

(3.1.153) but also enters abundant physiognomic encounters himself and even emerges as writer.

Hamlet is both *signifiant* and *signifié*, prompting acts of decipherments while creating characters both in the metaphoric and in the literal sense. On the one hand he designs his 'antic disposition' and instructs the actors prior to the performance of the 'Mousetrap'. On the other hand he intercepts Claudius' letter and rewrites it. Forging the king's hand, Hamlet secures the survival of his character. By the time the king recognises his handwriting (''Tis Hamlet's character' [4.7.49]), Hamlet's character should already have been extinguished. Its progression from the page to the face, or even to the stage, is completed when Hamlet re-enters the play shortly after the decipherment of his character. The recognition of the latter in writing brings the protagonist back to life via the graveyard and the *memento mori* scene prompted by the encounter with Yorrick's skull. The ability to take a hand in the construction of signs and documents both on a metaphorical (his performance of the 'antic disposition') and on a very literal level (the forging of Claudius' letter) together with a profound reading competence, which combines the understanding of written letters and the interpretation of facial characters, distinguishes Hamlet as 'physiognomist' in the play, which centres on his persona.

A similar exegesis, which points to the intimate connection of graphology and physiognomy with regard to the reception and production of 'documents' in their broadest sense, is enacted in *King Lear* when Edgar's character is recreated through what appears to be his 'hand'. With pretended reluctance, Edmund relinquishes a letter, which was penned by him but is foisted onto Edgar, to Gloucester, who demands him to confirm its author: 'You know the character to be your brother's?' (1.2.59). The act of forgery is successful in that it blurs Gloucester's perception of his son's hand-writing. When Edgar enters the scene, he seems to step from the page onto the stage even though he does not quite meet the image of the vicious character that has been sketched by his brother, Edmund, but nevertheless fulfils the role of manipulator and creator of characters by moving from the graphological to the physiognomic sphere whereby he turns from the son to the father, from the imprint to the stamp, and starts inscribing

signs of rage and anger into Gloucester's speech and correspond-
ingly also into his face: 'Found you no displeasure in him by word or
countenance?' (*King Lear* 1.2.142f.). Even though the roles of sub-
ject and addressee have changed and different media of inscription
(writing and speech) are involved, the characterisation is no less suc-
cessful. The forgery will not be discovered until the blotted Edgar has
begrimed his face and the misreading father has lost his sight.

While the right and the ability to intervene in the characterising
of the world and its inhabitants, and, if applicable, to alter the *sig-
natura rerum* seems to be reserved for the male subject, many of
Shakespeare's female figures emerge as diligent readers and most
cunning writers, thus qualifying for the position of physiognomists.
Nonetheless, we constantly have to remind ourselves that these
'female' readers are, of course, no others but male actors playing
women, which is problematic insofar as a female agent is authorised
not only by a male hand in writing but also by a male body onstage.
In order to assess the gender politics with regard to physiognomic
reasoning, however, the following readings will focus on the ques-
tion of how face-readers are distinguished as such within the logic
of the play. In this, the meta-theatrical dimension remains crucial,
especially with regard to the interaction of *dramatis personae*, actors,
and the theatre audience, which greatly contributes to Shakespeare's
physiognomic theatre.

Often physiognomists can be distinguished by their capability of
bridging the gap between the graphological and the physiognomic
realm as it is suggested by Lady Macbeth's consideration of her hus-
band's character, which reaches her first in a letter and then in per-
sona. With Lady Macbeth, one of the key female physiognomists in
Shakespeare's plays has been identified. Besides reading written and
facial characters, she engages in distributing signs in order to dis-
tort the legibility of the world by subverting traditional semiotics for
her purposes. While she shuns committing Duncan's murder herself,
she is the one to lead his followers on the wrong track by covering
the deed, or rather, by colouring it. Taking the treacherously bloody
knives from her husband, she returns to the death chamber in order to
bedaub the faces of Duncan's servants with blood and thereby desig-

nate them as the king's murderers: 'I'll gild the faces of the grooms withal, / For it must seem their guilt' (*Macbeth* 2.2.54f.). While Lady Macbeth's attempt to deceive the onlookers might be regarded as corroborating the attacks against the use of make-up as it was practised predominantly by women, the announced face-painting is not applied without foundation. Preceding the bloody deed, the porter has been pondering upon the connection of 'nose-painting' and drinking, pointing to a close correspondence between man's inner and outer disposition and raising somatic awareness in the audience. Against this background, the groom's painting is attributed a second layer, which, however, was applied by the same 'hand', Lady Macbeth, who has supplied the servants with plenty of wine to send them to sleep. On her return from Duncan's chamber, it must therefore be assumed— since both scenes take place offstage—the grooms' naturally reddened cheeks and Lady Macbeth's blood-mask mingle, displaying an image of drunkenness and 'guilt' (2.2.55), which does not fail to impress. Lennox indeed takes the painting for a testimony, indicating Duncan's murder. The blood-bedaubed face will continue to prompt misreadings. While the man on whose face Macbeth spots traits of blood has indeed killed Banquo, he appears more like a victim than a perpetrator in that he has acted on Macbeth's behalf and thus becomes yet another stooge of the murderous couple, just as the two 'gilded' grooms are.

Lady Macbeth's distribution of signs just like her diligent reading skills as well as the refined instruction of her husband is unmatched amongst Shakespeare's women, which might be explained by the fact that Lady Macbeth more than any other female figure in the plays estranges herself from her sex immediately after she appears onstage ('unsex me here / [...] Come to my woman's breasts, / And take my milk for gall' [1.5.39–46]), hardening her body to resist its soft and malleable nature and thus transforming her waxen substance into more rigid matter, which is fit to imprint rather than be imprinted. While behind her outer shell, her mind seems to decompose, and the irreconcilability of body and mind will eventually lead to her self-erasure, she succeeds in retaining her signifying power during the first half of the play.

Shakespeare's comedies seem to provide an even greater space for female subversions of man's textual dominion. Not only do cross-dressing and disguises onstage suggest a profound instability of categories such as class and gender, but women seem increasingly to take matters of characterisation into their own hands and more often than in the tragedies are met writing.

The most successful and, with regard to its conception and materialisation onstage, most enjoyable creation of a 'character' is Maria's letter to Malvolio, which contains a physiognomic manual on how to fashion himself before facing his mistress.

> I will drop in his way some obscure epistles of love, wherein by the colour of his beard, the shape of his leg, the manner of his gait, the expressure of his eye, forehead, and complexion, he shall find himself most feelingly personated. (*Twelfth Night* 2.3.138–41)

What authorises Maria to compose a letter, which is not signed by her but ascribed to Olivia, is the fact that her and her mistress' handwriting styles are confusingly similar: 'On a forgotten matter we can hardly make distinction of our hands' (2.4.142f.). Thus, strictly speaking, this is not a case of forgery. Nor is the character, which Maria is about to sketch, completely inaccurately drawn. Malvolio embraces the thought of appearing before Olivia in his yellow stockings, cross-gartered, and with a jolly smile on his face not least because the letter finally authorises him to follow and enact his desire: shortly before this scene, Malvolio has been day-dreaming of marrying his mistress and climbing up the social ladder: 'To be Count Malvolio!' (2.5.30). Thus, Maria's characterisation is no mere counterfeit devoid of any foundation but rather a translation of Malvolio's psychological state, which is finally allowed to surface.

As well as pointing to the art of character creation, the two scenes, the planning of the letter and Malvolio's interpretation of it, embrace an encounter, which contains most physiognomic material of the play, namely the dialogue between Cesario and Orsino, in which Viola-as-Cesario portrays her love, that is Orsino, as a woman while creating an image of herself in a fictitious sister (2.4.110–15). Fashioning both Orsino and herself as an 'other', Viola succeeds in confirming the existence of Cesario and support the credibility of her cross-dressing onstage. Viewed from a meta-theatrical level, however, her disguise as a man does not need confirmation as it displays the true sex of the actor incorporating 'Cesario'. While both Cesario's sister and 'his' alleged lover await translation, Maria's 'character' materialises onstage and does not remain 'a blank' (2.5.110). The space left behind by the mourning woman in Viola's account is filled by the smiling Malvolio in Maria's script. His wish-fulfilment, which turns his inside out, opposes the unrequited desire in Viola, whose translation of her inner being has yet to be authorised.

The encounter of a lovelorn woman and a lovelorn man, the first hiding her true feelings together with her character, the latter sending tokens of love, which meet rejection, is succeeded and, so it seems, over-compensated by Malvolio's reading of Maria-as-Olivia's letter, a scene that is reminiscent of Orsino's sending of the ring, which is discarded by Olivia, in that both the ring and the letter serve as love symbols. Maria's blueprint gulls Malvolio 'into a nayword' (2.3.125), fashions him with hideous attire, and makes him 'a common recreation' (2.3.125f.). Against this background, Viola's transformation is bound to take place offstage. What the male fashioning will turn the female body into, remains an open question and ultimately out of sight: At the end of the play, Viola leaves the stage following Orsino's order to put on some female attire, but does not return. This unsettling and unresolved scene ties in with the gender politics of the play, which ultimately challenge male authority and the predominance of man in the creation of characters. While it seems unlikely that Viola-as-Cesario rejects the transformation from Cesario to 'Orsino's mistress' (5.1.377), a persona which she has been longing for since she, the ocular proof has yet to be produced. The blank which is left by the non-appearance of this character, questions, if not subverts male power for signification and authorship and underlines the woman's role as agent, not recipient of signs and 'characters'.

With its cross-dressing, re-writings, and misreadings, *Twelfth Night* illustrates the instability of identity and texts not only by challenging male authorship while displaying the possible dangers of female authorship, but also by indicating a fundamental instability of texts,[1] be they literal or social, of class, gender, and ultimately of physiognomy. As Dympna Callaghan has rightly observed, writing in this particular play 'offers freedom from anatomical and class designations'[2]. Furthermore, it indicates selfness. By creating other characters both in the literal and metaphorical sense, the individual who produces signs and signatures confirms its own existence in the world by facing an 'other', be it a transcription of one's self as it is the case in a letter or autobiographical script, which centres the self, subjecting it to one's own critical eye, or the description of an 'other' that is identified as such in order to provide a foil, a background for the 'I' to view itself. This moment of self-perception and recognition, which connects to the imperative 'nosce te ipsum', becomes the prerequisite of performing successful readings and of facing and fashioning one's environment. The male figures, however, lack the ability to transform, translate, and transgress their 'characters': Malvolio is re-fashioned by Maria; Cesario designed by Viola as blueprint of her twin-brother Sebastian, and Orsino, one could argue, is wax in Olivia's hands, melting in her presences and wearing away due to his unrequited love.

It is especially in this play that parallel constructions of certain personae become visible on the surface level. In his RSC-production of *Twelfth Night* from 2007, Neill Bartlett has picked up on this idea in that *personae* find themselves in front of a mirror, predominantly before exiting the stage. They pause for a moment to look at their image, astonished, bewildered, even amused before spinning the mirror, stepping aside and taking their exit. This device adequately reflected the intertextuality between characters in a love-relationship (Orsino–Olivia, Viola–Orsino, Olivia–Viola), in the mourning of a brother (Olivia–Viola), unrequited love (Orsino–Malvolio, Olivia–Viola), disguise (successful and farcical) (Viola–Malvolio), handwriting (Maria–Olivia), and, last but not least, in outward appearance (Viola– [Cesario–] Sebastian).

---

1 Compare Karen Robertson, 'A Revenging Feminine Hand in *Twelfth Night*', in David A. Bergeron ed., *Reading and Writing in Shakespeare* (Newark/London: University of Delaware Press, 1996) 116–130, 127.

2 Dympna Callaghan, *Shakespeare without Women: Representing Gender and Race on the Renaissance Stage* (London/New York: Routledge, 2000) 42.

The predominance of female signifying agents is established as early as in the opening scene when Viola emerges as a diligent physiognomic reader, who compliments the caption on his 'fair behaviour' and 'a mind that suits / With this thy fair and outward character' (1.2.44–48). While her praise of this admirable alliance of beauty and virtue could also be regarded as rhetoric strategy, which is skilfully applied to win the captain over, the classical idea of *kalokagatheia* is fundamental to the physiognomic scheme of this particular play. Not only does Viola, whose soft and pretty features are missed by neither Orsino nor Viola, serve as a case in point: there is no counter-figure that could upset the unity of outer beauty and inner virtue. As the play proceeds, external features become more and more significant with regard to modes of identification and communication. The mole on the father's brow (5.1.235f.) is a token further supporting the family bond between Viola and Sebastian, who share 'one voice, one habit' and 'one face' (5.1.209); Orsino recognises Antonio by his face (5.1.45), the triangle Viola–Cesario–Sebastian, is based on physical alikeness, and at the pivotal points of the play, the view is directed onto physiognomy. Like the first encounter of Orsino and Viola, the meeting of Olivia and 'Cesario' evolves from a face-reading: in both cases, it is the persona falling in love that is 'read'. And very similar to Orsino's evaluation of Viola's features, Cesario's reading of Olivia at a first glance seems to support the predominance of man over the female body. At a second glance, however, this notion is highly misleading: Orsino's reading has to be put into perspective since the document presented to him has been modified and re-fashioned by Viola, and the evaluation of Olivia's features is not performed by a male, but by a female persona. Furthermore, the two scenes connect to each other with regard to the constellation of reader and 'document' in that it is the figure falling in love whose features are scrutinised, namely Viola, who has lost her heart to Orsino, and Olivia, who is attracted to Viola as Cesario. While Orsino directs his view onto Viola's face, subjecting his future servant to his gaze and thereby establishing his superiority, Viola as Cesario in the encounter with Olivia seizes the opportunity to take a closer look at the features of her rival as if to assure herself that the image drawn in words by Orsino is not unfounded.

The exposure of Olivia's face, which offers considerable dra-
matic potential and can be played out very effectively, is heightened
because it is delayed. The setting where the first meeting of the two
women takes place underscores the multiple layers which are to be
lifted in the course of this scene: Within the limited, enclosed space
in which the encounter takes place, a room in Olivia's house, Viola
as Cesario encounters a veiled woman, who claims to be the mistress
of the house and demands to be presented the text from the chapter
of 'Orsino's bosom' that is devoted to her. The precious message,
however, is not revealed until the portrait of the lady is uncovered.
The disclosure of her face, whereby Olivia reneges on her promise to
remain veiled for seven years (1.1.25–7) marks a critical moment in
the play, which makes the 'masking' of Viola all the more apparent
while posing a threat to the persona 'Cesario' at the same time. Her
adopted 'mask' is jeopardized whenever the two women come face to
face. The closest point to Viola's discovery is reached in their second
encounter when she confesses to her vis-à-vis, 'I am not what I am'
(3.1.139) as repartee to Olivia's doubts on her and her opponent's
'self' ('That you do think you are not what you are' [3.1.136]). This
reflection of her own and Viola's persona serves to prepare the great
uncovering in the final act when Cesario and Olivia will meet again
and their 'characters', i.e. Viola's identity and Olivia's true handwrit-
ing or rather the fact that it is identical with Maria's hand, will be
exposed.

'You are now out of your text' (1.5.204), Olivia remarks before
lifting her veil, alluding to the fact that Viola as Cesario has indeed
no commission from her master to converse with Olivia's face. Quite
on the contrary, Orsino ordered her to 'have audience' (1.4.18), not to
turn the scene into a spectacle. Exceeding her commission, Viola, for
one moment, is both out of her text and out of 'her' character Cesario.
She returns to both, however, when she urges Olivia not to let her
beauteous image waste away and 'leave the world no copy' (1.5.232).
While this request ties in with her task to win the lady for her master,
it is striking that in this case it is female features that are proposed
for printing, not male. The notion that women are pulling the strings
in this particular play, which is supported by printing and writing

politics, by Maria's forgery and the cross-dressing of the heroine, is furthermore strengthened by the fact that Viola does not change into female attire, as requested by Orsino: 'Let me see thee in thy woman's weeds' (5.1.268) but remains onstage dressed as Cesario until the play closes.

Her resistance to male authority, which is implied in the final scene, distinguishes Viola from, for instance, Portia, whose cross-dressing is no less successful, but derives from a male hand. Before entering Venice, Portia obtains both the attire and the legitimacy of acting as a young doctor before the court from her cousin, Doctor Bellario. While her change of roles is initiated by her writing, by the composing of a letter which will fashion her with the doctor's character, it is her cousin's and thus ultimately a man's hand, which calls her into her new attire: Portia's entrance in court is preceded by a letter, which is presumed to have been composed by Bellario. And yet, even though the reversed cross-dressing, i.e. the re-disguise of a man playing a woman who appears in the attire of a man at the Venetian court, is authorised by a male hand and, even though it is called into existence by a male voice, i.e. by the judge who reads the letter before granting its subject access to the court, it has been planned by a female figure, at least on the level of the plot. The 'learnèd doctor' (4.1.104) Bellario never materialises onstage except in translation, namely in the character he calls into being. Portia, however, thus 'translated' does not only take care of her own transformation but also recruits an accomplice, Nerissa, whom she urges to follow her and cross-dress like herself whereby the social scale is observed: 'I'll prove the prettier fellow of the two / And wear my dagger with the braver grace' (3.4.64f.), claims Portia, who emerges from the play as one of Shakespeare's strongest and most refined female characters, incorporating the Platonic ideal of *kalon k'agathon* and embodying an ideal combination of beauty, graciousness, virtue, and wit to perfection, which endures translation and is perceptible in her own persona as well as in her adopted identity, the figure of the young lawyer.

As the examples stated above indicate, the outline of a particular character, the act of rendering a human face in literature, the creation of a character on the page, and finally, the rewriting of documents are tasks that are frequently undertaken by female figures. Quite a few of Shakespeare's women not only resist descriptions and write back as if to challenge and undermine inscriptions imposed upon them but they ultimately supersede their male counterparts in terms of reading competence and the awareness of physiognomic texts. As already mentioned, Lady Capulet, for instance, transforms Paris' countenance into a 'book', which is not only created by 'beauty's' but also by her own pen. Thereby she provides the script for Juliet to recognise her destiny as covering letter to her husband's character, as ornamental binding which not only decorates but also defines and declares Paris' persona. Lady Capulet's portrayal is as much a description of Paris' character as it is a prescription for Juliet's reading. Similar to Lady Capulet, Lady Macbeth likens a face to a book and regards her husband's countenance as a document 'where men may read strange matters' such as Macbeth's fearful, anxious constitution. As suggested by the examples of Viola and Portia, also in the comedies, the major female characters show a significant awareness of the potential connected with non-verbal communication. This also applies to The Comedy of Errors, a play that to a far greater extent than Twelfth Night heavily relies on the confusion caused by the appearance of two sets of identical twins that were split at sea in a tempest. The two Antipholi and the two Dromios often enter the stage almost immediately after each other, causing bewilderment in Ephesus whenever they appear: 'Which is the natural man, / And which the spirit?' (*The Comedy of Errors* 5.1.334f.). Physiognomy seems to fail when it comes to deciphering identities, which seem unstable ('Am I myself?' [3.2.74]), and yet the audience is quite frequently reminded of the potential legibility of the human body. Dromio of Ephesus, for instance, alludes to the human power of inscribing the body when he compares the skin to a piece of parchment, drawing from the connection between graphology and physiognomy:

> If the skin were parchment, and the blows you gave were ink,
> Your own handwriting would tell you what I think. (3.1.13f.)

While the notion of the skin documenting the blows of everyday life as they are experienced by and through the body connects to the metaphor of branding, it is the temporary marks which Dromio refers to and which prove far more telling in this play than physiognomic (in the narrowest sense) features of the body. Significantly, it is women who show a greater insight into the potentialities of nonverbal communication. Thus Luciana instructs Antipholus of Syracuse in ways of how to make use of the 'speaking' body and apply certain features to his purpose when meeting his shamefully neglected 'wife' Adriana, who is in fact not betrothed to him but to his twin brother. Imagining the scene of their reunion, Luciana provides him with his 'text':

> Let not my sister read it in your eye.
> Be not thy tongue thy own shame's orator.
> Look sweet, speak fair, become disloyalty;
> Apparel vice like virtue's harbinger.
> Bear a fair presence, though your heart be tainted:
> Teach sin the carriage of a holy saint.
> Be secret-false. What need she be acquainted?
> […] 'Tis double wrong to truant with your bed,
> And let her read it in thy looks at board.
> Shame hath a bastard fame, well managèd.
> (3.2.9–19)

Where dissimulation meets success, appearances do matter: 'Though others have the arm, show us the sleeve' (3.3.23). In an almost Wrightean manner, Luciana lays out the tools for Antipholus' self fashioning, which are gratefully received:

> Teach me, dear creature, how to think and speak […].
> Are you a god? Would you create me new?
> Transform me, then, and to your power I'll yield.
> (3.2.33–40)

Subjected to the power of rhetoric, Antipholus seems wax in Luciana's hands and devoted to her as well as to her speech, which from her point of view has transformed a husband. Adriana, who has been expecting her impatiently, shares her physiognomic awareness and strongly believes in the correspondence of body and psyche[1] and directs her attention to pathognomic features on enquiring after Antipholus' reaction.

> Looked he or red or pale, or sad or merrily?
> What observation mad'st thou in this case
> Of his heart's meteors tilting in his face?
> (4.2.4–6)

The comparison between the face and the cosmos contributes to the notion of man's decipherability within a divine order of the world. Cleopatra refers to the same image when telling Dolabella her dream of the emperor Antony, whose face she likens to 'the heav'ns, and therein stuck / A sun and moon, which kept their course and lighted / The little O o'th'earth' (5.2.77–79). It is this expression of 'authority' that distinguishes a royal face, the expression of the king or the sun of the empire, to which also Kent alludes on being asked how he recognised kingly qualities in Lear's countenance. Whereas the cosmic order in Antony's and in Lear's face seems to have been kept, in Antipholus' face, heavenly bodies are expected to have engaged in a combat. In consideration of his imprudent and upsetting behaviour, his heart is bound to send conflicting emotions to the surface, 'meteors' that upset the otherwise harmonious expression of the face. At least this is Adriana's contention. Even though Antipholus' physical reaction is not commented on, by Luciana's report, however, one has to suppose that the reproaches brought up against him left him quite untouched. His apparent indifference to Adriana, who, as the audience is well aware of, mistakes him for his twin brother and his advancements to her sister, let her take refuge in a tirade of abuse to express her fury and her shame:

> He is deformèd, crookèd, old, and sere,
> Ill-faced, worse-bodied, shapeless everywhere,
> Vicious, ungentle, foolish, blunt, unkind,
> Stigmatical in making, worse in mind.
> (4.2.19–22)

The irony, of course, lies in the fact that behind the agreeable

---

1   Compare Adriana's belief in moral 'branding': *The Comedy of Errors* 2.2.131–37.

appearance of Antipholus of Syracuse there hides neither deceit nor viciousness.

While Luciana's control over her body and her insight into its rhetoric as well as Adriana's growing awareness for the potentialities of facial expressions support the predominance of women with regard to physiognomic principles and strategies, the theme of facial eloquence, like all major themes in Shakespeare, is inflected in the course of the action. The notion of man's mastery and conquering of the female body is not cut out of this play. On the contrary, the mapping of Nell's body in act three, scene two is unmatched in Shakespeare's oeuvre. The *contre-blazon* is performed by Dromio of Syracuse, who likens her body to parts of the globe, her nose with its blemished skin to America and the Indies 'all o'er embellished with rubies, carbuncles, sapphires' (3.2.132f.), the hard palm of her hand to Scotland and its rocky landscape, and her forehead that seems scarred badly, possibly displaying signs of syphilis, to France, 'armed and reverted, making war against her heir' (3.2.122f.). This multi-national body, which is explored by Dromio of Syracuse but has in fact already been conquered by his twin brother, lays claims to its 'discoverer' by identifying his private marks (a mole and a wart) in turn. Countering Dromio's 'reading' by a more refined and detailed scanning of his body, Nell turns the tables and puts her explorer (and his master) to flight, "Tis time, I think, to trudge, pack, and be gone' (3.2.151), before she can incorporate Syracuse into her *corpus mundi*. Nell, who is everybody and nobody at the same time, never appears onstage. She exceeds representation and until the end remains a *terra incognita* to Dromio of Syracuse and to the audience. Her absence from the stage furthermore calls Dromio's portrayal into question and leads his heavily prejudiced and highly comic notions of foreign, nationalised physiognomies *ad absurdum*.

The construction of masculinity and femininity in Shakespeare's plays is closely intertwined with the politics of reading and writing. While on the meta-theatrical level, the female body remains subjected by a company consisting of male actors wearing women's clothing and adopting their appearance, on the level of the play, constructions of gender are destabilised in that women are empowered to intervene in the signification of their bodies and thus undermine the patriarchal, male text either by erasing or tearing the characters composed by male hands (as in *The Two Gentlemen of Verona*), or by re-writing the script that has been ascribed to them. In the following chapter, the politics of physiognomic reading and writing as well as women's physiognomic 'eye' that governs the construction of characters onstage shall be further examined by focussing on figures that qualify as physiognomists in Shakespeare's plays and tracing their physiognomic scheme.

6 The Physiognomist in Shakespeare's Plays

Before identifying Shakespeare's physiognomists, the main characteristics of these figures need to be recapitulated. Considering the fact that it is the physiognomists who map the characters of their fellow-*personae*, the question arises as to what, if not who, does the job for them? As stated above, physiognomists can be regarded as extremely considerate and highly proficient perceivers of signs and signatures, who are not only familiar with the art of reading faces, but who are also very aware of ways in which to intervene in, and ultimately alter the bodily text of a particular persona. Due to their profound insight into physiognomy and physiognomic inference, it can be assumed that these figures are capable not only of deconstructing but also of constructing masks. Their superior knowledge of facial rhetoric enables them to frame their faces for all occasions and to hide their wickedness behind false 'smiles and affability' (*Julius Caesar* 2.1.82). While relying on the principle of physiognomic inference in their approaches to their fellow-beings, physiognomists seem to incorporate a physiognomic paradox, which combines the readable with the inscrutable or even the reader with the actor: their own external appearance more often than not remains in the dark. The strongest physiognomic 'readers' in Shakespeare's oeuvre appear up to a certain extent faceless in that they are only rarely subjected to physiognomic readings. The peculiar absence of their seemingly inscrutable faces heightens their supremacy as readers. The notion that their bodies lack description does not least arise from the want of a physiognomic antagonist, under whose gaze they could materialise.

There is usually only one figure in each play that qualifies as physiognomist. While at the outset of the action, two personae might be identified that appear equally capable of physiognomic readings, only one of them prevails. This is the case in *Julius Caesar*, which, as already mentioned, presents two physiognomic opponents, Caesar and Cassius, both of whom show a profound awareness of the significance of external signifiers. Furthermore, a third reader emerges in Brutus, who after the mirror scene starts to 'face' his environment and observes tokens of non-verbal communication. The role of the physiognomist, however, can finally be attributed to Cassius. His manipulative description of Brutus displays performative skills which exceed the scrutinising eyes of Brutus and Caesar, who fatally overlooks the signs pointing to the dangers lurking at the senate. A change of the physiognomist's persona happens in *Macbeth* and *Antony and Cleopatra* where it furthermore ties in with a shift of power from the female to the male perspective. Even though the outcome of this role change ultimately supports traditional gender politics in that the female is subjected to male imprinting, the female attempt to intervene in a greater semiotic scheme by means of a physiognomic reading and self-fashioning, as suggested above, can be read as an attempt to subvert and redefine traditional power relations.

As it will become apparent in the following close readings of selected plays, women are often in the front rank in Shakespeare's physiognomic theatre, not so much as objects to be imprinted or deciphered but as most prudent readers and, as the ability of reading and the skill of writing presuppose each other, as skilled actresses. Even though the emancipatory strife for participation in the signifying system seems more successful in the comedies—as the examples of Viola, Luciana, and Portia indicate—in that the advocates of female imprinting survive and, as in Viola's case, emerge from the play as the prime agent of self-fashioning, the tragedies and histories hold equally strong female readers: Lady Macbeth, Queen Margaret, Juliet, Desdemona, and first and foremost Cleopatra, who recurrently scrutinise faces, turn out to be extremely competent physiognomic readers with a strong awareness of their potential to manipulate the language of the human face and body. And yet, the question remains of to what extent female characters forfeit their femininity by engaging in the process of signification. Portia and Viola temporarily lose their womanly shape and change into mail attire in order to participate in the dynamic graphological and physiognomic interaction of 'characters'.

Neither Luciana nor Adriana, however, cross-dresses while gaining physiognomic competence but retain their womanliness throughout the play. Thus, in the following analysis of Shakespeare's physiognomists, one of the questions to be considered is to what extent female physiognomists are threatened in their female disposition, by adopting a reading and writing competence, which is traditionally attributed to man.

6.1 Facing the Macbeths

In the rough, war-dominated and predominantly masculine world of *Macbeth*, women seem pushed to the margins. The three uncanny figures who induct the audience into play by undermining the dualistic opposition of 'foul' and 'fair' lack distinctive female features and resist classification: 'You should be women, / And yet your beards forbid me to interpret / That you are so' (1.3.43–45). As will be confirmed in the 'martlet'-scene, Banquo's careful consideration of the mysterious appearances is predicated on a belief in the transparency of a world where the relation between signifier and signified is still valid. In view of the paradoxical appearance of the 'three weird sisters' (2.1.19), however, Banquo, unable to attach any meaning to these degenerated images of the three Fates, falls silent. Refraining from 'interpreting' the uncanny sight, he confers the physiognomic reading onto the audience.

Crossing the borders between the masculine and the feminine, between the supernatural and the natural, and between 'foul' and 'fair', the 'three weird sisters' open up a negative space, which seems to gradually absorb the traditional belief in the *signatura rerum* as well as eliminate feminine figures. Lady Macduff, who seems a last specimen of the frail female sex, is slaughtered in her castle at her first appearance in the play and Lady Macbeth disavows her natural disposition. Urging the spirits to 'unsex' (1.4.39) her, she hardens her body and her mind shortly before Duncan's murder to set free 'direst cruelty' (1.5.41). In Conall Morrison's production of *Macbeth*,[1] the peculiar absence of women is spotlighted: it opens with a savage

1   As it was staged in the Swan Theatre at Stratford in 2007.

prelude, showing Macbeth in a brutal raid, killing civilians, mothers and children and leaving behind a pool of blood. After he has left the scene, the bereaved mothers revive, unite, and turn into witches. Thus, it is Macbeth, who ultimately creates the 'weird sisters' and who, by unleashing violence, initiates the extinction of the female body. When Morrison's Macbeth picks up an infant, soothes it but then breaks its neck by a rapid turning of what seemed a tender hug, he is likened to Lady Macbeth, who will later claim her capability of killing a babe that she has given suck to. Thus in this particular production of the play, Lady Macbeth becomes the missing link between the three 'weird sisters' and Macbeth.

Insofar as Lady Macbeth engineers the assassination of the king, she implements the prophecy by the three mysterious women and ensures that her husband, who has been awarded the title 'Thane of Cawdor' and was predicted to become 'King' thereafter (1.5.6–8). Her alliance to the supernatural figures does not end here. Considering the fact that physiognomy was regarded a mantic art, which was declared a punishable offence as in the act released by Elizabeth, the connection between the masculinized women figures is intensified: like the 'weird sisters', who immediately identify Macbeth, Lady Macbeth 'reads' her husband's character before she paves the way for the witches prophecy to come true. Thereby, she promotes the abolishment of the dichotomy of heart and face, inner and outer being, 'foul' and 'fair' and instructs her husband not only in the art of how to assume a 'false face' to cover a 'false heart' (1.7.82) but also teaches him to 'look like the innocent flower, / But be the serpent under't' (*Macbeth* 1.5.63f.).

Already at her first appearance onstage, Lady Macbeth emerges as a most attentive observer that will be pulling the strings in the action to follow. Her physiognomic competence suggests itself when she enters with a letter, which bears her husband's 'character'. Gradually proceeding from the lineaments on the page to the expression of Macbeth's face, which appears before her shortly after she has finished reading the letter, she gives a foretaste of her literacy, 'Your face, my thane, is as a book where men / May read strange matters' (1.5.60f.). What matters these are and who placed them there remains disputable. Undisputable, however, is the complexity of facial features, which is also underscored by Lady Macbeth's reading. It is not a single page but a collection of documents, a volume that presents itself before her. The surface, therefore, resembles a transitory document, whose meaning lies beyond, or rather: beneath the exterior but can be disclosed *through* the facial text. Hence, the latter serves as an index for a more profound and complex content, which unfolds itself to the beholder provided that the latter knows how to read its lineaments.

The physiognomic encounter between Lady Macbeth and her husband, which merges the two concepts of graphology and physiognomy, holds up an inverted mirror to the first face-to-face-meeting between Duncan and Macbeth. While in the latter Macbeth seems to have been called onto the stage by the king's anti-physiognomic axiom, he now enters shortly after his 'character' was sketched for the audience. The parallel construction of the two scenes underscores the rivalry between Lady Macbeth and Duncan, which is based on different philosophies or world orders. While Lady Macbeth acknowledges the legibility of the human body, Duncan opposes physiognomic inference and questions the trustworthiness of countenances. However, this rejection of a body-psyche correspondence marks the beginning of his downfall as centre of a world whose semiotic structure is about to change. Lady Macbeth's reading of her husband's written and facial character invalidates the king's notion that 'there's no art / To find the mind's construction in the face' (1.4.11f.). What is remarkable with regard to these two positions is that Duncan, as the representative of the traditional, Tillyardian world order, does not subscribe to the doctrine of signs and their interpretability, whereas Lady Macbeth grounds her concept of a carefully planned and cautiously enacted physiognomic self-fashioning on the assumption that man is intrinsically legible. The chiastic structure, which suggests itself in this constellation, however, does not oppose the notion of transparency but ultimately serves to reinforce physiognomic reasoning and support the notion of an intimate interaction between man's body and his moral disposition, an interaction that Macbeth experiences at the first meeting with the three weird sisters when he feels the physical symptoms of fear taking control of his body (1.3.129–36).

In the course of the play, the action progresses from Duncan's denial of a neoplatonic correspondence of body and psyche to the emergence of the Machiavellian figure, Lady Macbeth, until it finally results in the making and fashioning of the usurper, Macbeth, whose dissimulative and manipulative powers—like those of his wife—derive from the acknowledgment of an ultimately legible world. If legibility generates illegibility, and if illegibility creates legibility, which is in accord with the principle of inversion as it is suggested in the dictum 'fair is foul and foul is fair', then these two poles frame the dramatic action and constitute beginning and end of *Macbeth*. In the last act, history threatens to repeat itself in that the traditional order seems to be recovered in a victory over a traitor and a 'day of success' (1.5.1.), which is reminiscent of Macbeth's triumph over the precedent Thane of Cawdor. The wheel of time and fortune whose continuous turning resonates in Macbeth's 'tomorrow, tomorrow, and tomorrow' (5.5.18), refers back to the first scene when the wheel comes full turn in the gloomy aphorism hovering over the play: 'Fair is foul, and foul is fair' (1.1.11). The potential circularity of the play is emphasised in Roman Polanski's film version of *Macbeth* (1971) as the three witches meet again in the final scene, which brings us back to the beginning of the play and thus to further 'toil and trouble' (4.1.35).

In the context of subversion and affirmation, of code-breaking and code-making, the face emerges as battlefield whereupon the persona is construed. In this process, the distinction between face and mask becomes complicated. The close connection between these two surfaces, which both point to something *beyond* the visible and act as ciphers awaiting a diligent reader to unfold their meaning, is suggested by the Greek expression *prosopon*, which can refer to both 'face' and 'mask'. With regard to Macbeth, however, their distinction is possible. As D. J. Palmer observed, of all Shakespearean characters, 'Macbeth in particular is required to give himself away, as it were, by his look'.[1] This is especially the case at the beginning of the play when Macbeth's performs readings of his body whereby he discov-

---

1   D. J. Palmer, '"A New Gorgon": Visual Effects in *Macbeth*', in John Russell Brown ed., *Focus on Macbeth* (London et al.: Routledge and Kegan, 1982) 58f.

ers symptoms of fear and horror, which do not escape his companion, Banquo, who notices that his partner is 'rapt' (1.3.142) or wrapped: Macbeth's mental enclosure caused by the predominance of the body over the soul that is confined to the physical vessel,[1] lasts until the banquet scene when for the last time, 'the very painting of [his] fear' (3.4.60), his pale cheeks and 'such faces' (3.4.66) that are prompted by terror and alarm reveal his natural, anxious, and vulnerable disposition. After the banquet scene, which has drawn the dinner guests' attention to the countenance and the strange behaviour of the king, the feasting on Macbeth's speaking body has ceased. The vision of the supernatural, the three weird woman-like figures, and the encounter with the dead, the ghost of Banquo haunting him at the banquet, seems to have numbed Macbeth's senses, leaving him with a frozen, unfeeling body, which thwarts the natural translation between inner and outer being. Hence, at the end of the play, the barren Macbeth has successfully extinguished his body's former legibility: 'no more sights' (4.1.171).

Before embarking on the closure of Macbeth's 'book', of his eloquent face, let us briefly review his physiognomic career: it is the awareness of his body's transparency of the uncontrolled translation of his thoughts and feelings onto the bodily surface, which necessitates and inaugurates Macbeth's transformation from an open book to an inscrutable mask. Duncan's sceptical view of physiognomic inference, which hearkens back to the dictum of the mysterious sisters, provides the background against which the symptomatic relation of body and mind becomes all the more obvious.

Notwithstanding Duncan's mistrust in the face of a man who has already been identified as traitor, which impedes the originality of his physiognomic reasoning, the transparency of surfaces remains in force until the action is shifted to Dunsinane. Approaching the castle, Duncan and Banquo perform a physiognomic reading of Macbeth's residence, whose pleasant aura commends its inhabitants:

> *Duncan*: This castle hath a pleasant seat. The air
> Nimbly and sweetly recommends itself
> Unto our gentle senses.

---

1   Compare Cicero, *Tusculanae* I 52.

Banquo: This guest of summer
The temple-haunting martlet, does approve
By his loved mansionry that the heavens' breath
Smells wooingly here.
(*Macbeth* 1.6.1–6)

As the audience was already granted a glimpse behind the castle's walls, they will dissociate from this fatal misconception of Dunsinane, where the floodgates have already been opened to deceit and dissimulation. In the previous scene Lady Macbeth not only subjected her husband to a physiognomic reading and thus confirmed the legibility of faces, but also laid the foundation for his facial self-fashioning and the art of wearing a flowering face to hide a serpent's heart (1.5.63f.). The foul interior, however, has not yet translated itself onto the surface but remains indiscernible as if adhering to Lady Macbeth's deceptive scheme. Even though they are equally misleading, Duncan's and Banquo's approaches to the aura surrounding the castle are in fact very different: while Duncan trusts his senses, Banquo attempts to substantiate the favourable impression of Macbeth's residence by referring to the infallible instinct of the martlet. While in heraldry, the martlet signifies nobility and braveness, it has also been regarded as a token of fine quarters since antiquity. Thus in *De Natura Animalum*, Aelianus records that the martlets nesting in the castle of Dionysos of Syracuse fled when the tyrant returned home.[1] The martlet's fine senses are confirmed in Braithwaite's *Survey of History*, which claims that 'the martin will not build but in fair houses'.[2] Suggesting a symbiosis of inner and outer appearance, which recommends the castle and its inhabitants, the martlet appears like a relic from an obsolete world order, indicating a correspondence of the external and the internal which is subverted by the castle's residents.

The reading of Macbeth's home is Banquo's last attempt at deciphering a physiognomy. Its failure prepares for the turning point from

1   Aelianus, *De Natura Animalum* X 34.
2   Richard Braithwaite, *Survey of History* (1638). Quoted from Horace H. Furness ed., *William Shakespeare: Macbeth*, New Variorum Edition (New York: Dover, 1963) 63. See also Peter M. Daly, 'Of Macbeth, Martlets and other "Fowles of Heaven"', *Mosaic: A Journal for the Comparative Study of Literature and Ideas* 12 (1978) 23–46, 30f.

a transparent to an opaque world, which is reached when the king is murdered at the 'pleasant seat' of Dunsinane. Proclaiming the news of Duncan's death, Macduff uses the same image as Banquo when he claims that 'most sacrilegious murder hath broke ope / The Lord's anointed temple and stole thence / the life of the building' (2.3.63–5). The ensouling of Macbeth's castle leads to the desouling of the king's body. Besides indicating a corruption of the divine order of the world, which is all of a sudden out of joint, the notion of the body as a dwelling occupied by divine presence ultimately suggests that it is the soul which forms the body and not vice versa as is implied by Richard Gloucester, for instance, who claims to be 'determinèd' to villainy by his deformated body. It is the martlet which bestows the 'temple' with its soul. By Banquo's twofold description of the castle, which refers to both the physical ('martlet') and metaphysical level ('breath'), Shakespeare succeeds in overcoming a dilemma, which elsewhere in his dramatic oeuvre sparks off the action. What remains veiled and resists representation in *Hamlet*, 'that within which passeth show' (*Hamlet* 1.2.85), becomes visible in *Macbeth* by a double translation. Even though Banquo interprets the external token correctly, the aura surrounding Dunsinane proves fatally misleading as the connection between seeming and being has already become brittle in a world where the *signatura rerum* are re- and overwritten by Lady Macbeth.

As if to heighten the audience's awareness for the bloody spectacle in act two, scene two and highlight Lady Macbeth's painting of the grooms' faces as documents of guilt[1], it is the colour of the cheeks that turns out to be most revealing in this particular play. Macbeth's fearful paleness forms a glaring contrast to the 'natural ruby' (*Macbeth* 3.4.113) of his wife's complexion. While the liaison of life and death becomes physically incorporated by the couple Macbeth, the distribution of colour is somewhat misleading. Rather than Lady Macbeth's red cheeks, it is Macbeth's wan face that points to the more animate body of the two in that the indices of fear displayed on his bodily surface point to a sound sensory perception,

---

1   Compare: 'I'll gild the faces of the grooms withal, / For it must seem their guilt' (*Macbeth* 2.2.54f.).

which Lady Macbeth lacks. As early as at the end of act one, scene five, Lady Macbeth denies her female body, imploring the gods to 'unsex' her, to thicken her blood, fill her body 'from the crown to the toe' with dire cruelty, free her of her womanly disposition, and make her immune to feelings of compassion and all other 'compunctious visitings of nature' (1.5.43). Considering the hardening of her body and the rejection of a sensitive female mind, it seems more than likely that the ruby colour on her cheeks is anything but natural but the outcome of a skilfully applied face-paint, which is but an artificial imitation of manly constancy, a perversion of the principle *semper eadem*, which breaks the tie between body and psyche. The document of life, which suggests itself in the 'natural ruby' of her cheeks, is a fake just like her female shape, which has been hollowed out and filled with the metal male characters are made of in order to compensate her husband's 'milky' nature ('full o'th'milk of human kindness' [1.5.15]). Counterbalancing Macbeth, Lady Macbeth has added weight to her body, creating a body that matters and that will eventually strike back at her to claim its share. The reunion of body and soul in the sleepwalking scene not only marks Lady Macbeth's loss of control over her 'self' and thus over her body but also indicates a shift of roles within the relationship to Macbeth regarding both the role of the physiognomist and the dichotomy of life and death. At his wife's suicide, Macbeth's body finally acquires the manliness and cruelty, which the lady has been striving for in her appeal to shut off her body and let the fountain of life run dry (1.5.38–48).

In comparison to Lady Macbeth, however, Macbeth seems to be still 'young in deed' (3.4.143) since the majority of the play is devoted to teaching him the art of wearing a flowering face over a serpent heart and hiding a dreadful deed behind an innocent façade. Macbeth's telling countenance with its 'blanched' (3.4.114) complexion, which openly communicates the horror that has taken possession of him, makes high demands on the actor playing this role. However, even though paling is not one of those features easily imitated onstage, its performance is not entirely impractical as the example of David Garrick suggests. The latter's empathetic acting caught Lichtenberg's attention, who admired the pathos communicated in every feature of his face. Playing Macbeth, Garrick is said to have grown pale at the sight of his bloodstained hands.[1] To achieve this reaction, he must have practiced the principle of *enargeia*, the art of imagining fear and horror, which enabled him to live out his role to an extent that made him feel Macbeth's passions and his shaking fear himself. This kind of imaginative strength that lies at the core of a natural style of acting is alluded to in Hamlet's advice to the players, which are encouraged 'to suit the action to the word'. No other actor has to be as skilled in arousing feelings of terror as the one playing Macbeth: Lily Campbell has already termed the play 'a study of fear'[2] and, throughout the first part of the play, Macbeth's face provides the data for this claim before the image of a shrouded, 'wrapped' soldier eventually culminates in the sight of an unfeeling, somehow deadened body, or rather a non-body which has become immune to external stimuli and remains untainted by emotions and 'the taste of fears' (5.5.9), which it knows only too well.

At the peak of his career as usurper and shortly before his downfall, Macbeth enacts a meticulous face-reading, whereby he traces the gradual blanching in a face that could have been his former self:

> *Macbeth*:   The devil damn thee black, thou cream-faced loon!
> Where gott'st thou that goose look?
> *Servant*:   There is ten thousand – […] Soldiers, sir.
> *Macbeth*:   Go, prick thy face and over-red thy fear,
> Thou lily-livered boy. What soldiers, patch?
> Death of thy soul, those linen cheeks of thine
> Are counsellors to fear. What soldiers, whey-face?
> […] Take thy face hence!
> (*Macbeth* 5.3.11–19)

Finally, it is Macbeth who perceives 'counsellors to fear' in another

---

1 Harald W. Fawkner, *Deconstructing 'Macbeth': The Hyperontological View* (Rutherford: Fairleigh Dickenson University Press and London/Toronto: Associated University Presses, 1990) 57. See also Dennis Bartholomeusz, *Macbeth and the Players* (Cambridge: Cambridge University Press, 1969) 61, and Michael S. Wilson, 'Garrick, iconic acting, and the ideologies of theatrical portraiture', *Word and Image* 6 (1990) 368–94.
2 Lily B. Campbell, *Shakespeare's Tragic Heroes: Slaves of Passion* (London: Methuen, 1962) 233. Compare *Macbeth* 1.3.129–36, 3.4.112–14, 4.1.101.

face and reiterates the different stages of paling from a creamy taint
to a lily- and linen-colour, which changes into a 'whey-face' that
Macbeth eventually bans from his sight.[1] If one reads the 'loon' not
only as a reference to a madman but also as an allusion to the bird,
whose plumage is black above and white beneath, points to the pro-
tagonist's two bodies, the fearful and yet unspotted soldier who strug-
gles to disrupt the connection between his inner being and his outer
appearance and the callous usurper, blackened by his deeds, who is
no longer in need of secrecy, but scrutinises other surfaces, which is
part of the strategy for masking himself. After the suicide of his wife,
Macbeth seems not only in control of physical impulses and the pas-
sions of his mind, but somehow appears to lack both a body and a
'within'. This 'within' and with it the notion of a conscience seems to
have been passed on from Macbeth to Lady Macbeth in the course of
their role change. The chiastic reversal of physiognomic competence,
on the one hand, and crisis of body and mind, on the other, whereby
Lady Macbeth's psyche increases as Macbeth's mask becomes real,
culminates in the strongest face-reading of the play, a reading, which
registers the opacity of the Macbeths, whose books both of the face
and the conscience are now closed.

The reading of the servant's face, Macbeth's obituary of his previ-
ous milky-natured body, substantiates the protagonist's role as *agens*
in the play: by beholding, seeing, and identifying an 'other', who is
a spitting image of his former self, without being seen, Macbeth con-
firms and substantiate his own being.[2] Exploring and exploiting an all
too familiar document of fear, he succeeds in affirming his recently
acquired mask. Facing the soldier, Macbeth seems to outface himself
– 'no more sights' (4.1.171). His 'invisibility', which arises from the
lack of descriptions of his face, shields him from his enemies. When
Macduff eventually calls him to a duel with the appeal, 'Tyrant, show
thy face' (5.8.1), Macbeth's fate is sealed. The encounter between the
loyal soldier and the traitor hearkens back to Macbeth's beheading of
Macdonald and thus brings the play full circle. The mask is torn, the

---

1   For a thorough reading of this scene, see Weston Babcock, 'Macbeth's "cream-
    faced loon"', *Shakespeare Quarterly* 4 (1953) 199–202.
2   Compare Philip Armstrong, *Shakespeare's Visual Regime: Tragedy, Psycho-
    analysis and the Gaze* (Basingstoke/New York: Palgrave, 2000) 167.

traitor's head openly displayed: mounted upon a pole, it becomes an apotropaic symbol, a trophy which makes the unbeholdable observable and takes away the horror from 'the new Gorgon' (2.3.69) that was born at Duncan's murder and eventually manifested itself in Macbeth's 'invisible' face.

6.2 Cleopatra, a New Gorgon

The image of the Gorgon and its connection to the physiognomist figure pave the way to the most powerful of Shakespeare's female readers—Cleopatra. Not only does her face defy description as the ekphrasis presented by Enobarbus suggests: her presence seems unsettling, her gaze piercing, and her wrath to be avoided: 'Herod of Jewry dare not look upon you / But when you are well pleased' (*Antony and Cleopatra* 3.3.3–4). The latter is not easily achieved. Except for her first appearance onstage, Cleopatra emerges as a rather discontented figure that is often met in rage and fury and hence shows certain features that can be termed Gorgonic.

While the figure of the Gorgon-Medusa is explicitly referred to in the play, it is, however, not attributed to Cleopatra. It is none other than herself, however, who evokes the mythological figure. Cleopatra ascribes it to Antony, of whom she claims, 'though he be painted one way like a Gorgon, / The other way's a Mars' (2.5.117f.). Even though the choleric and hot-tempered soldier might bear some resemblance to the snake-haired grimace, whose sight is petrifying, Cleopatra seems to have misplaced the mask. This is not to say that Antony does not show Gorgonic qualities. Considering the lovelorn Cleopatra, he must be granted an attractive and certainly captivating character. The alliance of Mars and Gorgon, however, should not be confined to Antony's persona but rather refers to the couple Antony and Cleopatra, or, on an even broader scale, the imperial world of Rome and the exotic realm of Egypt. In this particular scene, in which the mythological pair is evoked, Mars seems to prevail. At least this is suggested by the constrictive remark '*though* he be painted one way like a Gorgon', which alludes to Antony's marriage of Octavia despite his ties with the Egyptian queen. To regard the image of the Gorgon as referring to Antony instead of Cleopatra would miss the clues given in this particular scene and her outburst of jealousy, which indicates capriciousness and an inclination to fury, which fits the character of the Medusa far better than Antony's disposition, which, even though it shows strong choleric hints, it falls short of Cleopatra's ferocious nature.

Not only does she vent her wrath on her messenger delivering the news of Antony's marriage, threatening to 'spurn [his] eyes / Like balls before [her]' (2.5.63f.) and to 'unhair' (2.5.63) his head, she also repeatedly brings snakes into the picture: 'kindly creatures / Turn all to serpents! [...] So half my Egypt were submerged and made / A cistern for scaled snakes' (2.5.78–96). While Cleopatra sketches this horrific vision of a degenerated, false, and treacherous Egypt, thereby evoking a scenario that she herself would dread to come into being and that rather reflects the Roman perspective on her kingdom, she has been associated with a serpent before. Longing for her lover's return, she remembers Antony calling her 'my serpent of old Nile' (1.5.25), which is a playful and loving adaptation of his countrymen's sneer (2.7.25). The term of endearment is grounded on a highly ambiguous symbol. On the one hand, serpents were regarded as cunning and perfidious creatures, as emblems of evil, and authors of misery.[1] On the other hand, however, they became a symbol of renovation and regeneration, thus the rod of Asculapius was wound with a serpent. Besides, they were connected with wisdom and thus are often included in royal emblems: the Rainbow Portrait of Elizabeth, for instance, shows an embroidered snake on the queen's left sleeve.[2] Shakespeare might even have been aware of the fact that the cobra was regarded a royal symbol in Egypt and displayed on the headpieces of Pharaohs. Furthermore, the goddess Iris, Cleopatra identi-

---

1   These connotations are very prominent in *Macbeth*, for instance, where Lady Macbeth implores her husband to 'look like the innocent flower / But be the serpent under't' (1.5.63f.) See also 'this gilded serpent' (*King Lear* 5.3.84), 'a serpent heart' (*Romeo and Juliet* 3.2.73), 'think him a serpent's egg' (*Julius Caesar* 2.1.32). Cf. Dennis Biggins, 'Scorpions, Serpents, and Treachery in *Macbeth*', *Shakespeare Studies* 1 (1965) 29–36.

2   Cf. Roy Strong, *Gloriana: The Portraits of Queen Elizabeth* (London: Thames and Hudson, 1987) 156–59. See also Michael Neill ed., *The Tragedy of Anthony and Cleopatra* (Oxford: Oxford University Press, 2004) 174 n.25.

fies herself with, wearing her garment on the public stage (3.6.16–8), was also associated with a serpent, or more precisely: an asp. The latter, 'the pretty worm of Nilus' (5.2.238f.), will eventually act as the queen's ally in the staging of her death.

The notion that the image of the Gorgon can be read as a reflection of Cleopatra is moreover supported by the figure of Narcissus that is evoked shortly before the queen sketches the anamorphic picture of Antony. Even though attributed to her opponent the messenger, whom Cleopatra chides, 'hadst thou Narcissus in thy face, to me / Thou wouldst appear most ugly' (2.5.97f.), the image of the lovelorn figure, pining away in the yearning for an 'other', who is but a simulacrum and likeness of one's self, bears a strong resemblance to the Egyptian queen. It combines the notion of her 'infinite variety' (2.2.241), which arises from the numerous projections she faces especially from the Roman front, and her paradoxical attraction. Despite her somewhat intangible and absent body, which does not quite seem to materialise, Cleopatra succeeds in ensnaring her beholders. As Jonathan Gil Harris remarks on rereading the play, using the Narcissus myth, Cleopatra is 'in thy face' more than any other character, 'possessed of a corporeality that seems to cry out for recognition', and yet 'her body has an odd habit of disappearing altogether at precisely those moments when it seems most overwhelmingly present'[1].

The conflation of self and other suggested by the image of Narcissus, which represents a moment of self-alienation in which the 'I' is confronted with the foreigner within it, with 'the other' that is its own unconscious,[2] prepares Cleopatra's self-reflection, or rather, self-projection onto an alleged 'other'. The mutual dependence of self and mirror is translated into the anamorphic image, which couples Gorgon and Mars. Torn between the two kingdoms and captivated by their mutual love, both protagonists have their share in the attributes connected with the mythological figures, whose alliance supports the

1   Jonathan Gil Harris, 'Narcissus in thy face: Roman Desire and the Difference it Fakes in Antony and Cleopatra', Shakespeare Quarterly 45/4 (1994) 408–25, 417.
2   See Julia Kristeva, Strangers to Ourselves, trans. by L. S. Roudiez (London: Harvester Wheatsheaf, 1991) 181–83.

love relationship in which, it was believed, the lovers recognise each other in their mirror images.[1]

The allusion to the Gorgon-Medusa is underscored in act three when Cleopatra replies to Alexas' comment, 'Herod of Jewry dare not look upon you' (3.3.2), declaring, '[t]hat Herod's head / I'll have' (3.3.4f). When shortly afterwards, she turns to her messenger, commanding him to step closer to her ('come thou near' [3.3.6]), the threat is obvious. For the second encounter with the queen, however, the messenger is well-prepared in that experience has taught him not to displease his mistress. Similar to Sophocles' *Antigone* where the messenger emphasizes his part in the capturing of Antigone in order to be spared another of Kreon's furious outburst, which he endured at delivering the message of Polyneikas' burial, the second report by the messenger is tailored to fit Cleopatra's expectations. To her delight, her servant sketches a rather unfavourable portrait of Octavia, which, as one might suspect, appears as a counter-image to the queen, whose beauty is all the more gleaming in comparison to her 'other' and clearly outshining her rival in Antony's love.

Considering her 'dwarfish' (3.3.16) figure with a forehead diminished to Cleopatra's liking ('as low as she would wish it' [3.3.33]) and a creeping gait (3.3.18), the image of Octavia can hardly hold a candle to Egypt's sovereign, whose petrifying glance the servant implements in his reading, claiming that Octavia's 'motion and her station are as one' (3.3.19), letting her appear like 'a statue' rather than 'a breather' (3.3.21).

Whereas these features serve, support, and ultimately satisfy Cleopatra's desire for self-fashioning, Octavia's character seems too beautiful to be so easily dispatched. Even though her low voice, which distinguishes her from yet another rival, 'shrill-tongued Fulvia' (1.1.34), as well as her brown hair, which indicates a perfect mixture

---

1   '[...] love causeth him that doth love to engrave and imprint in his heart, that face and image which he loveth: so that the heart of him that loveth is made like to a looking glasse, in which the image of the party beloved shineth and is represented. Therefore when he that is loved, beholdeth and acknowledgeth himselfe in him that loveth him' (Pierre de La Primaudaye, *The French Academy*, trans. by Thomas Bowes (London: Edmund Bollifan, 1618) II 484, as well as Plato, *Phaidros* 252d–253a. See also *Romeo and Juliet* 3.5.57–9 and *As You Like It* 3.5.54–6.

of bodily fluids, are not explicitly identified as positive attributes, they suggest a more favourable image than Cleopatra would approve of. And yet the queen is satisfied by her messenger's reading and, with regard to Antony, concludes 'he cannot like her long' (3.3.14). The peculiar absence of Cleopatra's features, which becomes all the more striking as Octavia's face gains shape in the course of the messenger's account, catches our ear, or rather, our eye, since this particular play seems to rely heavily on visual perception, deciding the rivalry of eye and ear in favour of the visual. At the outset of the first scene, we are greeted by Philo with the request to 'behold and see' (1.1.13), a request that combines the sensory with the cognitive perception. Whereas in the gloomy world of *Macbeth*, faces are intrinsically visible and legible, in *Antony and Cleopatra*, the majority of which is set 'in the public eye' (3.6.12), the protagonist's face remains largely out of sight. One could argue that Shakespeare leaves some room for the reader's imagination to fill in the vacancy and possibly project his mental portrait of the queen onto the boy-actor's face. The fact that the play repeatedly reminds the audience of the fact that what is displayed onstage is merely a show and Cleopatra is but represented by the very same 'squeaking' boy-actor, which she fears would distort her image, underscores the alleged indescribability and aloofness of her appearance. It is also feasible, however, that Shakespeare refrained from corroding the mythological beauty ascribed to this figure, which seems rather unfounded. While Plutarch praises the 'sweetness of her tongue'[1], and describes her as being 'at the age when a woman's beauty is at the prime and she also of best judgement'[2], he admits that 'her beauty (as it is reported) was not [...] such as upon present view did enamour men with her: but so sweet her company and conversation that a man could not possibly be taken'[3]. In avoiding describing her external appearance, Plutarch skirts around Cleopatra's physiognomy. More substantial information about her external appearance is provided by numismatic portraits of the time, which depict the Egyptian queen with a rather

---

1   Plutarch, 'Marcus Antonius', in Charles F. Tucker Brooke, ed., *Shakespeare's Plutarch* (London: Chatto and Windus, 1907) Vol. 2, 37.
2   Ibidem, 38.
3   Ibidem, 40.

haughty, ruthless, and unflattering physiognomy. Her face seems of an angular shape (and thus the exact opposite of Octavia's portrayal in the play), her nose was sharply bent, her forehead protruding, and her eyes seemed to retreat from the face while sending out an almost threatening glance.[1]

Hence, the question remains whether Cleopatra was as beautiful as indicated by Enobarbus' ekphrastic praise. Both historical sources and surviving portraits suggest the opposite. The rather unfavourable images might have been one reason why, with the exception of Enobarbus' reference to her 'delicate cheeks' (2.2.210), Shakespeare chose to omit any clues regarding Cleopatra's physiognomy. Instead, he creates a vacancy, a blank space for beauty to be imagined. After all, splendour defies description:

> Beauty (unlike ugliness) cannot really be explained: in each part of the body it stands out, repeats itself, but it does not describe itself. Like a god (and as empty), it can only say: *I am what I am.* The discourse, then, can do no more than assert the perfection of each detail [...].[2]

And Cleopatra is, similar to Desdemona, 'indeed perfection' (2.3.24), judging from Enobarbus' nondescription wherefrom the queen emerges as outshining deity, 'o'er-picturing [...] Venus' (2.2.206). While Roland Barthes' comment on the inexplicability of beauty will become even more significant in relation to Desdemona as Barthes, in this context, refers to art as the 'code underlying all beauty' and Desdemona's alabaster face suggests artifice, it seems to hit the mark with regard to Cleopatra's peculiar facelessness. Beauty is unfeasible; it can be circumscribed but never fully accounted for by words, or, as Barthes remarks, '[t]here is only one way to stop the replication of beauty: hide it, return it to silence, to the ineffable, to aphasia, refer the referent back to the invisible.'[3]

Drawing on Barthes, Catherine Belsey constitutes Cleopatra's seductive power not simply in her absence but rather in an 'imagined,

---

1 Compare Edelgard Brunelle, *Die Bildnisse der Ptolemäerinnen* (Frankfurt a.M.: University of Frankfurt, 1976) 106.
2 Roland Barthes, *S/Z*, trans. by Richard Miller (London: Cape, 1975) 33.
3 Ibidem, 33f.

promised, deferred presence'. 'The play locates her *at a distance*,'[1] she writes, and physiognomy becomes a means of creating this gap, which opens up between Cleopatra's persona and her environment, between the figure and its deficient embodiment by the boy-actor, between actor and audience, and even, one could argue, also between Shakespeare's adaptation and the historical image.

On Shakespeare's stage, Cleopatra's beauty becomes a myth, a promise, an imagination, which is as unattainable as it is fascinating. The fusion of the seductive, uncanny, and enthralling beauty, 'something both magical and mythical'[2], supports the connection to the Gorgon-Medusa, who can also be regarded as a deferred beauty: Medusa's awful appearance is the outcome of a metamorphosis. As is told in Ovid's *Metamorphoses*, which Shakespeare might have read in the original and most probably in George Sandy's translation, Medusa, who was renowned for her beauty, was raped by Neptune in Minerva's temple. The enraged goddess thereupon transformed the maiden's beautiful hair into a nest of serpents and decreed that anyone looking at her would be petrified.[3]

As suggested above, however, the association of the Medusa figure with Cleopatra grounds itself first and foremost on their mutual face-lessness: while the former lacks a physiognomy in that she cannot be beheld, or rather, nobody that faced her could report her features, the latter, as physiognomic eye of the play, seems to lack an antagonist who is capable of facing her. The notion of her unbeholdable face is not extinguished but rather underscored by the two 'readings' provided of her external appearance, one of which is performed by Cleopatra herself while the other is undertaken by Caesar. While the first view of her face remains highly dubious since it is a self-portrayal, Caesar's facing of the queen is far more revealing and highly significant in terms of the overall dramatic structure. His physiognomic encounter with Cleopatra marks a moment of conquest in that the

1 Catherine Belsey, 'Cleopatra's Seduction', in Terence Hawkes ed., *Alternative Shakespeares* (London/New York: Routledge, 1996) Vol. 2, 38–62, 42.
2 James L. Hill, 'The Marriage of True Bodies: Myth and Metamorphoses in *Antony and Cleopatra*', *REAL – The Yearbook of Research in English and American Literature* 2 (1984) 211–37, 217.
3 Ovid, *Metamorphoses* IV 793–802.

exotic alien figure is finally subjected to Roman power. This scene
deviates significantly from Shakespeare's main source for this play,
from Plutarch's account in his *Vitae*: in contrast to Shakespeare's
adaptation in which Cleopatra dreads her exposure to the sneer-
ing gaze of the Romans, Plutarch's 'Life of Caesar' claims that the
queen finally entered the city of Rome. However, she does so as
statue, turned into stone, by her enemy, petrified by Caesar's gaze,
and exposed to Roman eyes. In Plutarch's account, Cleopatra her-
self has become a monument while in Shakespeare she retreats to
one in order to hide from the Roman, from Antony in a playful game
of hide-and-seek, which she loses in Plutarch on an even broader
scope in that she is submitted to the gaze of the Romans. While the
play ends before Caesar's triumphal return to his *polis*, the undermin-
ing of the queen's authority, her embarrassment before her subordi-
nates, and above all her subjection to Caesar's face-reading, where
the gazing 'I' and its inferior are inverted, not only allow for the scru-
tinising of Cleopatra's countenance, but also set the stage for a finale,
which somehow connects to Plutarch's version. This is not to say that
Shakespeare assumed a pre-knowledge of the *Vitae* in his audience,
which is not required for the understanding of the play. A spectator
familiar with Plutarch, however, the *Lives* could serve as a supple-
ment, almost an act six, which follows up on Caesar's order '[a]nd
then to Rome' (5.2.355) and hence serve as a fruitful appendix to
Shakespeare's *Antony and Cleopatra*.

6.3 *Othello* and the Physiognomy of the Mind

What makes *Othello* an interesting case for the analysis of physiog-
nomic subtexts in Shakespeare's drama is not its seeming adherence
to racial stereotypes, which are invoked only to be broken down in
the course of the play as the figure which draws the attention turns
out to be the ocular proof of the fallibility of physiognomic infer-
ence. What makes a physiognomic reading of the play a fruitful ven-
ture is firstly the alliance of two physiognomic antipodes, namely
Othello and Desdemona, and, secondly, the physiognomic combat
which Desdemona and Iago engage in. With the couple Othello and

Desdemona and the adversaries Desdemona and Iago, the audience is confronted with two opposing extremes each on the physiognomic scale. Whereas Othello and Desdemona answer for very different notions of the legibility of the human body, Desdemona and Iago correspondingly represent the phyisognomists in the play, while they follow very different schemes of physiognomic reading.

As these two constellations of readers and 'their' documents suggest, the art of physiognomy in this particular play is approached from very different angles whereby both its advantages and its perils come into view, urging the audience to engage in the mutual 'reading' and 'writing' that is performed onstage. The most prominent eye-catcher of the play is undoubtedly Othello, whose exotic appearance engenders mistrust in the streets of Venice, which is not least due to the inscrutability of his face: every attempt to subject Othello's countenance to a physiognomic reading seems to bounce off his black visage[1] where emotional reactions such as blushing and paling cannot be displayed. Notwithstanding the inscrutability of his complexion, the inhabitants of Venice continue to gaze at his body, which is clearly demarcated and thus identifiable as alien, as the dreaded 'other' by its dark complexion which according to common stereotypical indicates a fiendish, base, and monstrous character. As well as being a great story teller holding numerous tales of other nations, foreign races, and unknown cultures, tales and narratives that captivate Desdemona (*Othello* 1.3.144–65), Othello becomes a projection screen for obloquies and slander. While Desdemona's face is received as a testament to her modesty, purity, and virtuous mind until the final act, Othello's obscure visage arouses suspicion and raises hackles. Its natural opacity seems blotted even more by prejudiced ascriptions whereas Desdemona's face remains spotless throughout the play. She has a clear aspect and a fair mind, which corresponds to

---

1   Even though Ernst Honigmann proposes a contrasting colour to 'raven-black' Aaron and suggests a 'tawny front' for Othello, it seems likely that the actor playing Othello (who would have been Richard Burbage in Shakespeare's production) was playing the part with heavy dark make-up, which would support the contrasting images of black and white which are constitutive especially for this play. (Cf. Ernst A. Honigmann, *Shakespeare: Seven Tragedies Revisited: The Dramatist's Manipulation of Response* [Basingstoke et al.: Palgrave, 2002] 27–31).

her light skin. Her 'fair paper', however, will eventually be smudged by Othello, who searches in vain for the word 'whore' on its surface and, blinded by Iago's cunning and effective misreadings, raises the knife against the innocent body as if to belatedly inscribe upon it the stigma it ought to bear.

When Othello directs his attention to Desdemona's physiognomy, it is Othello's first attempt to perform a face-reading on his own. Even though the inscrutability of his face would potentially qualify him as a physiognomist figure, the 'reader' Othello only appears on the margins of the play. Rather than directing his view onto other faces, he finds himself in the place of the document that is being scrutinised or emerges as misreader in the play, who falls into the semiotic traps laid out for him. It seems as if he is denied access to a mutual code, which his environment has agreed on behind his back. Before scrutinising Desdemona's fair paper, Othello's vision has been blurred by Iago's manipulative eye, which prompted his first fatal misreading. On hearing Desdemona accused, Othello demands the 'ocular proof' (3.3.365), which Iago can present: making physiognomy his accomplice by drawing from the already ambivalent reaction of laughing, the 'manipulator of signs'[1] blurs Othello's vision and sets a snare for him. Adequately prepared with his visual senses attuned to treachery and deceit, Othello misinterprets Cassio's laughter and in 'his unbookish jealousy' takes his 'smiles, gestures and light behaviours / Quite in the wrong' (4.1.99–101). Positioned out of earshot, Othello has to rely on nonverbal signifiers he receives. His naïve approach to the scene and his fateful misreading render him even more a negative inversion of Desdemona. While the latter casts serious doubts on the semiotic character of external appearances even though her own features support the art of physiognomic inference, Othello walks straight into Iago's trap and believes his eyes even though his unimpeachable persona wrapped in dark skin demands a more reflected reasoning.

It is the arrangement of the spectacle which confirms Iago's function as actor-manager within the play. Moreover, it is striking that

---

1   Stephen Greenblatt, *Renaissance Self Fashioning: From More to Shakespeare* (Chicago et al.: University of Chicago Press, 1980) 238.

Iago's face-readings anticipate pathognomic reactions that are yet to take place and could serve as stage-directions,[1] which feeds into his role as intra-theatrical director. When Iago draws the attention onto facial features, he does this for three reasons: a) to instruct his vis-à-vis in the art of how to fashion one's outer appearance, b) to motivate a misreading (he blurs Othello's vision), and c) to antici-pate a misreading which he has carefully prepared (the reading of Othello's black visage, for instance). There is hardly a scene which is not commented on by Iago, who takes the audience by the hand to lead them through 'his' play. After his first intrigue at Brabantio's house went out of hand, Iago develops from a cunning schemer and skilful role-player, who through his own facelessness can adopt mul-tiple persona,[2] to a theatrical director *avant la lettre*, whereby the human face becomes his favourite stage for his mischief. His quali-ties as actor-manager are already suggested in the first scene when he casts Roderigo, urging him to get a false beard for himself (1.3.334) in order to fit his allotted role. By this device, Roderigo's appear-ance is aligned with Othello's and Cassio's who are equally furnished with this particular token of masculinity and authority by Iago. In his determination to play off Cassio's 'smooth dispose' (1.3.379) against Othello's 'free and open nature' (1.3.381), Iago eventually monopo-lises the direction and reaches the peak of his manipulative scheme in the delusion of Othello.

Directed and misled by Iago (4.1.80f.), Othello line by line draws a false picture of the scene displayed before him: 'Look how he laughs already. [...] Now he denies it faintly, and laughs it out' (4.1.108–11). Due to their superior knowledge, however, the audience can distance themselves from Othello's blind and premature reasoning. And yet, at the same time, they get entangled in Iago's net of cunning and deceit just like him in that they are prompted to alienate a figure that

---

1   Compare Ernst A. J. Honigmann, *Shakespeare, Seven Tragedies Revisited: The Dramatist's Manipulation of Response* (Basingstoke et al.: Palgrave, 2002) 105: 'Iago also speaks for Shakespeare. Attempting to manipulate the other characters, Iago is the dramatist inside the play'

2   'Confident in his shaping power, Iago has the role-player's ability to imagine his nonexistence so that he can exist for a moment in another and as another' (Stephen Greenblatt, *Renaissance Self Fashioning: From More to Shakespeare* [Chicago: University of Chicago Press, 1980] 235).

is in fact part of the audience in this particular scene. The watching Othello, who is put in the place of the spectator as the audience's pendant, shares their perspective and holds up a mirror to the theatre-goers in the globe, who reject his fateful misreading. As an effect, the audience starts to disintegrate until the alienation process is brought to an abrupt end when Othello is released from his position as reader and the gap between the theatre goers and the personae onstage is re-established.

Iago's manipulation of Othello's reading skills paves the way for the tragic misapprehension of Desdemona's features. Just like Romeo, who overlooks the tokens of life in Juliet's face, Othello distrusts Desdemona's external appearance and engages in a desperate search for the character Iago has ascribed to her. In his fatal disregard of external signifiers, however, he follows Desdemona's initial appeal to transcend man's outer appearance and behold the true face in the inside of the body, in man's psyche instead of his body ('I saw Othello's visage in his mind' [1.3.251]). Amongst Shakespeare's female physiognomists, Desdemona is exceptional: unlike her fellow female readers she denies the legibility of the human face and pleads for the recognition of 'the other' below the surface. According to this reading, Othello's fair soul complements her own fair skin whereby the correspondence between outer and inner man is restored through his linkage to Desdemona. It is striking, however, that the strongest advocate of the 'physiognomy of the mind' serves as a prime example of the validity of physiognomic inference. Desdemona's alabaster skin is one of the leading *topoi* of the play and becomes all the more striking as the precious material is only referred to once in the tragedies.[1] As far as Desdemona's external appearance openly communicates her 'modest', blameless nature, she supports the classical concept of *kalokagathia* in that she embodies the conjunction between the good and the beautiful. Desdemona's antiphysiognomic axiom, however, seems to have rubbed off on her environment. If one factors out the persona of Othello, whose black but morally immacu-

---

1   Elsewhere in Shakespeare's oeuvre, the term is used to denote exceptional beauty, which exceeds nature and evokes the notion of an artifice or the divine (cf. *The Rape of Lucrece* 419 and *The Merchant of Venice* 1.1.84).

late figure supports Desdemona's maxim, descriptions of external signifiers are remarkably rare, especially when it comes to her own looks. Even though she is described as 'modest' (2.3.22) and 'divine' (2.1.74), her external appearance to a great extent remains in the dark. The gap left by her body, whose 'alabaster' skin is the only feature commented on, calls for a close consideration of the term 'alabaster'. While the material is usually connected with lucidity, it also has a static, immobile quality to it, which seems irreconcilable with the versatile surface of the human countenance: statues, for instance, are made of alabaster. The stillness of Desdemona's face would account for the scarce references to her looks. It does not, however, oppose a physiognomic reading but rather eliminates pathognomic expressions, which impede the analysis of man's innermost 'character'. Thus it is alleged by Lavater, who favoured static portraits for his physiognomic investigations into the human 'character' and claimed that the most telling faces are the faces of the dead. According to the Swiss clergyman, solely an akinesic countenance whose features are untroubled by any kind of movement could provide data reliable enough to serve as a true index of the mind. Against this background, the term alabaster ultimately supports the notion of Desdemona's legibility in that it refers a certain stillness of features, which ensures that the reader is not distracted by temporary passions that churn up the face, but can scrutinize its pristine character. Furthermore, the reference to her 'alabaster' skin alludes to Desdemona's apotheosis as statues were carved from this material. Similar to Cleopatra, therefore, 'divine Desdemona' is elevated to the status of a goddess, beggaring all description (2.1.62–4).

Cassio's panegyric and ekphrastic portrayal, which is reminiscent of Enobarbus' account of Cleopatra (*Antony and Cleopatra* 2.2.197–224), offers the closest view of Desdemona even though it skirts around physical signifiers: 'She is indeed perfection" (*Othello* 2.3.24) and 'in th'essential vesture of creation / Does tire the engineer' (2.1.65f.). Whether she has pushed her creator towards his limits, leaving him exhausted in view of his masterpiece ('tire' in the sense of 'exhaust') or is an appearance fit to 'attire' her inventor, her external appearance seems to be breathtaking. As such it bears a strong resemblance to the figure Cleopatra, a resemblance which is grounded on the essential indescribability of their bodies, which lets both personae to a great extent appear as gaps in nature, defying description.

Both readings of the verb 'tire', however, celebrate Desdemona as the crown of creation. Her pre-eminent status implied by Cassius' deification underscores the peculiar remoteness of her figure, which seems as alien to her fellow men as Othello's appearance even though it is received more favourably. While Desdemona is not demonised but idealised, she serves as projection area just like the Moor even though her character will not be smudged until the final act. Against the background of her white skin, Othello's dark complexion and painted-black character become even more apparent, as Emilia observes shortly after Desdemona's death: 'The more angel she, and you the blacker devil' (5.2.140). The exact opposite also holds true: The blacker the man on her side, the more splendid and spotless seems Desdemona's face. As Janet Adelman has argued, '[...]' 'whiteness' emerges as a category only when it is imagined as threatened by its opposite'.[1] By allying herself with Othello, Desdemona not only draws attention to her whiteness, but she can also stage herself as a flawless and unimpeachable character. A cunning scheme on her part, which makes use of the semantically highly charged opposition between black and white is implied by Iago's notion of a 'white devil', which counters the traditional association of white-good and black-evil. Considering Iago's own role-play and his status as manipulator and schemer in the play, the question arises whether the alliance with Othello was as much a strategic move as it was an act of love.

That Desdemona is capable of shaping her role and fashioning herself is indisputable. On her first appearance onstage at the outset of the play, she emerges as 'the strongest, the most heroic person in the play'[2]. Rebelling against her father's will and challenging traditional views of her fellows, she formalises her relationship to the Moor.

---

1   Janet Adelman, 'Iago's Alter Ego: Race as Projection in *Othello*', *Shakespeare Quarterly* 48/2 (1997) 125–44, 129f.
2   William Shakespeare, *Othello*, ed. by Ernst A. J. Honigmann (London: Arden, 2002) 43.

She succeeds even though Iago has had enough time to paint Othello black before the denunciated Moor appears onstage for the first time. Prior to Othello's entrance, Iago webs a catching net of libel, prejudices, and deceit, which culminates in the derogatory outcry 'an old black ram / Is tupping your white ewe' (1.1.88f.). From the outset of the play, the audience is thus sensitised to a physiognomic subtext, which will be eliminated by Desdemona only to be reinforced by the physiognomic data provided by her body and face. By using the term 'alabaster', however, Shakespeare succeeds in maintaining certain ambivalence towards the expressiveness of appearances and adds a further layer to the proposed legibility of the heroine.

In a stage production, this notion of a double-layered countenance can be played out quite effectively. Iago's denunciation of the 'divine' heroine and the concept of the 'white devil' which is fair without and foul within, gains ground if the actor playing Desdemona appears in a whitened, mask-like face. This would not only underscore the visible (and audible) contrast of Othello and Desdemona but also highlight the area of tension between alterity and identity as it is incorporated by the two figures, both individually and as a couple.

This tension is furthermore reflected in the different settings of the play, which progresses from 'the place of urbanity and civilization' to a 'place of wildness, passion, and rebellion',[1] from urban Venice to unruly Cyprus. On a second glance, this dichotomy, which ties in with the dichotomy of black and white, of darkness and light, turns out to be even more complex. Taking into consideration that the name Cyprus derives from Kypruis, or Venus, the goddess of the island, the setting supports the principle of inversion, which is introduced by the dichotomy of Desdemona's anti-physiognomic axiom and her lucid physiognomic text. For Venus is not only the goddess of love and thus a symbol of passion but also the incorporation of utmost beauty. According to Enobarbus' ekphrastic account, the Cleopatra is 'o'er-picturing Venus' (*Antony and Cleopatra* 2.2.206) outshining the goddess by her breathtaking appearance, which leaves 'a gap in nature' (2.2.224). The alignment of Desdemona with Venus and

---

1   Compare Marjorie Garber, *Shakespeare After All* (New York: Pantheon Books, 2004) 589.

consequently also with Cyprus would feed into Iago's allegations. In contrast to the great schemer of the play, who declares his dissimulation onstage and openly refrains from wearing his heart on his sleeve, however, it remains questionable whether at all and, if so, to what extent Desdemona uses her physiognomic insight for her own self-fashioning.

In Cassio's unfeasible attempt to sketch the portrait of the divine, a neo-platonic belief suggests itself in which beauty and virtue are interlinked and for whose preservation Cassio remains responsible. His apotheosis of Desdemona continues when the praised finally appears onstage in flesh and blood: 'Hail to thee, lady, and the grace of heaven, / Before, behind thee, and on every hand / Enwheel thee round!' (*Othello* 2.1.86–8). His spiritual circumscription, however, will be shattered by Iago's comment 'You are pictures out of door' (2.1.112). Inverting the image, debasing Cassio's eulogy and lowering the sanctifying tone to an ordinary and profane level by aligning the divine colouring to common face-painting, Iago not only challenges Cassio, but also provokes Desdemona, who hereafter enters a physiognomic combat with her defamer. From the audience's perspective, however, Iago's affront fails in view of the context it is uttered in. Not only since, due to their superior knowledge of Iago's vicious mind, they would support Cassio's portrayal, which has Desdemona as the incorporation of utmost beauty, virtue, and innocence, but it is Iago himself who paves the way for a favourable reception of Desdemona when he involves Emilia in the image. Like Othello, whose blackness is coupled to Desdemona, making her whiteness gleam all the more intensively, Emilia serves as a contrastive foil to the heroine. Thus, the rebuke of these pictures, which have been exposed to a hostile environment and are unprotected 'out of doors', can be read as being directed towards two different, if not opposing concepts of women in the play: on the one hand, it is the common practice of face-painting which is at stake here. Depending on the staging of the play, the make-up of the actor embodying Emilia might even support the notion that her face, unlike Olivia's or indeed Desdemona's, endures neither wind nor weather and covers the true features with a thick layer of white lead almost. On the other hand, however, the coupling with Emilia emphasises Desdemona's elevated status as it establishes a contrastive opposition between an artificial appearance and a work of art, which is likewise exposed not only to an unsympathetic environment, but first and foremost to Iago's blasphemous comments. Her divine likeness remains one of the main *topoi* of the play and is referred to again when Othello pauses in his rage at the sight of her body, awestruck by its splendour and perfection.

> [...] Yet I'll not shed her blood,
> Nor scar that whiter skin of hers than snow,
> And smooth as monumental alabaster.
> (*Othello* 5.2.3–5)

The Pygmalion motif[1] suggested here, which raises hopes for a happy ending, is turned into its opposite as indicated by the adjective 'monumental', which alludes to a funerary monument rather than suggesting a resurrection. When Desdemona awakes, she looks into the visage of her murderer, not of her creator. Just as in the *Metamorphoses*, however, the female body remains formidable Othello succeeds in inscribing its surface and destroying the image in his endeavour to discover the 'whore' beneath the dazzling surface. His confidence to finally have assigned her true character to her ('she was a whore' [5.2.141]) and thereby prevent other man to be lured on to destruction by her seemingly innocent appearance ('Yet she must die, else she'll betray more men' [5.2.6]) cuts the audience to the quick, all the more so, as his tragic misreading hits a figure that has been pleading for a cautious handling of physiognomic axioms and has emerged as a most diligent facial reader herself.

Desdemona's somehow ungraspable body, her missing portrait, which also leaves a 'gap in nature' and a blank in the book of creation together with her confident intervention in the traditional semiotic scheme, and her profound sensitivity to the eloquence of the human body distinguish her as physiognomist in this particular play. Even though it seems otherwise at first, her claim that she 'saw Othello's visage in his mind' (1.3.251) does not oppose this role. When Desdemona urges the beholders to overlook Othello's

---

1   Compare Ovid, *Metamorphoses* X 243–97.

dark complexion, she does not deny the significance of bodily signi-
fiers, but rather turns against dogmatizing the 'art of physiognomy'
in favour of a differentiated, anti-racist, and astounding execution of
physiognomic readings. In contrast to Duncan's dictum in *Macbeth*,
Desdemona does not claim that the human body is illegible on prin-
ciple, but rather dispels the common prejudice against the coloured
and the foreign. Her insightful knowledge of human nature, which
grounds itself in the 'art of physiognomy' (*The Rape of Lucrece*
1394f.) becomes apparent when she sides with Cassio, whose hon-
ourable disposition she defends:

> For if he be not one that truly loves you,
> That errs in ignorance and not in cunning,
> I have no judgement in an honest face.
>   (*Othello* 3.3.48–50)

Not until the peak of her own physiognomic illegibility, does
Desdemona direct her view towards pathognomically motivated
movements in Othello's face. This confirms the hypothesis that the
illegibility of one's own face is the prerequisite for disclosing another.
As expected, Desdemona recognises tokens of rage and fury in his
countenance and the gnawing on his lips and does not miss the por-
tents (5.2.48). However, she holds back from relating these physical
reactions to herself: 'I hope / They do not point on me' (5.2.48f.). Her
misapprehension points to the *topos* of blind love.[1] This love, how-
ever, does not undermine Desdemona's position as physiognomist,
because Othello's passions in this particular scene are, after all, not
overlooked but, one could argue, deliberately ignored.

   While Desdemona emerges as the more diligent reader in that she
puts the art of physiognomy into perspective, pointing out the perils
of facial readings and character-writings, she does not remain uncon-
tested in her physiognomic scheme. Shakespeare includes a second
physiognomist figure in this play, which from the very first scene
counters Desdemona's sophisticated approach to human appearances:
Iago. The Machiavellian schemer, unlike Desdemona, openly sub-

---

1   Compare *Othello* 4.3.18–20: 'My love doth so approve him / That even his stub-
bornness, his checks, his frowns – / [...] have grace and favour in them'.

scribes to dissimulation ('I am not what I am' [1.1.65]) and represents a deteriorated formation of the Burkhardtian individual,[1] who aspires to authorisation of, and by, itself and draws on the reservoir of natural signs and symbols, a semiotic Eden, which has been made accessible to man and engages in an autonomous, deceiving and often ruthless self-fashioning (1.3.317f.). Iago's manipulative scheme grounds itself on a world that is, on principle, legible. He uses the trust of his fellowmen in nonverbal signifiers for creating a net of cunning devices to lead them astray. The physiognomic combat between Othello's supposed allies, Iago and Desdemona, who are his severest opponents, psychologically and physically, commences in act two, scene one and sensitises the audience to the physiognomic subtext, which is pivotal to the play. Even before Othello comes into view in person, two conflicting readings battle on his face: Iago's hostile depiction, which nourishes stereotypes of blackness, is challenged by Desdemona's plea for transcendence of appearances. Having successfully defeated Iago in his first attempt to denunciate Othello, the physiognomic contest is resumed in the beginning of act two.

Countering Iago's mocking remark ('You are pictures out of door' [2.1.112]), Desdemona challenges him: 'What wouldst write of me, if thou shouldst praise me?' (2.1.120). Thereby the appeal to get a picture of her is directed as much to her opponent as to the audience, who having been sensitised to the value and the perils of physiognomic inference are asked to participate in character-readings and, if necessary, counter the readings performed onstage. When Iago hesitates to answer, Desdemona once more goes on the offensive, pretending a dissimulation, which – as is obvious to the audience – is completely unfounded: 'I am not merry, but I do beguilen / The thing I am by seeming otherwise. / Come, how wouldst thou praise me?' (2.1.125–27).[2] Her question remains unanswered. The silence, however, contributes to the notion of her indescribable, ungraspable, and incomparable figure, which words cannot account for. Furthermore,

---

1   See Jacob Burckhardt, *The Civilization of the Renaissance in Italy (1860)*, trans. by S. G. C. Middlemore (New York: Random House, 2002) esp. 93–120.

2   Considering the context of Desdemona's remark, it seems unlikely that it has to be read as an 'aside' as suggested by E. A. J. Honigmann (William Shakespeare, *Othello*, ed. by Ernst A. J. Honigmann [London: Arden, 2002] 170).

the incommensurability of language is one of the key problems phy-
siognomy has to deal with. The multifaceted play of features super-
sedes the capacity of verbal portrayal in its complexity; words fall
short of the interplay of multiple movements that are surging onto the
facial surface simultaneously and fail to capture an image of utmost
beauty such as it is incorporated by Desdemona.

Instead of formulating an answer, Iago turns to caricaturing the
Socratian method of maeutics by referring to the great effort that is
needed to turn his inside out (2.1.130f.). Having thus struck a blow
against the principle of *kalokagathia* and its ocular proof, Desdemona,
Iago finally 'delivers':

> If she be fair and wise, fairness and wit,
> The one's for use, the other useth it. [...]
> If she be black, and thereto have a wit,
> She'll find a white that shall her blackness fit. [...]
> She never yet was foolish that was fair,
> For even her folly helped her to an heir.
> (*Othello* 2.1.132–39)

The cryptic play on words and inversion of the connotations com-
monly associated with the colours black and white does not bedaz-
zle Desdemona: 'These are old fond paradoxes, to make fools laugh
i'th'alehouse' (2.1.140f.). However, Iago does not negate the inter-
action between beauty and wit, but seems to follow Cassio's reason-
ing and expand on it by reinforcing the alliance of outer and inner
being. Drawing on the traditional connotations of 'fair and foolish'
and 'black and witty',[1] which were commonly used to decipher the
female body and which Desdemona proposes as a further challenge
to her opponent, however, Iago frames yet another attack: by seem-
ingly subverting these connotations, he in fact confirms their valid-
ity. Pretending to breaking down the symbiosis of fair (in the sense of
beautiful, fair-skinned, or blonde) and foolish, he turns to a wordplay
on the phrase folly, which can refer to either 'foolishness' or 'unchas-
tity' and thus supports rather than mitigates the negative associa-

---

1   Compare Thomas Wright, for instance, who refers to the English proverb: 'Faire
     and foolish, little and lowde, / Long and lazie, black and prowde' (Thomas Wright,
     The Passions of the Minde in Generall [London: Helme, 1620] 42).

tion. Iago's comment on the dichotomy of black and white, however, proves far more revealing than his levelling of opposing criteria and his sexual innuendo. In the inversion, Iago's favourite scheme, of the relation between Desdemona and Othello, he claims that a woman who is both black and witty will get for herself a wight or 'white' 'that shall her blackness fit' (2.1.136).

What at first glance appears as a confusion of the colours black and white, however, turns out to be a sequel to the claim that Othello 'is far more fair than black' (1.3.289). Against this background, the blackness in Iago's aphorism is attributed to Desdemona, whose dark mind, thus it is implied, longs for a dark cover in order to restore the natural correspondence between the inner and the outer appearance. The couple would thus connect to the marital as it is sketched by Lady Capulet in *Romeo and Juliet* where the metaphor of the book that seeks for a cover which elevates its content substantiates the alliance between Paris and Juliet: 'This precious book of love, this unbound lover, / To beautify him only lacks a cover' (*Romeo and Juliet* 1.3.89f.). In Iago's reasoning, however, it is not the woman who resembles the cover to the book, but Othello takes over this task and thereby re-establishes the correspondence between outer and inner being. While the couple complements each other, Iago suggests, the alliance is part of a greater plot to deceive the onlookers. For in the presence of her husband, the alabaster skin of 'divine Desdemona' (*Othello* 2.1.74) seems whiter than ever. According to Iago's reading, which ties in with his notion that identities are established by the confrontation of contrastive opponents (5.1.19f.), which serve as a negative mirror for demarcation to the 'other', Desdemona's liaison with Othello is part of a greater strategy whereby the appraised beauty wittily fashions herself as counter-image to her husband, who becomes the visible proof of what it means to be 'almost damned in a fair wife' (1.1.20).

As suggested above, Desdemona complements Othello in her somewhat unsettling facelessness. Hence, in the alliance of the two 'others', the white maid and the black Moor, which appear equally as strangers to Venetian society, a sense of sameness is evoked, which ties in with concepts of Elizabethan psychology. Love was regarded as an act of recognition of oneself in the other and consequently as an incorporation of the other in one's self.[1] This union, however, dissolves when the two protagonists begin to face each other and it is Othello, who initiates the deterioration of their relationship by confronting Desdemona, calling her to his face and subjecting her to his view, blinded by Iago's allegations:

> Let me see your eyes,
> Look in my face [...]. What art thou?
> [...] Turn thy complexion there,
> [...] Ay, here look grim as hell.
> (4.2.26–66)

Estranged from its other half, the document under scrutiny complies with Othello's reading, which hearkens back to Iago's aphorism. Bereft of its cover, the 'fair paper, this most goodly book' (4.2.73) is expected to reveal its content, and yet, its pages retain their pure and unspotted colour, resisting the inscription 'whore' (4.2.74), which Othello searches for in vain. While the attempt to recover a signifying system in which body and mind correspond is doomed to fail, not least due to the spotlessness of Desdemona's complexion, whose semiotic value is fatally neglected by Othello's blurred vision.

Not until Othello has stabbed the 'manipulator of signs', whose soul, infused with malevolence and resentment, seems a perfect counterpart to Othello's complexion or rather the negative connotations connected with it whereas Desdemona's fair face was a perfect image of the Moor's mind, and not until he has shattered both the external and internal mirror of himself, does he raise his dagger against what can finally be established as his self. It has often been considered remarkable that Othello has two death speeches before he finally stabs himself. The doubling of this highly dramatic moment is essential, however, in order to evoke a sense of self-recognition, which allows for the formation of Othello's identity.[2] His first attempt is disturbed by

---

1   Pierre de La Primaudaye, *The French Academy*, trans. by Thomas Bowes (London: Edmund Bollifan, 1618) II 484.

2   For the concept of identity and the formation of the self see Bruce Wilshire, *Role Playing and Identity: The Limits of Theatre as Metaphor* (Bloomington: Indiana University Press, 1982) esp. 152.

the arrival of the captured Iago. Othello's attack of the schemer, who has played a major part in his denunciation and Desdemona's disgrace, is essential for the re-membering, the reconstruction, recognition, and also the erasure of his own body and soul, which is his 'self'. In his second death speech, Othello succeeds in establishing a sense of identity by differentiating himself from an 'other'. Positioning his persona in relation to those who loved unwisely but too well and were destroyed by jealousy, to the base Indian, and to a malignant and turbaned Turk that resembles both Iago and the Moor, Othello estranges himself from the image imposed on his figure by his environment. Thus, Othello exits the stage not in self-judgement but in self-reflection with the request to remember him as himself and not an 'other' and to 'speak of me as I am' (5.2.351). Insofar as Othello's obituary, which he proposes to posterity by providing guidelines of how he wishes to be remembered, does not contain any physiognomic material, it adheres to Desdemona's plea for transgressing of external features. When the alien figure finally takes his memento into his own hands, the play is brought full circle and the audience is finally granted an insight into Othello's mind.

Thus, at the end of *Othello*, the concept of otherness is turned upside down. Not only does Othello distinguish himself from 'others' and thus seems to eventually integrate into Venetian society, but he also identifies the true 'white devil' whereby he refrains from external signifiers: 'I look down towards his feet, but that's a fable' (5.2.292). While the play sets off with a clear distinction between self- and otherness that was bound to skin colour, which was taken to be a 'sign of inferiority or degeneracy' and 'natural identity'[1], the alleged 'other' finally emerges as a truthful reflection of the self. Against the expectations of the audience, otherness as it was identified in the alien figure of Othello does not serve as a means to confirm and establish selfness: it rather serves as a rhetorical strategy to belie the self, which strives to appear different from the *Fremdkörper*, the disturbingly foreign body, by projecting its own character onto the alien figure. This was Iago's strategy. For him, physiognomy becomes a highly manipulative tool, a double-edged sword that enables him to both identify

---

1   Homi K. Bhabha, *The Location of Culture* (London et al.: Routledge, 1994) 80.

and construct otherness. Iago's concept of identity relies on differentiation and demarcation of alleged alien figures such as Othello and Cassio: 'If Cassio do remain, / He hath a daily beauty in his life / That makes me ugly' (5.1.18–20). A black face like Othello's, on the other hand, served him to conceal his own malign and evil disposition and provided the foundation for the 'white devil' that could make mischief without being spotted. When Iago falls silent under his accusations, again the play comes full circle with the final scene mirroring the first when it was Othello who was not given a voice to oppose his portrayal. While Iago's physiognomy, however, continues to remain in the dark, his character is exposed by two letters, one of which bears his handwriting while the other confirms his part in Desdemona's denunciation. Where physiognomic characters fail, the epistemological value of characters on the page is recovered. The documents, which serve to rapidly and without further ado unfold Iago's machinations, remain as fragments of a greater scheme, which was carefully composed and directed by Iago, whose role as actor manager is thus confirmed.

Throughout the play, Othello's identity, his blackness, and his blackening, greatly depend on the portrayal by Iago, who used him as the pseudo-other for both the audience and himself. Against the foil of the Moor, Iago succeeded in fashioning himself as 'other' that eventually turns out to incorporate the black soul which he projects onto the Moor. Hence, in the final scene, the blank space which opens up between the alleged 'fair devil' Desdemona and the devilish-black but flawless Othello, is taken up by the 'other', by Iago. The conflation of self- and otherness as well as the incorporation of a black soul and a white body in the figure of Iago obliges the audience to revise their concepts of the technologies of the self. Foreignness is finally recognised as an element of the self, as an uncanny part of that within, which can be skirted around, but ultimately defies translation.

6.4 Much Ado about Masking

A play that involves masks onstage seems to deprive physiognomy of its data in that it replaces the natural visor by an artificial, static case, which displays stereotypical features that indicate a certain type-character. But when Shakespeare employs the manifest mask as prop, it has quite a different effect. In the presence of the mask, which adds to the ambivalence already attached to the human countenance that can be either a legible face or (metaphorically speaking) deceptive visage, faces that remain uncovered appear all the more legible. If facial features are covered up, the desire to behold a readable countenance and scrutinize its design is fuelled rather than squelched. The masked ball in *Romeo and Juliet* and the revellers in *Much Ado About Nothing* predicate this longing to transgress the visor and behold what seems to be its opposite but emerges as its counterpart. In any case, the masquerade serves to hone the audience's senses for the moment of the visage's exposure. When the mask is donned, the surface that comes into view appears to be a truthful mirror of the mind, displaying 'that within' which Hamlet claims to locate beneath his 'inky cloak'. Even though it appears paradoxical at first, masking in Shakespeare's drama becomes a strategic device for creating readable faces and characters.

Accordingly, the moment the mask is donned can be regarded as an appeal to the audience to approach and decipher the physiognomic document, which comes into view quite abruptly to display a person's character. While the spectator is free to accept or reject the offer to perform a fruitful physiognomic reading, the *dramatis personae* will eventually perish due to their scepticism towards the legibility of the human face, as is the case in *Romeo and Juliet* and *Much Ado About Nothing*. The employment of masks, both material and metaphorical, is a decisive factor in determining the degree of human legibility in a particular play. Whereas metaphors of masking in Shakespeare's drama indicate a potential allusiveness of the meaning of faces and points to the intrinsic dialectic property of the *prosopon*, the presence of the material mask onstage points to the legibility of faces. In short, this means that where there are masks in Shakespeare's plays, faces are legible in principle. Accordingly, where material visors fail to appear, they are compensated by the deceptive quality of the human face. For this hypothesis, *Romeo and Juliet* serves as a prime example, since, especially in this play, characters turn out to be what they seem.

It has often been overlooked that the two lovers encounter each other through masks. When Romeo first catches sight of Juliet, he does so in disguise. Mercutio's appeal for masking, 'a visor for a visor' (*Romeo and Juliet* 1.4.30), confirms that the faces of the Montagues are covered when they enter the residence of the Capulets. This enables them to get access to hostile territory and mingle with the other guests at the mask-ball while remaining incognito. Even though it is left to the director to decide upon the moment when the masks are donned, an encounter of Romeo and Juliet in masks would challenge, even caricature the notion of love at first sight in this particular scene. The almost spiritual moment when the pilgrim's journey comes to an end on the arrival at the shrine, the saintly encounter which leads to the shared sonnet, however, would not necessarily be impaired by the presence of masks, which could underscore the ritual dimension of the play. Even though there are no records which could elucidate the performance practice in Shakespeare's globe, one could argue that in accordance with the *Commedia dell'Arte* the *innamorati* might have been the only figures onstage not wearing masks. However, Mercutio's appeal to replace a visor by a visor seems to include Romeo, which would contradict this claim. In any case, the mask serves as a device which ultimately supports the notion of a transparent and ultimately legible world. Romeo's and Juliet's faces, for instance, give a deep insight into the passions of their minds. Whereas the audience does not miss the eloquence of their countenances and knows how to read their physiognomies, the *dramatis personae* fatally disregard these most significant and telling tokens. Of all characters onstage, it is Romeo who performs the most fatal misreading of Juliet's face, which leads to the tragic outcome of the play.

In *Much Ado About Nothing*, there is a similar misapprehension of external features even though a tragic ending is avoided by the resurrection of Hero, who collapses under the accusations of fraud and unchastity. When Claudio charges her before the altar on their wedding day, he uses her blushes against her, which according to his reasoning indicate 'guiltiness, not modesty' (4.1.40). Enraged and blinded by false premises that have been infused by Don John, Claudio threatens to belatedly inscribe Hero with what he assumes to

be her true character: 'Out on thee, seeming! I will write against it!'
(4.1.54). Claudio's desire for inscribing the unspotted countenance
with its supposedly true character is reminiscent of Othello's blind
rage against the 'fair paper' which awaits the stamp 'whore' on its
surface (*Othello* 4.2.73f.). The metaphors of physiognomic writing
culminate in the blackening of Hero: 'she is fallen / Into a pit of ink'
(*Much Ado About Nothing* 4.1.138f.). Like in *Othello*, however, the
coupling of 'foul' and 'fair' (4.1.102) does not only lack a foundation
but also a persona to connect to.

Even though Claudio's misconception turns out to be less tragic
than Romeo's misapprehension of Juliet's ruby cheeks and crimson
lips, in both cases, the rash misreading of physiognomic data, which
is prompted by blushing, serves as a prelude to the (once) belov-
ed's demise, to social denunciation and physical death respectively.
In Shakespeare's comedy, death is substituted by a temporary faint,
which allows for the nuptial scene to be reiterated in which the sup-
posedly dead Hero is resurrected. A further parallel between the two
plays suggests itself in the wooing, which is performed under the
shelter of a mask. In *Much Ado About Nothing*, however, the mask-
ing does not only initiate the love relationship, but also adds a fur-
ther dimension of disguise to the play in that Claudio refrains from
wooing for Hero himself, but lets the Prince take over his role and
court her on his behalf. It is striking that Don Pedro's visor is the
only one to meet success in this carnevalesque scene. Hero seems
to fall for the mask, which is the prerequisite for the false allega-
tions brought against the prince by his brother, namely the assump-
tion that he has won Hero for himself and has thus deceived Claudio.
The other characters, however, see through these conniving machi-
nations. Ursula's exposure of Antonio (2.1.94–101) paves the way
for recognition through the mask. It is unlikely that Beatrice does not
recognise Benedick when she engages in her mocking tirade of his
persona and calls him the king's jester since Beatrice emerges as the
strongest reader figure in the play.

It is Beatrice who spots Claudio's 'jealous complexion' (2.1.257)
before anybody else and thus serves to translate non-verbal signifi-
ers both for her fellow personae onstage and for the spectators in the

theatre who find in her a reliable ally. She has brought Claudio before
Don Pedro, who fails to decipher the signs of bitterness and is depend-
ent on the reading performed by Beatrice, who steps into the physiog-
nomic breach by translating Claudio's sentiment, which makes him
as 'civil as an orange' (2.1.256). While the prince approves the read-
ing and shows some physiognomic competence himself (1.1.90), he
will eventually contribute to a most fateful rating of facial features
side-by-side with Claudio. Thus Beatrice remains quite unchallenged
in her position as interpreter and continues to pull the strings in the
play. Placed amongst the lovelorn Claudio and an astoundingly col-
ourless Don Pedro, she starts directing a coltish game of love and
cuts the silence by telling the dumbstruck Claudio and Hero the next
move.

> Beatrice: Speak, Count, 'tis your cue. [...]
> Beatrice (*to Hero*): Speak, cousin. Or, if you cannot, stop his
>   mouth with a kiss, and let not him speak, neither.
>   (2.1.266–371)

While lacking a Machiavellian mind, Beatrice shows the same qual-
ities of an actor-manager as Iago. As far as her own legibility is con-
cerned, she can be attributed the status of physiognomist in that she
maintains an elusive character, not unlike Cleopatra. Her predication
to be 'sunburnt' (2.1.279) does not imply physical unattractiveness but
allows for her demarcation as 'the other', which will finally recog-
nise its counterpart in Benedick, who celebrates his distinctiveness to
Claudio, for instance, by the proclamation of misogynistic views and
his rigorous refusal to marry. Beatrice's dark complexion furthermore
serves to mark off the spirited, frisky, and unruly 'cousin' from Hero,
whose white skin is susceptible to blushing and as such becomes a tes-
timony to the purity of her body. On the female front, there is no coun-
terpart that could keep up with her wittiness and, one might assume,
her beauty. Following Benedick's contrastive portrayal of Beatrice and
Hero, which is designed to mock Claudio's affections, it seems likely
that these figures were played by two boy-actors of opposing appear-
ance ('as the first of May' and 'the last of December' [1.1.156f.]), the
one blond and tall, the other dark and short:

Why, i'faith, methinks she's too low for a high praise, too brown
for a fair praise, and too little for a great praise.
(1.1.138–40)

The character of Hero is sketched as rather common, colourless
and simple-hearted. As such, she matches Claudio perfectly. Both
figures are highly susceptible to the malicious plays that are staged
before their eyes and tailored to their naïve, receptive minds while
strongly relying on heterogeneous ascriptions. However, both Hero
and Claudio fall short of the features accredited to them. The osten-
sible praise of Claudio's 'turned orthography' (2.3.18), for instance,
reveals itself as a projection of Benedick's own loquacity, a transfer-
ral of an essential part of Benedick's 'self' onto his vis-à-vis. The
latter serves as a reflective mirror, in whose presence Benedick's per-
sona gains shape. Instead of doing justice to his love-struck friend,
this device foreshadows his own loquacity, which will intensify as
his affections for Beatrice develop. Claudio, however, remains rather
tongue-tied until his marriage day. The tirade prompted by the threat
to his honour, is as much out of character as it is out of place. What
furthermore contributes to Claudio's is the fact that he falls for Don
Pedro's machinations twice. Before witnessing Hero's 'affair', he
is hoodwinked at the masked ball even though he assumes to have
veiled his identity successfully. When Don John approaches him as
Benedick, Claudio plays along whereupon his opponent starts deni-
grating the prince, alleging that he won Hero not for his companion
but for himself.

After the masked ball, Don Pedro's scheme runs its course while
being mirrored by the light-hearted and jocular coupling of Beatrice
and Benedick, which almost all characters engage in. While the mask-
ing does not impede physiognomic readings, it inaugurates a precari-
ous play, in which signs and tokens are exploited for teasing trickery
and spiteful deceit. The two plays-within-the-play that are delivered,
however, follow very different patterns. Whereas the portrayal of the
lovelorn couple Benedick and Beatrice serves to translate their inner-
most affections for each other, which have been seething under the
surface awaiting their translation, the mischievous manipulation of
external signifiers as it is performed under the guidance of Don John

is completely unfounded. It only gains grounds due to a fundamental mistrust in the art of physiognomy, which could clear Hero of the allegations made against her.

As suggested earlier, it is not despite, but rather because of the presence of masks that characters emerge as being ultimately legible. Even villains fail to conceal their 'selves', but are easily recognized by their 'deformed' (3.3.125), abhorrent, and repulsive appearance. The semiotic subtext of the play is astoundingly simple: Don John openly admits his inability to cover his melancholic disposition (1.3.10f.) and becomes the malcontent par excellence. Even though urged by his comrade, Conrad, to control and curb his passions (1.3.15f.), he does not succeed in concealing the nefarious influence that Saturn exerts on him. The sight of his countenance lets Beatrice cringe: 'How tartly that gentleman looks. I never can see him but I am heartburned an hour after' (2.1.3f.). With regard to the observations made above one can conclude that the mask sustains, rather than undermines, the notion of a decipherable world in which physiognomy proves a valuable tool for characterisation. This notion is furthermore supported by the employment of the mask in *A Midsummer Night's Dream*, a play in which not only a performance but also the rehearsal is staged.

When Flute refuses to play Thisbe since he has 'a beard coming' (*A Midsummer Night's Dream* 1.2.39f.), Quince appeases him, referring to the possibility of covering his face: 'That's all one: you shall play it in a mask' (1.2.43). These visors, however, are farcical for their potential for concealment is eroded by the players themselves who are anxious to spotlight the fictitiousness of the masks.

> *Bottom*:   Nay, you must name his name, and half his face must be seen through the lion's neck, and he himself must speak through, saying thus, or to the same defect: 'ladies', or 'fair ladies [...].
> If you think I come hither as a lion, it were pity of my life. No, I am no such thing. I am a man, as other men are [...].
> (*A Midsummer Night's Dream* 3.1.32–40)

It is remarkable that no other than Bottom pleads for breaking the illusion since he is not only in danger of losing himself in a multiple role-play and longs to take over the parts of lover, beloved, and roaring lion at the same time, but shortly afterwards enters the stage in the mask of an ass. The metamorphosis of the fatuitous weaver, whose character is 'translated' onto the surface and suddenly becomes visible to the naked eye, takes the zoomorphic device of physiognomy *ad absurdum*. While the physiognomic farce displayed in the over-stretched portrait of Bottom's character raises the audience's awareness for a self-subversive and highly ironic physiognomic scheme, it also points to the multiple levels of play in a world which shifts between the magical and the theatrical. Released from his metamorphosis with his ass-head donned, Bottom makes a distinction between the imaginative and the real, which is fundamental to the play in that it affirms rather than denies the indissolubility of the two. He identifies his excursion to the animal world as a dream: 'It shall be called "Bottom's Dream", because it hath no bottom' (4.1.208f.). Locating his persona in a sphere outside the imaginary while taking on the position of the author, Bottom authorises himself as a figure which resides in what is to be regarded as the 'real' world according to the logic of the play, which is, however, *A Midsummer Night's Dream*. By adding a further imaginative level to the play, which appears as a dream-within-a-dream, the world of Bottom, the weaver, is presented as the 'real'. Hence, the doubling of the imaginative in the course of the play emerges as a dramatic device for aligning the theatrical world with the *theatrum mundi*, the theatre of the world. And yet, we are reassured by Bottom himself that his reasoning is devoid of any foundation 'because it hath no bottom' (4.1.209). What is founded, however, is the play-within-the-play which follows shortly after Bottom's resurrection as weaver and stages him as protagonist. Bottom's role as Pyramus, however, re-establishes the connection to his dream in that the 'sweet-faced' (2.1.79) lover provides the exact counterpart of the ass-headed man who is adored by the deluded Titania. Even though the character of Bottom's dream has been declared as a simulacrum bearing no connection to any reality, seems to linger on as the play proceeds. While the monstrous ass-head has disappeared, Bottom's folly remains. His character seems to have weathered its 'translation' and continues to exist on the verbal stage whereupon a face can be heard: 'I see a voice. [...] I can hear my Thisbe's face' (5.1.190f.). Again, it is Bottom whom Shakespeare picked to announce the shift from the visual to the verbal 'stage'. While the confusion of the auditory and the visual senses alludes to the limits and potentialities of physiognomic portrayal in Shakespeare's plays it reinforces Shakespeare's theatrical scheme, which heavily relies on verbal scenery both to embellish the stage and to characterise his personae. As suggested above, Bottom's reversed metamorphosis does not impede physiognomic readings but rather encourages them in that his character remains the same even though it retreats into verbal scenery. Furthermore, the figure of the weaver not only crosses the boundaries between the visual and the verbal, but also inaugurates the (con-)fusion of the imaginary and the real. This is supported by the figures of 'the golden ass' and Pyramus which he embodies in turn, reviving characters from Apuleius and Ovid to life. The progression from page to stage, which entails a literary metamorphosis of the classical figures, which is coupled with Bottom's attempt at self-authorisation, contributes to the assimilation of the 'imaginary' and the 'real', which reaches its peak when Bottom adopts the position of the spectator, or rather, the audience and gives advice on how to receive a play, namely to 'hear' faces and to 'see' voices.[1]

As the masking and metamorphosis in *Romeo and Juliet*, *Much Ado About Nothing*, and *A Midsummer Night's Dream* suggest, the 'agony of the real'[2] seems to be overcome by duplicating the levels of disguise and modes of play through masks and plays-within-the-play. The doubling of the level of play becomes a key device for dismantling characters and faces and creating a sense of the real in *Hamlet*. At the corrupt court of Denmark, it is the mimesis of mimesis which is used for establishing meanings in a world dominated by false appearances and which leads to the discovery of the king's murderer in a setting in which the boundaries between imitation and reality become blurred: 'I mine eyes will rivet to his face' (*Hamlet* 3.2.78). Through the reflection of the art and artifice of playing, the cover of the illusionary is prised open. Similarly to the face which

---

1   For the physiognomic value of the voice, see chapter 4.6.
2   See Jean Baudrillard, *Agonie des Realen*, trans. by Lothar Kurzawa and Volker Schäfer (Berlin: Merve, 1978) 6f.

appears behind a mask, the performance of the *Mousetrap* leads to the erosion of difference between reality and mere representations of reality on the level of *Hamlet*, the play. If the play-within-the-play, which follows the 'script' provided by the ghost at the outset of the scene, can establish a sense of the real and discover the machinations of Claudius, Hamlet's antic disposition has a similar effect. Once the protagonist has adopted a different persona and with his 'antic disposition' undermines the *simulatio* expected from a 'glass of fashion and the mould of form' (3.1.152), faces become legible. There is indeed 'method' (2.2.203) in Hamlet's play in that it is designed to outface and dismantle his fellow-actors, that is the personae surrounding him on the courtly stage, which are preoccupied with their self-fashioning.

The first victim to come before him is Polonius, the great believer in appearances and ironic pendant of the *cortegiano*. Even though Polonius unfolds the catalogue of self-fashioning to his son Laertes, he fails to comply with his own instructions. As suggested in Gertrude's appeal 'more matter with less art' (2.2.96), his behaviour is factitious, his acting unsuccessful. Unable to differentiate between the illusionary and the real ('I was killed i'th'Capitol' [3.2.94]), Polonius emerges as the antagonist of Hamlet, who subjects him to a highly ironic but somehow most adequate evaluation of his character. When Polonius enters the room and finds Hamlet delved into reading, we find a similar progression from page to stage as in *Macbeth*, even though Hamlet's assessment of the character materialising before his eyes is coloured by the 'antic disposition' he put on:

> [...] the satirical slave says here that old men have grey beards, that their faces are wrinkled, their eyes purging thick amber or plum-tree gum, and that they have a plentiful lack of wit, together with most weak hams. (*Hamlet* 2.2.196–99)

Transferring the written portrayal onto Polonius, who seems to have sprung off the page, Hamlet rehabilitates the axiom of physiognomic legibility for the play. Protected against the scrutinizing gazes of his environment, he more and more engages in physiognomic encounters: he sees through Rosencrantz and Guildenstern who both show 'a kind of confession in [their] looks' (2.2.272f.), ponders upon the potentialities of acting (2.2.534–60), presents images of the king and his usurper to his mother and thereby prompts her self-reflection, instructs the actors in the art of acting, challenges Laertes to outdo or rather: to outface him in the sorrow for Ophelia, and finally leaves the stage by putting the theatre-goers, who have accompanied him throughout the play, back into their places in front of the stage by addressing them as spectators: 'You that look pale and tremble' (5.2.276). The physical reaction, which anticipates a cathartic effect, brings the play full circle in that it connects to Horatio's terrified response to the ghost's appearance: 'you that tremble and look pale' (1.1.51) while pointing to the 'invisible strings'[1] between actor and spectator.

Furthermore, Hamlet's masking does not utterly oppose his character. The 'antic disposition' (2.1.173), a burlesque of the smiling villain, is quite compatible with a melancholic mind. Since in antiquity, 'madness' (3.1.187), 'transformation' (2.2.5), and 'distemper' (2.2.55) are intertwined with atrabiliousness. The term *mania* is often coupled with *melancholia*,[2] thus for instance in the concept of the *furor poeticus* as it is alluded to in *A Midsummer Night's Dream* when Theseus aligns 'the lunatic, the lover, and the poet' (5.1.7) and refers to the 'fine frenzy' (5.1.13) which has taken possession of the poet. Hamlet's 'antic disposition' combines the creative spirit and pronounced sensibility of a genius, and a melancholic mind, both of which are Saturnalian qualities. The negation of these qualities, as is indicated by the replacement of the melancholic-manic character with a grotesque-'antic' disposition, brings the masking as backlash to a decoded and decoding world to perfection. Overstretching the limits of simulation and dissimulation, Hamlet serves as an inverted mirror that not only reflects the personae around him but also dismantles the foul play at court. Hamlet's mask, which goes hand in

---

1 Lawrence Olivier regarded actors and spectators as being connected by 'invisible strings'. See Meridith A. Skura, *Shakespeare the Actor and the Purpose of Playing* (Chicago et al.: University of Chicago Press, 1993) 12.

2 The compability of these two character traits is asserted by Aristotle, who claims that even renowned philosophers, poets, and artists were melancholics (*Problemata XXX* 1 953a19–15). Relating to Aristotle, Marsilio Ficino also refers to the connection between *melancholia* and *mania* (*De vita triplici* I 5).

hand with a critical reflection of the art of playing as it is pronounced in the Hecuba scene and in Hamlet's instruction of the players to 'suit the action to the word, the word to the action' (*Hamlet* 3.2.16f.), furthermore becomes a means of differentiation. It does not express conformation but marks both the desire for, and the beginning of individualisation. Under the antic disposition, Hamlet outmanoeuvres his fellow-actors and gradually disintegrates from the courtly play surrounding him. In his contra-discursive adaption, he pretends to participate in the role-play as performed at court while undermining its constitution and exposing the masks of his fellowmen.

Considering the subversive function of masks and the imagery of masking in Shakespeare's drama, it seems worth considering whether his plays could potentially be staged, using masks. Even though the comedies appear most suitable for a performance in masks, especially since some of these plays seem to require masking as part of the plot, the visor is not necessarily out of place in the tragedies. Apart from the masked ball in *Romeo and Juliet*, which due to its appearance in the first part of the play which follows the structure of a comedy must be regarded as an exception to the rule, Shakespeare's tragedies seem essentially void of onstage masking. As Franz-Patrick Steckel's production of *Timon of Athens* has shown,[1] however, the mask can prove an effective prop to draw the attention to the paradox of the *prosopon*, of the expressive surface which can be covered as well as disclosed, encoded or decoded. The tension arising between the verbal and visual images of the face not only serves to sensitise the theatre-goers to the verbal portrayal of characters, but also points to the limits of representing physiognomic and pathognomic features onstage.

Amongst Shakespeare's tragedies, it is especially *Timon of Athens* which calls for the employment of masks in that there are only three explicit references to the facial features in the entire play.

---

1 Frank-Patrick Steckel directed *Timon of Athens* at the Schauspielhaus at Bochum in 1990. A detailed description of the production was presented by Walter Bachem ('Das Maskenspiel der Repräsentation: Shakespeares *Timon von Athen* in der Inszenierung von Frank-Patrick Steckel', in Günter Ahrends et al. ed., *Theater im Revier, Kritische Dokumentation* (Trier: Wissenschaftlicher Verlag Trier, 1991) Vol. 2, 15–35.

Countenances seem to fade in the Athenians' corporative role-play in which nothing is as it seems. Not until the protagonist transforms from philanthropist to misanthropist and not until the action is shifted from the flawed polis to bowling wilderness, does a legible face come into view. And yet, as Steckel's production indicates, the masks of men remain; impossible to be donned, they can only be replaced by new visors in the adaption of a new role. In this respect, Steckel's masks resemble constants in a world which is in flux and develops from the illegible to the legible, from the artificial to the natural, from polis to wilderness while simultaneously fuelling the desire to behold the 'beyond'. In tint and design, the masks clearly communicate their characters: Timon's 'varnished friends' (4.2.36) appear in colourful apparel, which opposes the wan grey of the visors and clothes worn by his allies. Timon himself appears in a broad mask which is grey on the one side and blue on the other. From the very beginning, he is thus introduced as an ambivalent figure, which incorporates two opposite personae, the philanthropist and the misanthrope, and provides the 'ocular proof' to Apemantus' claim:

> The middle of humanity thou never knewest, but the extremity of both ends. (4.3.300f.)

As pendant to the fool,[1] the cynic, 'the dog' (1.1.203), Apemantus takes over the position of an outsider, which is indicated by the mask he wears: the smooth and grey cuboid covering his head is the most prominent mask in the play and not only distinguishes the satirist through his looks, but also through his voice: it reverberates in an eerie, dunning tone in the 'mask', which is closed to all four sides except two vents indicating eyes and mouth. While almost all voices seem distorted to some extent (the voices of Timon's flatterers, for instance, sound shrill and distasteful), none is as distinct as Apemantus' due to the roomy sounding body it resonates in and which seems to have absorbed all other voices. As cynical commentator Apemantus first and foremost serves as mirror reflecting its environment while remaining an enigma, whose smooth surface, unlike the corrugated masks surrounding him, resists physiognomic descriptions and thus

---

1   'Here comes the fool with Apemantus' (*Timon of Athens* 2.2.45).

appears, as Karl Klein has already observed, as a 'black box'[1]. While Apemantus' persona seems to feed from the masks it encounters, it also partakes in the creation of characters in a maieutic manner. Within the walls of Athens, Apemantus stands by Timon ('Let me stay at thine apperil, Timon' [1.2.32]) as if to support the development of his misanthropic traits until his ward has finally adopted them to utmost perfection, making the presence of Apemantus superfluous in that he seems to have assumed his likeness (4.3.218). Timon, the misanthropist, can be regarded a 'printout' of Apemantus in that hypocrisy and flattery seem to bounce off him just as they have done when hitting the smooth surface of Apemantus' cubicle. Both figures share a certain facelessness, which qualifies them for the positions of phyisognomists. In the first half of the play, however, this role is taken over by Apemantus, who is not only the main observer in the play (1.2.33) but also the only figure that appears onstage reading:

> *Page*:   Prithee, Apemantus, read me the superscription of
>   these letters. I know not which is which.
> *Apemantus*: Canst not read?
> *Page*:   No.
> *Apemantus*: There will little learning die then that day thou
>   art hanged. This is to Lord Timon, this to Alcibiades.
>   (2.2.74–9)

First and foremost, it is Timon that is spelt out before him, the character that will perform his first own reading as misanthropist when he has advanced to become the soulmate of Apemantus.

As the plot progresses, the discrepancy between seeming and being increasingly comes to the fore. The confusion of 'foul' and 'fair' and the mistaking of 'fair' for 'foul' splits Shakespeare's play into two parts. Even though Timon falls for appearances, he demonstrates a certain awareness of man's hypocrisy when he acknowledges, at the opening of the play, the possibility of pretence and mere façade and realises that man can be 'but outside' (1.1.163). In Steckel's adaptation, the exterior of Timon's persona, however, serves as a truthful mirror of the two souls residing in his breast, which will emerge

---

1   William Shakespeare, *Timon of Athens*, ed. by Karl Klein (Cambridge: Cambridge University Press, 2001) 47.

one after the other. As philanthropist, Timon lays his trust in outward shows, which at times seems a willing suspension of disbelief as for instance in his encounter with the painter: 'Painting is welcome' (1.1.160). Timon's enthusiastic exclamation prompted by his portrait, which one would assume to be flattering, not only inaugurates the schemes of masking and dissimulation, which will eventually lead to his estrangement from both his city and mankind in general, but also declares the painter winner of the *paragone*. Timon's commendation of painting, however, does not last long. The lynchpin of the play when the misanthrope starts to emerge, is an act of cleansing directed against his 'varnished friends' (4.2.36). When they gather around the table, Timon reveals the content of the promising dishes, which do not contain any delicacies, but stones and pure water, which the host sprinkles in the faces of his guests. The re-baptism of those 'most smiling, smooth, detested parasites' (3.7.86) amounts to a ritual act of sublimation and purgation, which is directed not only at the false faces of his flatterers but also at Timon himself. When he distances himself from his 'glass-faced flatterers' (1.1.59), he also becomes estranged from his own persona and his image as it was reflected in the faces of his opponents.

> [...] Therefore be abhorred
> All feasts, societies, and throngs of men,
> His semblable, yea, himself, Timon disdains.
>   (4.3.20–2)

When the drops of water hit their faces, their smooth outside should be disturbed and set in motion, yet the masks in Steckel's production retain their constant and static aspects, pointing to the continuance of social and personal role-play, which is untouched by Timon's outbreak. Thus, having left the *polis* Steckel's Timon can merely undress but he cannot don his mask. Furthermore, his blue-white-grey striped body, which comes into view, suggests his confinement even in wilderness where he incorporates the living paradox of a misanthropist. Like in *King Lear* where it is Edgar who withdraws into the wilderness and disguises himself as Poor Tom by tearing his clothes and begriming his face, the naked body accentuates the masked countenance, which refuses to communicate with its beholder. What reveals itself in the masked negation of masquerade is the desire to outmanoeuvre this restrictive prop of society, which degrades the individual to a persona, to a mask and confines it to a specific social role. If in Steckel's production the mask persists even in wilderness, the discourse between inner and outer being is kept alive in the face of the impossibility of cancelling the visor and eventually dissolving it into a countenance that is legible in principle, as is the case in *Romeo and Juliet*. The quest for an 'honest man' (4.3.515) becomes the quest for a decipherable face and remains a desideratum throughout the play. Aloof from Athens, masks begin to become brittle. Layer by layer, the face is gradually disclosed. In this, the denunciation of female make-up is the first step. Thus beneath Timandra's ruby cheeks, Timon diagnoses a foul interior, which corresponds to the first symptoms of syphilis, which show in her beginning boldness (4.3.159) and her cankered nose (4.3.156). Painting and wigs seem to be the last resort.

> [...] thatch your poor thin roofs
> With burdens of the dead [...]
> Wear them, betray with them; whore still;
> Paint till a horse may mire upon your face.
> (4.3.144–48)

While Timon has warned Alcibiades not to pay any regard to physiognomic tokens such as the white beards of old men, the smooth cheeks of virgins and the innocent smile of infants, which he dismissed as utterly delusive, the correspondence between body and psyche seems rehabilitated in view of the eroded appearances of the two women. Debunked as mere 'paintings', they form a strong contrast to their companion, Alcibiades, who, even without being portrayed, evokes the image of beauty and, in Timon's view, also loyalty for he will make war against Athens. The restoration of physiognomic inference, which suggests itself in the appearance of Alcibiades and the eroded exterior of the two women proceeds when the two rogues enter the scene. They are immediately identified as such by Timon ('Now, thieves' [4.3.406]), who appreciates their unveiled wickedness: '[...] thanks I must you con / That you are thieves professed, that you work not / In holier shapes' (4.3.418–20).

The encounters with Alcibiades, the two corrupted women and finally with the three genuine bandits prepare for the pivotal face-reading of the play, which discloses the 'one honest man' in the play.

> Let me behold thy face.
> [...] I do proclaim
> One honest man.
>   (4.3.485–89)

It is the first time the view is directed straight onto the human face and it is Timon's most loyal and devoted servant Flavius who is subjected to the scrutinising eye of his master, who notices his tears ('What, dost thou weep?' [4.3.475]). Flavius' crying which is reminiscent of the cleansing ritual at the last banquet, supports the notion of his legibility which prompts Timon's pronouncement of a new species of 'honest man'. And yet, this one specimen is only a ray of hope in the face of the corrupted society it is born into. As Timon is well aware, it is in danger of extinction which is why he, on the one hand, commissions him to 'farewell, and thrive' (4.3.524), but, on the other, forbids any contact with his fellow-beings: 'Ne'er see thou man, and let me ne'er see thee' (4.3.528). Steckel's masks, in this context, which obstruct the view and interpose a barrier between faces and their beholder(s), add a further level to Timon's advice and, for the first time, appear as having a positive connotation in that they protect their wearer from adverse influences.

Timon's advancement to the role of physiognomist in the play, which he takes over from Apemantus (4.3.218) and which is coupled to the emergence of his misanthropist character, entails an act of self-authorisation. While having been 'read' by Apemantus (2.2.79) and by the thieves, who recognise him as the printout of the misanthropist character as it is sketched in Athens: 'Tis his description' (4.3.403), Timon finally succeeds in recreating his character by translating it and putting it on display in an epitaph composed by himself:

> Here lies a wretched corpse,
> Of wretched soul bereft.

Seek not my name. A plague consume
You wicked caitiffs left!
Here lie I, Timon, who alive
All living men did hate.
Pass by and curse thy fill, but pass
And stay not here thy gait.
(5.5.71–8)

This self-portrayal is not only an act of self-authorisation, but, on a meta-dramatic level, it also pays tribute to the literary character of Timon, which Shakespeare took from Plutarch.[1] In Shakespeare's play, however, Timon's character does not reach its recipients in the original, but as a copy. The two translations of Timon's persona performed by himself and by the soldier, who transcribes the epitaph to his wax plate, are significant both in that they mark two important stages in the process of establishing a character for posterity: its initiation, authorisation, and capturing in writing, on the one hand, and its reception, translation and transmittance, on the other. The latter is emphasised in Shakespeare's plays, since the soldier, who claims of himself not to be able to decipher the epitaph ('what's on this tomb / I cannot read' [5.4.3f.]), does not emerge as being illiterate. He is not only able to identify the place described to him (5.4.1) but he can actually read some of the words that are written on the tomb:

Timon is dead, who hath outstretched his span;
Some beast read this; there does not live a man.[2]

The reading has constructive and, at the same time, degrading effect. For not only does the epitaph construe its reader, it also bestialises its recipient in the act of reading. These immensely powerful words, however, are lost in translation. The focus of the latter is shifted towards the reproduction of the text and the recreation of the character Timon, who can finally be described even though it can never be pegged. The soldier carves the unknown symbols in wax. In opposition to the imperishable stone which bears Timon's writ-

---

1 See Geoffrey Bullough ed., *Narrative and Dramatic Sources of Shakespeare* (London et al.: Routledge and Paul, 1966) Vol. 6, 242.
2 *Timon of Athens* 5.2.3f. This passage is taken from the folio-edition (1623).

ing, the soft and volatile surface structure of the wax plate cannot retain the character for long, which heightens the gap between (transient) copy and original. Creating his own epigram, the misanthrope secures both the survival of his figure and its future reception. In this respect, Shakespeare is indebted to the classical genre of the epigram: on the one hand, the epigram serves to maintain a geographical reference while marking the permanent site of the person whose decease it laments. On the other hand, however, it is designed and designated for translation, for communication, for being picked up and carried away into the world to herald the sad news of its author's decease. In *Timon* Shakespeare draws from the twofold function of the epigram. While pretending to degrade its reader (and thus imparting Timon's character) and urging him to move on and not linger at the tomb ('pass by and curse thy fill, but pass / And stay not here thy gait' [5.5.77f.]), it inscribes itself into 'the tables' of his memory. The mnemotechnical coup secures the character's persistence. Thus, Timon lingers on in the world which has segregated him as a persona, as a mask which can be picked up again at any time by anybody, be it a poet, a producer, or a critic.

While *Timon of Athens* seems to lend itself to an experimental production which brings back the visor into the theatre, other plays do not seem quite as adequate for this venture. As far as Steckel's production raises the audience's awareness for the nonverbal subtext and physiognomic content, it is a significant contribution to the reception of Shakespeare's drama and prompts a rereading of individual plays with special focus on the pivotal role that is attributed to the (self-) fashioning of the human face.

7 Conclusion

Considering the pivotal role of the human face and its rhetoric in Shakespeare's plays, one is tempted to invert Duncan's dictum and conclude this study by asserting that there *is* an art to find the mind's construction in the face. The aphorism holds true insofar as it emphasises the '*art* of physiognomy' (*Lucrece* 1394f.). As suggested by the various readings performed in the present study, Shakespeare's plays take both the artificiality of faces and the artistry of their interpretation centre stage and explore how to do things with physiognomy. The readings presented in the previous chapters are by no means exhaustive. Especially with regard to the history plays and Shakespeare's sonnets, the dynamic between body and mind and the significance of physiognomic subtext(s) would provide a fruitful venture which is yet to be undertaken. What this study aimed at, however, was to open up a new vista on Shakespeare's theatrical scheme by drawing attention to the physiognomic discourse that emerges in his plays and sheds some new light on his stage techniques as well as his control of audience response. Physiognomic or anti-physiognomic axioms, which are often raised at the outset of a play, serve to sensitise the audience and sharpen their views for the multifarious play of features on the actor's faces. Even though the construction of characters heavily relies on verbal scenery, physiognomies ultimately arise at the intersection of the verbal, visual, and imaginative stage. In this, the active participation of the audience is essential in that they contribute to the construction of personae by filling in the blanks of the performance and conflate the visual representations onstage with the verbal make-up to compose a coherent image of a particular character.

In accordance with the three 'stages' whereupon the face is portrayed, three levels of physiognomic discourse can be identified, which become relevant in the construction of physiognomic characters. The first level is indebted to the communication between

Shakespeare and his recipients insofar as the dramatist employs certain (un)equivocal facial features in order to convey a very specific character to the spectator. Thereby, a certain previous knowledge of physiognomic axioms can be assumed not only since basic physiognomic inference has become a common tool for deciphering fellowmen, but also because the art of face-reading was revived and controversially discussed at the time his plays were first performed. The second level, which for an early modern audience coincided with the first, also includes the *dramatis personae* and comprises the translation of characters from the page onto the stage. The translation is twofold in that it entails not only the embodiment of characters onstage but also the transmission of physiognomic data through verbal make-up, which the *personae* ascribe to each other in mutual face-readings. The conflating or conflicting portrayals on the verbal and visual 'stage' serve to activate the audience, who are encouraged to enter the physiognomic dialogue and to review critically as well as, whenever necessary, counter the readings presented to him. Finally, on the third level the meta-theatrical scope comes into view. Like the 'antic disposition' in *Hamlet*, or the masked ball in *Much Ado About Nothing*, which allude to, or employ, a mask as prop onstage, physiognomy serves to spark a critical and constructive discussion of theatrical devices. Through the focus on the art of simulation and dissimulation and the presentation of the face as *prosopon*, which can reveal as well as conceal a character, the theatrical world of the Globe is approximated to the *theatrum mundi*. Ultimately, therefore, Shakespeare's plays hold up a mirror to a highly volatile medium of non-verbal communication, which is as central to the theatre as it is fundamental to everyday life. Whereas for the former, however, the legibility of the actors' faces is a prerequisite since the audience's perception or impression of characters onstage to a great extent depends on non-verbal communication.

As indicated by the physiognomic inventory, Shakespeare's character portrayals comply with physiognomic manuals of his time. Instead of rigidly adhering to the interpretations offered in these physiognomies, however, Shakespeare uses the manuals as a creative source, which he expands and alters according to his purposes.

Therefore an inventory of features employed by Shakespeare can only serve as a starting point to tackle the physiognomic subtext underlying his drama and to shed some new light on Shakespeare's theatrical grammar. Furthermore, it served to establish contrastive relations and 'counter-bodies', whose rival appearance also points to an opposition in character. The face in Shakespeare's plays is more than just the sum of its parts. It is the product of multiple descriptions and ascriptions whereby the persona subjected to the reading can either be present or absent. In addition to physiognomic perception and the face under scrutiny, there is always also a spectator who attends the portrayal. This role, which is typically fulfilled by the audience, can also be assigned to a persona onstage.

It is the act of reading, receiving, and revising, on the one hand, and the process of transcribing, staging, and dramatising the face, on the other hand, and hence the translation from the visual into the verbal and vice versa, which constitutes Shakespeare's physiognomic scheme. Thereby, the interaction of graphology and physiognomy, which suggests itself in the progression of characters from the page to the stage, lays the foundation for a complex physiognomic discourse. In Shakespeare's plays, characters become mobile. Like Gutenberg's letters, they remain versatile insofar as they can adapt to diverse contexts, merge with other characters to establish (new) meaning(s), and are forever positioned anew on the (meta-)theatrical stage. Some of Shakespeare figures, however, (on the level of plot) intervene in 'their' texts in order to authorise themselves and take care of their own reception. The ability to read and stage facial features is intertwined with the ability to receive and produce signs and thus presupposes, in a very literal sense, the ability to read and write. Edgar's composition of a character, which he presents Gloucester to read, and Lady Macbeth's 'translation' of a character from the page onto the stage are both instances which confirm the interrelation of graphology and physiognomy and indicate the rise of physiognomist figures in Shakespeare's plays. The latter can be distinguished by a profound awareness of facial rhetoric, which emerges in multiple face-readings inaugurated by these *personae*. As shown in the analysis of individual plays, Shakespeare's greatest readers are women

who quite frequently take on the role of physiognomist and thereby
subvert male authority and challenge male authorship. A further qual-
ity of these physiognomists is their resistance to heteronomic descrip-
tion, which is why most of these personae seem peculiarly faceless.
What becomes apparent, especially with regard to Cleopatra, whose
face remains out of view until it is conquered by Caesar in the final
act, and also with reference to *Hamlet*, is the fact that physiognomists
need a stage.

Focussing on the performance of facial features as part of a courtly
simulatio or deceitful *dissimulatio*, Shakespeare's plays expose the
means of theatrical play. In a critical reflection of the actor's *persona*
as it is enacted in *Hamlet*, the art of playing and the correspondence of
the 'action' and the 'word' is under scrutiny. Considering the multiple
masks he adopts, Hamlet seems to represent the archetypical 'actor'
in a play, which frequently points the audience to its meta-theatri-
cal scope. However, Hamlet never seems to fulfil the roles assigned
to him. Nevertheless, Fortinbras remembers him as someone who
'had he been put on / [...] would have proved most royally' (*Hamlet*
5.2.341f.). Considering the fact that the actor does not survive the
play, the semiotic crises in which the connection between *signifiant*
and *signifié* can finally be overcome. The prospect of a semiotic order
in which the correspondence of inner and outer, of seeming and being
can be rehabilitated, however, is shifted into a space and time outside
the play, not only in *Hamlet* but also in other plays. Thereby physio-
gnomy persists as a challenge which incites the audience to continue
their readings beyond Shakespeare's drama while, at the same time,
urging them to read and re-read his plays all over again.

8 Selected Bibliography

Adelman, Janet, 'Iago's Later Ego: Race as Projection in *Othello*', *Shakespeare Quarterly* 48/2 (1997), 125–44.

Allen, Cameron, 'Symbolic Color in the Literature of the English Renaissance', *Philological Quarterly* 15 (1936), 81–92.

Anderson, Ruth L., *Elizabethan Psychology and Shakespeare's Plays* (Iowa: University of Iowa Press, 1927).

Arcandam, *The most excellent profitable, and pleasant Booke of the famous Doctor and expert Astrologian Arcandam [...] With an Addition of Physiognomy*, trans. William Worde (London: Orwin, 1592).

Arden, Annabel, 'Gesture, language, and the body', in: Lynette Hunter ed., *Shakespeare, Language and the Stage: The Fifth Wall, Approaches to Shakespeare from Criticism, Performance and Theatre Studies* (London: Arden Shakespeare, 2005), 61–88.

Pseudo-Aristoteles, *Physiognomonica*, ed. Sabine Vogt (Berlin: Academie Verlag, 1999).

Aristotle, *Minor Works*, trans. W. S. Hett (London/Cambridge [Mass.]: Harvard University Press, 1936).

Armstrong, Philip, *Shakespeare's Visual Regime: Tragedy, Psychoanalysis and the Gaze* (Basingstoke et al.: Palgrave, 2000).

Aughterson, Kate, *Renaissance Woman: A Sourcebook: Constructions of Femininity in England* (London/New York: Routledge, 1995).

Ayers, Philipp K., 'Reading, Writing, and *Hamlet*', *Shakespeare Quarterly* 44/4 (1993), 423–39.

Babcock, Weston, 'Macbeth's "cream-fac'd loon"', *Shakespeare Quarterly* 4/2 (1953), 199–202.

Bachem, Walter, 'Das Maskenspiel der Repräsentation: Shakespeares *Timon von Athen* in der Inszenierung von Frank-Patrick Steckel', in: Günter Ahrends et al. ed., *Theater im Revier: Kritische Dokumentationen* (Trier: WVT, 15–35), Vol. 2, 15–35.

Baker, Susan, 'Personating Persons: Rethinking Shakespearean Disguises', *Shakespeare Quarterly* 43/3 (1992), 303–16.

Bakhtin, Mikhail, *The Dialogic Imagination: Four Essays*, translated by Carly Emerson and Michael Holquist (Austin et al.: University of Texas Press, 1981).

Baldo, Jonathan, *The Unmasking of Drama: Contested Representation in Shakespeare's Tragedies* (Detroit: Wayne State University Press, 1996).

Bamborough, John, *The Little World of Man* (London et al.: Longmans, Green & Co, 1952).

Banks, Carol, '"You are pictures out of doore...Saints in your injuries": Picturing the Female Body in Shakespeare's Plays', *Women's Writing* 8/2 (2001), 295–311.

Barash, Moshe, 'Renaissance Hieroglyphics', in: Aleida and Jan Assmann ed., *Hieroglyphen: Stationen einer anderen abendländischen Grammatologie* (München: Fink, 2003), 165–90.

Barish, Jonas, *The Antitheatrical Prejudice* (Berkeley et al.: University of California Press, 1981).

Barker, Francis, *The Tremulous Private Body: Essays on Subjection* (London/New York: Methuen, 1984).

Barroll, John L., *Artificial Persons: The Formation of Character in the Tragedies of Shakespeare* (Columbia: University of South Carolina Press, 1974).

Barthelemy, Anthony G., *Black Face Maligned Race: The Representation of Blacks in English Drama from Shakespeare to Southerne* (Baton Rouge et al.: Louisiana State University Press, 1987).

Barthes, Roland, *S/Z*, translated by Richard Miller (London: Cape, 1975).

Bate, Jonathan, *Shakespeare and Ovid* (Oxford: Clarendon Press, 1993).

Baudrillard, Jean, *Die Agonie des Realen*, translated and edited by Lothar Kurzawa and Volker Schäfer (Berlin: Merve, 1978).

Baumbach, Sibylle, *'Let me behold thy face': Physiognomik und Gesichtslektüren in Shakespeares Tragödien* (Heidelberg: Winter, 2007).

Belsey, Catherine, *The Subject of Tragedy: Identity and Difference in Renaissance Drama* (London/New York: Routledge, 1985).

Bergeron, David M. ed., *Reading and Writing in Shakespeare* (Newark/London: University of Delaware Press, 1996).

Bevington, David, ed., *Action is Eloquence: Shakespeare's Language of Gesture* (Cambridge [Mass.] et al.: Harvard University Press, 1984).

Bhabha, Homi, *The Location of Culture* (London et al.: Routledge, 1994).

Bloom, Gina, '"Thy Voice Squeaks": Listening for Masculinity on the Early Modern Stage', *Renaissance Drama* 29 (2000), 39–71.

Bloom, Harold, *The Invention of the Human* (New York: Riverhead Books, 1998).

Braden, Gordon, 'Shakespeare's Petrarchism', in James Schiffer ed., *Shakespeare's Sonnets: Critical Essays* (New York et al.: Garland Publishing, 1999), 163–183.

Brook, Peter, *The Empty Space* (New York: Avon, 1969).

Brown, Carolyn E., 'Juliet's Taming of Romeo', *Studies in English Literature* 36 (1996), 333–355.

Brown, John R., 'On the Acting of Shakespeare's Plays', in Gerald E. Bentley ed., *The Seventeenth-Century Stage: A Collection of Critical Essays* (Chicago et al.: University of Chicago Press, 1968), 41–54.

Brown, John R., *Shakespeare and the Theatrical Event* (Basingstoke/New York: Palgrave Macmillan, 2002).

Bullough, Geoffrey ed., *Narrative and Dramatic Sources of Shakespeare*, 8 vols. (London et al.: Routledge and Paul, 1957–75).

Bulman, James C., *Shakespeare, Theory, and Performance* (London et al.: Routledge, 1996).

Burckhardt, Jacob, *The Civilization of the Renaissance in Italy (1860)*, trans. S. G. C. Middlemore (New York: Random House, 2002).

Burton, Robert, *The Anatomy of Melancholy* (Oxford: Lichfield and Short, 1621).

Butler, Judith, *Gender Trouble: Feminism and the Subversion of Identity* (New York et al.: Routledge, 1999).

Calbi, Maurizio, *Approximate Bodies: Gender and Power in Early Modern Drama and Anatomy* (London et al.: Routledge, 2005).

Callaghan, Dympna, *Shakespeare Without Women: Representing Gender and Race on the Renaissance Stage* (London et al.: Routledge, 2000).

Camden, Carroll, 'The Mind's Construction in the Face', *Philosophical Quarterly* 20/3 (1941), 400–412.

Carruthers, Mary J., *The Book of Memory: A Study of Memory in Medieval Culture* (Cambridge: Cambridge University Press, 1990).

Castiglione, Baldassare, *The Booke of the Courtier, from the Italian of Count Baldassare Castiglione: Done in English by Sir Thomas Hoby* (London: Seres, 1561).

Cerasano, Susan P. and Marion Wynne-Davies ed., *Gloriana's Face: Women, Public and Private, in the English Renaissance* (Detroit: Wayne State University Press, 1992).

Clarke, Angus G., 'Metoposcopy: An Art to Find the Mind's Construction in the Forehead', in Patrick Curry ed., *Astrology, Science, and Society: Historical Essays* (Woodbridge et al.: The Boydell Press, 1987), 171–195.

Clausen, Wendell, 'The Beginnings of English Character-Writing in the Early Seventeenth Century', *Philological Quarterly* 25 (1946), 32–45.

Cocles, Bartolommeo della Rocca, *A Brief and Most Pleasaunt Epitomye of the Whole Art of Phisiognomie, Gathered out of Aristotle, Rasis, Formica, Loxius, Phylemo, Palemo,, Consiliator, Morbeth the Cardinal and Others Many Moe*, trans. by Thomas Hill (London: Iohn Waylande, 1556).

Cole, Toby and Helen Krich Chinoy ed., *Actors on Acting: The Theories, Techniques, and Practices of the Great Actors of all Times as Told in Their Own Words* (New York: Crown, 1970).

Culpeper, Jonathan, *Language and Characterisation: People in Plays and Other Texts* (Harlow: Longman Higher Ed., 2001).

Cummings, Brian, 'Animal Passions and Human Sciences: Shame, Blushing and Nakedness in Early Modern Europe and the New World', in: Erica Fudge et al. ed., *At the Borders of the Human: Beasts, Bodies and Natural Philosophy in the Early Modern Period* (Basingstoke: Macmillan, 1999), 26–50.

Daileader, Celia R., *Racism, Misogyny, and the 'Othello' Myth, Interracial Couples from Shakespeare to Spike Lee* (Cambridge et al.: Cambridge University Press, 2005).

Daly, Peter M., 'Of Macbeth, Martlets and other "Fowles of Heaven"', *Mosaic: A Journal for the Comparative Study of Literature and Ideas* 12 (1978), 23–46.

Darwin, Charles, *The Expression of the Emotions in Man and Animals*, ed. Francis Darwin (London: Pickering, 1989).

De Grazia, Margreta, 'Imprints: Shakespeare, Gutenberg and Descartes', in Terence Hawkes ed., *Alternative Shakespeares*, Vol. 2 (London et al.: Routledge, 1996).

Della Porta, Giambattista, *De Humana Physiognomonia, Libri IV* (Vici Aequensis: G. Cacchi, 1586).

Della Porta, Giambattista, *Die Physiognomie des Menschen*, transl. and ed. Will Rink (Radebeul/Dresden: Madaus, 1929).

Dessen, Alan C., *Elizabethan Drama and the Viewer's Eye* (Chapel Hill: University of North Carolina Press, 1977).

——, *Recovering Shakespeare's Theatrical Vocabulary* (Cambridge: Cambridge University Press, 1995).

Diehl, Huston, 'Horrid Image, Sorrid Sight, Fatal Vision: The Visual Rhetoric of *Macbeth*', *Shakespeare Studies* 16 (1983), 191–203.

Dolan, Frances E., 'Taking the Pencil out of God's Hand: Art, Nature, and the Face-Painting Debate in Early Modern England', *Publication of the Modern Language Association* 108 (1993), 224–239.

Döring, Tobias, *Performances of Mourning in Shakespearean Theatre and Early Modern Culture* (Basingstoke/New York: Palgrave Macmillan, 2006).

Drakakis, John, '"Fashion it Thus": *Julius Caesar* and the Politics of Theatrical Representation', in Graham Holderness et al. ed., *Shakespeare: The Roman Plays* (London et al.: Longman, 1996), 32–44.

Drew-Bear, Annette, 'Face-Painting in Renaissance Tragedy', *Renaissance Drama* 12 (1981), 71–93.

——, *Painted Faces on the Renaissance Stage: The Moral Significance of Face-Painting Conventions* (Lewisburg et al.: Bucknell University Press, 1994).

Dusinberre, Juliet, *Shakespeare and the Nature of Women* (Basingstoke/London: Palgrave Macmillan, 1996).

Earle, John, *Microcosmographie, or A Peece of the World Discovered in Essayes and Characters* (London: William Stansby, 1630).

Eco, Umberto, *History of Beauty*, trans. by Alastair MacEwen (New York: Rizzoli, 2004).

Eisenstein, Elisabeth, *The Printing Press as an Agent of Change: Communication and Cultural Transformations in Early-Modern Europe* (Cambridge et al.: Cambridge University Press, 1979).

Ekman, Paul, *Emotions Revealed: Recognizing Faces and Feelings to Improve Communication and Emotional Life* (New York/London: Times Books, 2007).

Ekman, Paul et al., 'Conceptual Ambiguities', in Paul Ekman ed., *Emotion in the Human Face* (Cambridge: Cambridge University Press, 2001).

Elam, Keir, *The Semiotics of Theatre and Drama* (London et al.: Routledge, 1980).

——, '"Understand Me by My Signs": On Shakespeare's Semiotics', *New Theatre Quarterly* 1 (1985), 84–96.

——, '"In What Chapter of his Bosom?": Reading Shakespeare's Bodies', in Terence Hawkes ed., *Alternative Shakespeares*, Vol. 2 (London et al.: Routledge, 1996), 140–163.

——, 'Language and the Body', in: Sylvia Adamson et al. ed., *Reading Shakespeare's Dramatic Language: A Guide* (London: Thomson, 2001), 173–188.

Enenkel, Karl et al. ed., *Modelling the Individual: Biography and Portrait in the Renaissance* (Amsterdam/Atlanta: Rodopi, 1998).

Enterline, Lynn, *The Tears of Narcissus: Melancholia and Masculinity in Early Modern Writing* (Stanford: Stanford University Press, 1995).

——, *The Rhetoric of the Body from Ovid to Shakespeare* (Cambridge et al.: Cambridge University Press, 2000).

Erne, Lukas, *Shakespeare as Literary Dramatist* (Cambridge et al.: Cambridge University Press, 2003).

Evans, Elizabeth C., *Physiognomics in the Ancient World* (Philadelphia: American Philosophical Society, 1969).

Everett, Barbara, 'The Fatness of Falstaff', *Proceedings of the British Academy* 76 (1991), 109–128.

Fawcett, Mary L., 'Arms/Words/Tears: Language and the Body in *Titus Andronicus*', *English Literary History* 50 (1983), 261–277.

Ferguson, Margaret et al. ed., *Rewriting the Renaissance* (Chicago: University of Chicago Press, 1986).

Fernie, Ewan, *Shame in Shakespeare* (London et al.: Routledge, 2002).

Ferry, Anne, *The 'Inward' Language: Sonnets of Wyatt, Sidney, Shakespeare, Donne* (Chicago: University of Chicago Press, 1983).

Fisch, Harold, 'Character as Linguistic Sign', *New Literary History* 21 (1990), 593–606.

Fisher, Will, 'The Renaissance Beard: Masculinity in Early Modern England', *Renaissance Quarterly* 54/1 (2001), 155–187.

Foucault, Michel, *The Order of Things: An Archaeology of the Human Sciences* (repr. London: Routledge, 1991).

——, 'Technologies of the Self', in L. H. Martin et al. ed., *Technologies of the Self* (Amherst: University of Massachusetts Press), 16–49.

Fowler, Elizabeth, *Literary Character: The Human Figure in Early English Writing* (Ithaca/London: Cornell University Press, 2003).

Freedmann, Barbara, *Staging the Gaze: Postmodernism, Psychoanalysis, and Shakespearean Comedy* (Ithaca/London: Cornell University Press, 1991).

Frey, Siegfried, 'Lavater, Lichtenberg, and the Suggestive Power of the Human Face', in: Ellis Shookman ed., *The Faces of Physiognomy: Interdisciplinary Approaches to Johann Caspar Lavater* (Columbia: Camden House, 1993), 64–103.

Fülleborn, Georg Christoph, 'Abriss einer Geschichte und Litteratur der Physiognomik', in: ibidem ed., *Beyträge zur Geschichte der Philosophie* (Züllichau/Freystadt: Frommann, 1797) Vol. 2, 1–188.

Garber, Marjorie, 'Macbeth: The Male Medusa', in: Susanne Wofford ed., *Shakespeare's Late Tragedies: A Collection of Critical Essays* (Upper Saddle River: Prentice Hall, 1996), 74–103.

Garner, Shirley N., '"Let Her Paint an Inch Thick": Painted Ladies in Renaissance Drama and Society', *Renaissance Drama* 10 (1989), 123–39.

Gent, Lucy, *Picture and Poetry 1560–1620: Relations between Literature and the Visual Arts in the English Renaissance* (Leamington Spa: Hall, 1981).

Gent, Lucy and Nigel Llewellyn ed., *Renaissance Bodies: The Human Figure in English Culture c. 1540–1660* (London: Reaktion Books, 1990).

Gibbons, Brian J., *Spirituality and the Occult: From the Renaissance to the Modern Age* (London et al.: Routledge, 2001).

Goldberg, Jonathan, 'Hamlet's Hand', *Shakespeare Quarterly* 39/3 (1988), 307–327.

——, *Writing Matter: From the Hands of the English Renaissance* (Stanford: Stanford University Press, 1990).

Gosson, Stephen, *The Schoole of Abuse, Conteining a plesaunt Invective against Poets, Pipers, Plaiers, Jesters and such like Caterpillers of a Commonwelth* (London: Dawson, 1579).

Grady, Hugh, *Shakespeare, Machiavelli, and Montaigne: Power and Subjectivity from 'Richard III' to 'Hamlet'* (Oxford: Oxford University Press, 2002).

Green, Douglas E., 'Interpreting "her martyr'd signs"': Gender and Tragedy in *Titus Andronicus'*, *Shakespeare Quarterly* 40/3 (1989), 317–326.

Greenblatt, Stephen, *Renaissance Self Fashioning: From More to Shakespeare* (Chicago/London: University of Chicago Press, 1980).

——, *Shakespearean Negotiations: The Circulation of Social Energy in Renaissance England* (Oxford: Clarendon Press, 1988).

Grote, David, *The Best Actors in the World: Shakespeare and His Acting Company* (Westport et al.: Greenwood Press, 2002).

Gurr, Andrew, 'Hearers and Beholders in Shakespearean Drama', *Essays in Theatre* 3 (1984), 30–45.

——, *The Shakespeare Company, 1594–1642* (Cambridge: Cambridge University Press, 2004).

—— and Mariko Ichikawa, *Staging in Shakespeare's Theatres* (Oxford: Oxford University Press, 2000).

Hall, Joseph, *Characters of Vertues and Vices in two Bookes* (London: Bradwood, 1608).

Hall, Peter, *Exposed by the Mask: Form and Language in Drama* (London: Oberon Books, 2000).

Hammerschmidt-Hummel, Hildegard, 'What did Shakespeare Look Like? Authentic Portraits and the Death Mask: Methods and Results of the Tests of Authenticity', *Symbolism: An Introductional Journal of Critical Aesthetics* 1 (2000), 41–79.

Harris, Jonathan Gil, '"Narcissus in thy face": Roman Desire and the Difference it Fakes in *Antony and Cleopatra'*, *Shakespeare Quarterly* 45/4 (1994), 408–425.

Hawthorne, Nathaniel, 'Recollections of a Gifted Woman', in George P. Lathrop ed., *The Complete Works of Nathaniel Hawthorne*, Vol. 7 (Boston et al.: Houghton, Mifflin, 1883), 113–147.

Hazard, Mary E., *Elizabethan Silent Language* (Lincoln et al.: University of Nebraska Press, 2000).

Heffernan, James A. W., *The Museum of Words: The Poetics of Ekphrasis from Homer to Ashbury* (Chicago: The University of Chicago Press, 1993).

Henning, Standish, 'Branding Harlots on the Brow', *Shakespeare Quarterly* 51/1 (2000), 86–89.

Heywood, Thomas, *An Apology for Actors* (London: 1612, repr. New York/London: Garland, 1972).

Hill, Thomas, *The Contemplation of Mankinde, Contayning a singuler Discourse after the Art of Phisiognomie, on all the Members and Partes of Man, as from the Heade to the Foote, in a more ample Maner than hytherto hath beene published of any* (London: Seres, 1571).

Hill, James L., 'The Marriage of True Bodies: Myth and Metamorphosis in *Antony and Cleopatra*', *REAL – The Yearbook of Research in English and American Literature* 2 (1984), 211–237.

Hillman, David, 'The Inside Story', in Carlo Mazzio and Douglas Trevor ed., *Historicism, Psychoanalysis, and Early Modern Culture* (New York: et al.: Routledge, 2000).

—— and Carla Mazzio ed., *The Body in Parts: Fantasies of Corporeality in Early Modern Europe* (New York et al.: Routledge, 1997).

Höfele, Andreas, 'Man, Woman and Beast in Timon's Athens', *Shakespeare Survey* 56 (2003), 227–235.

Holahan, Michael, '"Look, her lips": Softness of Voice, Construction of Character in *King Lear*', *Shakespeare Quarterly* 48/4 (1997), 406–431.

Holderness, Graham et al. ed., *Shakespeare: Out of Court: Dramatizations of Court Society* (Basingstoke et al.: Macmillan, 1990).

Honigmann, Ernst A.J., *Shakespeare, Seven Tragedies Revisited: The Dramatist's Manipulation of Response* (Basingstoke et al.: Palgrave, 2002).

Huarte, Juan, *Examen de Ingenios = The Examination of Mens Wits in whicch, by discouering the Varietie of Natures, is shewed for what*

Profession each one is apt, and how far he shall profit therein, trans. by Richard Carew (London: Islip, 1594).

Hughes-Hallet, Lucy, *Cleopatra: Histories, Dreams and Distortions* (London: Bloomsbury, 1990).

Hulse, Clarke, 'Shakespeare's Sonnets and the Art of the Face', *John Donne Journal* 5 (1986), 3–26.

Hunt, Marvin, 'Be Dark but Not Too Dark: Shakespeare's Dark Lady as a Sign of Colour', in James Schiffer ed., *Shakespeare's Sonnets: Critical Essays* (New York/London: Garland Publishing, 1999), 369–389.

Hunter, Lynette and Peter Lichtenfels ed., *Shakespeare, Language and the Stage: The Fifth Wall: Approaches from Criticism, Performance and Theatre Studies* (London: Arden Shakespeare, 2005).

ab Indagine, Johannes, *The Book of Palmestry and Physiognomy, Being brief Introductions, both natural, pleasant and delectable, unto the Art of Chiromancy, or manual Divination and Physiognomy, with Circumstances upon the Faces of the Signes* (1537), transl. by Fabian Withers (London: J. Cottrel, 1651).

Ingleby, Clement M., *Shakespeare, the Man and the Book: Being a Collection of Occasional Papers on the Bard and his Writings*, Vol. 1 (London: J. Allen, 1877).

James, Heather, 'The Politics of Display and the Anamorphic Subjects of *Antony and Cleopatra*', in Susanne L. Wofford ed., *Shakespeare's Late Tragedies: A Collection of Critical Essays* (Upper Saddle River: Prentice Hall, 1990), 208–35.

James VI and I, *The first Daemonologie* (1597), ed. George B. Harrison (repr. New York: Barnes and Noble, 1966).

Jose, Nicholas, '*Antony and Cleopatra:* Face and Heart', *Philological Quarterly* 62 (1983), 487–504.

Kantorowicz, Ernst H., *The King's Two Bodies: A Study in Mediaeval Politcal Theology* (Princeton: Princeton University Press, 1957).

Keevak, Michael, *Sexual Shakespeare: Forgery-Authorship-Portraiture* (Detroit: Wayne State University Press, 2001).

Kiefer, Frederick, *Writing on the Renaissance Stage: Written Words, Printed Pages, Metaphoric Books* (Newark: University of Delaware Press, 1996).

——, *Shakespeare's Visual Theatre: Staging the Personified Characters* (Cambridge: Cambridge University Press, 2003).

Kirsch, Arthur, *The Passions of Shakespeares Tragic Heroes* (Charlottesville/London: University Press of Virginia, 1990).

Klibansky, Raymond et al., *Saturn and Melancholy* (London et al.: Nelson, 1990).

Kozikowski, Stanley J., 'Fortune and Men's Eyes in *Romeo and Juliet*', *Concerning Poetry* 10 (1977), 45–49.

Krieger, Murray, *Ekphrasis: The Illusion of the Natural Sign* (Baltimore et al.: Johns Hopkins University Press, 1992).

Kristeva, Julia, *Strangers to Ourselves*, trans. L. S. Roudiez (London: Harvester Wheatsheaf, 1991).

de La Primaudaye, Pierre, *The French Academy*, trans. Thomas Bowes (London: Edmund Bollifan, 1586).

Lavater, Johann C., *Essays on Physiognomy*, trans. Thomas Holcroft (London: J. Robinson, 1844), 4th ed.

Lavater, Johann C., *Physiognomische Fragmente zur Beförderung der Menschenkenntnis und Menschenliebe – Eine Auswahl*, ed. by Fritz Aerni (Waldshut–Tiengen: Aerni, 1996).

Lee, John, *Shakespeare's 'Hamlet' and the Controversies of Self* (Oxford: Oxford University Press, 2000).

Legatt, Alexander, 'Shakespeare and the Actor's Body', *Renaissance and Reformation* 10/1 (1986), 95–107.

Leishman, James B. ed., *The Three Parnassus Plays (1598–1601)* (London: Nicholson & Watson, 1949).

Lemnius, Levinus, *The Touchstone of Complexions, Generallye appliable, expedient and profitable for all such, as be desirous and carefull of theyr bodyly Health, Contayning most easy rules & ready tokens, whereby every one may perfectly try, and thoroughly knowe, aswell the exacte State, Habite, Disposition, and Constitution, of his Body outwardly: as also the Inclinations, Affec-*

tions, Motions, and Desires of his Mynde inwardly, trans. Thomas Newton (London: E. Allde, 1581).

Lemnius, Levinus, *The secret Miracles of Nature in four Books: Learnedly and moderately treating of Generation, and the Parts thereof, the Soul, and its Immortality, of Plants and living Creatures, of Diseases, their Symptoms and Cures, and many other Rarities* (London: Jo. Streater, 1658).

Levy, Eric P., "'Nor th'exterior nor the inward man": The Problematics of Personal Identity in Hamlet', *University of Toronto Quarterly* 68 (1998/99), 711–727.

Lichtenberg, Georg Christoph, 'Über Physiognomik; wider die Physiognomen (1778)', in: Wolfgang Promies ed., *Georg Christoph Lichtenberg, Schriften und Briefe*, Vol. 3 (Darmstadt: Wiss. Buchgesellschaft, 1972), 256–295.

Machiavelli, Niccolo, *The Prince*, trans. Harvey C. Mansfield (Chicago: University of Chicago Press, 1985).

MacKenzie, Clayton, 'Antony and Cleopatra: A Mythological Perspective', *Orbis Literarum* 45 (1990), 309–329.

Magnusson, A. Lynne, "'I paint him in the character": Prose Portraits in Coriolanus', *English Language Notes* 25/2 (1987), 33–36.

Manferlotti, Stefano, 'Macbeth and the Implied Director', in: Dieter Stein and Rosanna Sornicola ed., *The Virtues of Language: History in Language, Linguistics and Texts: Papers in Memory of Thomas Frank* (Amsterdam/Philadelphia: Benjamins, 1998), 167–176.

Maus, Katharine Eisaman, *Inwardness and Theater in the English Renaissance* (Chicago/London: University of Chicago Press, 1995).

McAlindon, Thomas, *Shakespeare and Decorum* (London: Macmillan, 1973).

Meagher, John C., *Pursuing Shakespeare's Dramaturgy: Some Contexts, Resources, and Strategies in His Playmaking* (Madison: Fairleigh Dickinson University Press, 2003).

Miles, Geoffrey, 'How Roman Are Shakespeare's "Romans"?', *Shakespeare Quarterly* 40 (1989), 257–283.

——, *Shakespeare and the Constant Romans* (Oxford: Clarendon Press, 1996).

de Montaigne, Michel, *Montaigne's Essayes*, trans. John Florio, 3 vols. (repr. London: Dent, 1910).

Moulton, Ian Frederick, '"A Monster Great Deformed": The Unruly Masculinity of Richard III', *Shakespeare Quarterly* 47 (1996), 251–268.

Mulcaster, Richard, *The first Part of the Elementarie which entreateth chefelie of the right Writing of our English Tung* (London: Vautroullier, 1582).

Murphy, James J. ed., *Renaissance Eloquence: Studies in Theory and Practice of Renaissance Rhetoric* (Berkeley et al.: University of California Press, 1983).

Murray, Peter B., *Shakespeare's Imagined Persons: The Psychology of Role-Playing and Acting* (Lanham: Barnes & Noble, 1996).

Napier, A. David, *Masks, Transformation, and Paradox* (Berkeley et al.: University of California Press, 1986).

Nolen, Stephanie, *Shakespeare's Face* (London: Piatkus, 2003).

Orgel, Stephen, *Impersonations: The Performance of Gender in Shakespeare's England* (Cambridge: Cambridge University Press, 1997).

——, *Imagining Shakespeare: A History of Texts and Visions* (Basingstoke/New York: Palgrave Macmillan, 2003).

Palmer, D.J., '"A New Gorgon": Visual Effects in *Macbeth*', in John Russell Brown ed., *Focus on Macbeth* (London et al.: Routledge & Kegan Paul, 1982), 54–69.

Parker, Patricia, *Literary Fat Ladies: Rhetoric, Gender, Property* (London/New York: Methuen, 1987).

Parrot, W. Gerrod, 'The Psychologist of Avon: Emotion in Elizabethan Psychology and the Plays of Shakespeare', in Barbara Landau et al. ed., *Perception, Cognition, and Language* (Cambridge [Mass.]/London: Bradford Books, 2000), 231–243.

Parsons, Philip, 'Shakespeare and the Mask', *Shakespeare Survey* 16 (1963), 121–131.

Paster, Gail K., *The Body Embarrassed: Drama and the Disciplines of Shame in Early Modern England* (Ithaca: Cornell University Press, 1993).

——, *Humoring the Body: Emotions and the Shakespearean Stage* (Chicago/London: University of Chicago Press, 2004).

Pollard, Tanya, 'Beauty's Poisonous Properties', *Shakespeare Studies* 27 (1999), 187–210.

——, *Drugs and Theater in Early Modern England* (Oxford: Oxford University Press, 2005).

Porter, Martin, *Windows of the Soul: Physiognomy in European Culture 1470–1780* (Oxford: Clarendon Press, 2005.

Puttenham, George, *The Arte of English Poesie* (1589), ed. Gladys D. Willcock and Alice Walker (Cambridge: Cambridge University Press, 1936).

Quintilian, *The Orator's Education*, transl. and ed. Donald A. Russell (Cambridge [Mass.]: Harvard University Press, 2001).

Rackin, Phyllis, *Shakespeare and Women* (Oxford: Oxford University Press, 2005).

Reusch, Franz H. ed., *Die Indices librorum prohibitorum des sechzehnten Jahrhunderts* (Tübingen: 1886; repr. Nieuwkoop: de Graaf, 1970).

Rosand, David, '"Troyes Painted Woes": Shakespeare and Pictorial Imagination', in Stephen Orgel ed., *Shakespeare and the Arts* (New York et al.: Garland Publishing, 1999) 215–43.

Royster, Francesca T., 'White-limed Walls: Whiteness and Gothic Extremism in Shakespeare's *Titus Andronicus*', *Shakespeare Quarterly* 51 (2000), 432–455.

Rutter, Carol Chillington, *Enter the Body: Women and Representation on Shakespeare's Stage* (London/New York: Routledge, 2001).

Salgado, Gamini, *Eyewitnesses of Shakespeare: First Hand Accounts of Performances 1590–1890* (London: Sussex University Press, 1975).

Salomon, Nanette, 'Positioning Women in Visual Convention: The Case of Elizabeth I', in Betty S. Travitsky and Adele F. Seeft ed.,

Attending to Women in Early Modern England (Newark et al.: University of Delaware Press, 1994), 64–95.

Saunders, Richard, *Physiognomie and Chiromancie, Metoposcopie, the symmetrical Proportions and signal Moles of the Body, fully and accurately handled, with their natural-predictive Significations* (London: Brooke, 1653).

Sawday, Jonathan, *The Body Emblazoned: Dissection and the Human Body in Renaissance Culture* (London/New York: Routledge, 1995).

Schiffer, James, 'Mnemonic Cues to Passion in *Hamlet*', in Barbara J. Baines, *Renaissance Papers* (Raleigh: Southeastern Renaissance Conference, 1995), 65–79.

Schoenbaum, Samuel, *William Shakespeare: Records and Images* (London: Scolar Press, 1981).

Schoenfeldt, Michael, 'The Matter of Inwardness – Shakespeare's Sonnets', in James Schiffer ed., *Shakespeare's Sonnets: Critical Essays* (New York/London: Garland Publishing, 1999), 305–324.

Scholz, Susanne, *Body Narratives: Writing the Nation and Fashioning the Subject in Early Modern England* (Basingstoke et al.: Macmillan, 2000).

Serpieri, Alessandro, 'Reading the Signs: Towards a Semiotics of Shakespearean Drama', in John Drakakis ed., *Alternative Shakespeares* (London et al.: Routledge, 1985), 119–143.

Shumaker, Wayne, *The Occult Sciences in the Renaissance: A Study in Intellectual Patterns* (Berkeley et al.: University of California Press, 1972).

Skura, Meridith Anne, *Shakespeare the Actor and the Purpose of Playing* (Chicago/London: University of Chicago Press, 1993).

Slater, Ann P., *Shakespeare the Director* (Sussex et al.: Harvester Press, 1982).

Smeed, John W., *The Theophrastan Character: The History of a Literary Genre* (Oxford/New York: Clarendon, 1985).

Smith, Bruce R., *Shakespeare and Masculinity* (Oxford: Oxford University Press, 2000).

Smith, Ian, 'White Skin, Black Masks: Racial Cross-Dressing on the Early Modern Stage', *Renaissance Drama* 32 (2003), 33–67.

Spevack, Martin ed., *The Harvard Concordance to Shakespeare* (Cambridge [Mass.]: Belknap Press, 1973).

States, Bert O., *Hamlet and the Concept of Character* (Baltimore/London: Johns Hopkins University Press, 1992).

Stern, Tiffany, *Making Shakespeare: From Stage to Page* (London et al.: Routledge, 2004).

Stimilli, Davide, *The Face of Immortality: Physiognomy and Criticism* (Albany: State University of New York Press, 2005).

Stubbes, Philip, *The Anatomie of Abuses containing a Discouerie, or briefe Summarie of such notable Vices and Corruptions, as nowe raigne in many Christian Countreyes of the Worlde, but (especially) in the Countrey of Ailgna* (London: Richard Iones, 1584).

Swain, Simon, *Seeing the Face, Seeing the Soul: Polemon's 'Physiognomy' from Classical Antiquity to Medieval Islam* (Oxford: Oxford University Press, 2007).

Taylor, Charles, *Sources of the Self: The Making of Modern Identity* (Cambridge: Cambridge University Press, 1989).

Taylor, Gary, 'Feeling Bodies', in Jonathan Bate et al. ed., *Shakespeare in the Twentieth Century: Proceedings of the Sixth World Shakespeare Congress* (Newark/London: University of Delaware Press, 1998).

Thompson, Ann and John Thompson, '"To Look So Low as Where They Are": Hand and Heart Synecdoches in *Othello*', *Southern Review: An Australian Journal of Literary Studies* 19 (1986), 53–66.

———, *Shakespeare: Meaning and Metaphor* (Brighton: Harvestor Press, 1987).

Thorndike, Lynn, *A History of Magic and Experimental Science*, 8 vols. (New York et al.: Macmillan, 1923–58), Vol. 6 (1941), Vol. 8 (1958).

Thorne, Alison, *Vision and Rhetoric in Shakespeare: Looking through Language* (Houndmills/Basingstoke: Macmillan, 2000).

Torrey, Michael, "'The plain devil and dissembling looks": Ambivalent Physiognomy and Shakespeare's *Richard III*', *English Literary Renaissance* 30/2 (2000), 123–153.

Twycross, Meg and Sarah Carpenter, *Masks and Masking in Medieval and Early Tudor England* (Aldershot: Ashgate, 2002).

Vaughan, Virginia M., *Performing Blackness on English Stages, 1500–1800* (Cambridge: Cambridge University Press, 2005).

Vickers, Brian, "'The Power of Persuasion": Images of the Orator, Elyot to Shakespeare', in James J. Murphy ed., *Renaissance Eloquence: Studies in the Theory and Practice of Renaissance Rhetoric* (Berkeley et al.: University of California Press, 1983), 411–435.

Walpole, Horace, *Historic Doubts on the Life and Reign of King Richard the Third* (London: J. Dodsley, 1768).

Walker, Susan and Peter Higgs, *Cleopatra of Egypt: from History to Myth* (Princeton: Princeton University Press, 2001).

Weimann, Robert, *Author's Pen and Actor's Voice* (Cambridge: Cambridge University Press, 2000).

Weiss, Wolfgang, "'There is Language in her Eye, her Cheek, her Lip": Körper und Körpersprache in *Troilus and Cressida, All's Well That Ends Well* und *Measure for Measure*', *Shakespeare Jahrbuch* 125 (1989), 196–208.

White, Martin, *Renaissance Drama in Action: An Introduction to Aspects of Theatre Practice and Performance* (London et al.: Routledge, 1998).

Wickham, Glynne et al. ed., *English Professional Theatre: 1530–1660* (Cambridge: Cambridge University Press, 2000).

Wigginton, Waller B., "'One way like a Gorgon": An Explication of *Antony and Cleopatra*, 2.5.116–17', *Papers on Language and Literature* 16 (1980), 366–375.

Williams, Neville, *Powder and Paint: A History of the Englishwoman's Toilet* (London et al.: Longmans, Green & Co., 1957).

Wilshire, Bruce, *Role Playing and Identity: The Limits of Theatre as Metaphor* (Bloomington: Indiana University Press, 1982).

Wilson, Thomas, *The Arte of Rhetorique* (1553) (repr. Amsterdam: Da Capo, 1969).

Wright, Thomas, *The Passions of the Minde in Generall* (London: Helme, 1620).

Humanities Insights